Collected Poems

Books by

Edna St. Vincent Millay

POEMS

The Buck in the Snow
Second April
Renascence
A Few Figs from Thistles
The Harp-Weaver
Poems Selected for Young People
Fatal Interview
Wine from These Grapes
Conversation at Midnight
Huntsman, What Quarry?
Make Bright the Arrows
The Murder of Lidice
Collected Sonnets
Collected Lyrics
Mine the Harvest
Collected Poems
Flowers of Evil, from the French of Charles Baudelaire
with George Dillon

PLAYS

The King's Henchman
The Lamp and the Bell
Aria da Capo
Three Plays
The Princess Marries the Page

Letters of Edna St. Vincent Millay,
edited by Allen Ross Macdougall

Collected Poems

EDNA ST. VINCENT MILLAY

Edited by Norma Millay

HARPER**PERENNIAL** MODERN**CLASSICS**

NEW YORK • LONDON • TORONTO • SYDNEY • NEW DELHI • AUCKLAND

CONTENTS

Y

From *The Buck in the Snow*

From *Poems Selected for Young People*

From a Very Little Sphinx

From *Mine the Harvest*

SONNETS

From *Renascence*

From *A Few Figs from Thistles*

From *Second April*

xix

From *Wine from These Grapes*

From *Mine the Harvest*

FOREWORD

Y

The first edition of Edna St. Vincent Millay's *Collected Poems* was published in 1956 by the poet's younger sister Norma, who served as Millay's literary executor from 1950 until her death in 1986 at age ninety-two. A devoted "keeper of the flame," Norma had previously published *Mine the Harvest* (1954), a selection of poems written from 1939 to 1950, and several unpublished early poems she discovered, scrawled in longhand, in Millay's writing notebooks.

In the nine books of poetry Millay published in her lifetime, the lyrics were placed at the beginning of the book, the sonnets at the end. (The exception is *Fatal Interview*, which is comprised of sonnets only.) In editing *Collected Poems*, Norma created a similar arrangement: the book begins with the lyrics from individual books, reprinted in chronological order, followed by the sonnets. This new edition, which preserves Norma's ordering system, also includes an index of titles and first lines and several other new features.

A thirty-two-page P.S. section provides the reader with a richly textured introduction to Millay's life and the inspiration for her work. It includes a biographical critical essay, a collection of photographs from the Millay Society archives, and excerpts from the poet's personal letters to family, friends, and her beloved editor Cass Canfield, chairman of the board of Harper & Brothers.

"The faults as well as the virtues of this poetry are my own," Millay wrote to Mr. Canfield in 1946. The virtues of her work have defied the differences in generations, and her poems—often traditional in form but timeless in their message—continue to attract an ever-expanding audience of readers.

Elizabeth Barnett and Holly Peppe
Literary Executors, Edna St. Vincent Millay
New York City, December 2010

From *RENASCENCE*

Y

All I could see from where I stood
Was three long mountains and a wood;
I turned and looked another way,
And saw three islands in a bay.
So with my eyes I traced the line
Of the horizon, thin and fine,
Straight around till I was come
Back to where I'd started from;
And all I saw from where I stood
Was three long mountains and a wood.

Over these things I could not see:
These were the things that bounded me.
And I could touch them with my hand,
Almost, I thought, from where I stand!
And all at once things seemed so small
My breath came short, and scarce at all.

But, sure, the sky is big, I said:
Miles and miles above my head.
So here upon my back I'll lie
And look my fill into the sky.
And so I looked, and after all,
The sky was not so very tall.
The sky, I said, must somewhere stop . . .
And—sure enough!—I see the top!
The sky, I thought, is not so grand;
I 'most could touch it with my hand!
And reaching up my hand to try,
I screamed, to feel it touch the sky.

I screamed, and—lo!—Infinity
Came down and settled over me;
Forced back my scream into my chest;
Bent back my arm upon my breast;
And, pressing of the Undefined
The definition on my mind,
Held up before my eyes a glass
Through which my shrinking sight did pass

Until it seemed I must behold
Immensity made manifold;
Whispered to me a word whose sound
Deafened the air for worlds around,
And brought unmuffled to my ears
The gossiping of friendly spheres,
The creaking of the tented sky,
The ticking of Eternity.

I saw and heard, and knew at last
The How and Why of all things, past,
And present, and forevermore.
The Universe, cleft to the core,
Lay open to my probing sense,
That, sickening, I would fain pluck thence
But could not,—nay! but needs must suck
At the great wound, and could not pluck
My lips away till I had drawn
All venom out.—Ah, fearful pawn:
For my omniscience paid I toll
In infinite remorse of soul.

All sin was of my sinning, all
Atoning mine, and mine the gall
Of all regret. Mine was the weight
Of every brooded wrong, the hate
That stood behind each envious thrust,
Mine every greed, mine every lust.

And all the while, for every grief,
Each suffering, I craved relief
With individual desire;
Craved all in vain! And felt fierce fire
About a thousand people crawl;
Perished with each,—then mourned for all!

A man was starving in Capri;
He moved his eyes and looked at me;
I felt his gaze, I heard his moan,
And knew his hunger as my own.

I saw at sea a great fog bank
Between two ships that struck and sank;
A thousand screams the heavens smote;
And every scream tore through my throat.

No hurt I did not feel, no death
That was not mine; mine each last breath
That, crying, met an answering cry
From the compassion that was I.
All suffering mine, and mine its rod;
Mine, pity like the pity of God.

Ah, awful weight! Infinity
Pressed down upon the finite Me!
My anguished spirit, like a bird,
Beating against my lips I heard;
Yet lay the weight so close about
There was no room for it without.
And so beneath the weight lay I
And suffered death, but could not die.

7

Long had I lain thus, craving death,
When quietly the earth beneath
Gave way, and inch by inch, so great
At last had grown the crushing weight,
Into the earth I sank till I
Full six feet under ground did lie,
And sank no more,—there is no weight
Can follow here, however great.
From off my breast I felt it roll,
And as it went my tortured soul
Burst forth and fled in such a gust
That all about me swirled the dust.

Deep in the earth I rested now.
Cool is its hand upon the brow
And soft its breast beneath the head
Of one who is so gladly dead.
And all at once, and over all
The pitying rain began to fall;
I lay and heard each pattering hoof
Upon my lowly, thatchèd roof,

And seemed to love the sound far more
Than ever I had done before.
For rain it hath a friendly sound
To one who's six feet under ground;
And scarce the friendly voice or face,
A grave is such a quiet place.

The rain, I said, is kind to come
And speak to me in my new home.
I would I were alive again
To kiss the fingers of the rain,
To drink into my eyes the shine
Of every slanting silver line,
To catch the freshened, fragrant breeze
From drenched and dripping apple-trees.
For soon the shower will be done,
And then the broad face of the sun
Will laugh above the rain-soaked earth
Until the world with answering mirth
Shakes joyously, and each round drop
Rolls, twinkling, from its grass-blade top.

How can I bear it, buried here,
While overhead the sky grows clear
And blue again after the storm?
O, multi-coloured, multi-form,
Belovèd beauty over me,
That I shall never, never see
Again! Spring-silver, autumn-gold,
That I shall never more behold!—
Sleeping your myriad magics through,
Close-sepulchred away from you!
O God, I cried, give me new birth,
And put me back upon the earth!
Upset each cloud's gigantic gourd
And let the heavy rain, down-poured
In one big torrent, set me free,
Washing my grave away from me!

I ceased; and through the breathless hush
That answered me, the far-off rush
Of herald wings came whispering
Like music down the vibrant string
Of my ascending prayer, and—crash!
Before the wild wind's whistling lash

The startled storm-clouds reared on high
And plunged in terror down the sky!
And the big rain in one black wave
Fell from the sky and struck my grave.

I know not how such things can be;
I only know there came to me
A fragrance such as never clings
To aught save happy living things;
A sound as of some joyous elf
Singing sweet songs to please himself,
And, through and over everything,
A sense of glad awakening.
The grass, a-tiptoe at my ear,
Whispering to me I could hear;
I felt the rain's cool finger-tips
Brushed tenderly across my lips,
Laid gently on my sealèd sight,
And all at once the heavy night
Fell from my eyes and I could see!—
A drenched and dripping apple-tree,
A last long line of silver rain,

A sky grown clear and blue again.
And as I looked a quickening gust
Of wind blew up to me and thrust
Into my face a miracle
Of orchard-breath, and with the smell, —
I know not how such things can be! —
I breathed my soul back into me.

Ah! Up then from the ground sprang I
And hailed the earth with such a cry
As is not heard save from a man
Who has been dead, and lives again.
About the trees my arms I wound;
Like one gone mad I hugged the ground;
I raised my quivering arms on high;
I laughed and laughed into the sky;
Till at my throat a strangling sob
Caught fiercely, and a great heart-throb
Sent instant tears into my eyes:
O God, I cried, no dark disguise
Can e'er hereafter hide from me
Thy radiant identity!

Thou canst not move across the grass
But my quick eyes will see Thee pass,
Nor speak, however silently,
But my hushed voice will answer Thee.
I know the path that tells Thy way
Through the cool eve of every day;
God, I can push the grass apart
And lay my finger on Thy heart!

The world stands out on either side
No wider than the heart is wide;
Above the world is stretched the sky,—
No higher than the soul is high.
The heart can push the sea and land
Farther away on either hand;
The soul can split the sky in two,
And let the face of God shine through.
But East and West will pinch the heart
That can not keep them pushed apart;
And he whose soul is flat—the sky
Will cave in on him by and by.

The room is full of you!—As I came in
And closed the door behind me, all at once
A something in the air, intangible,
Yet stiff with meaning, struck my senses sick!—

Sharp, unfamiliar odours have destroyed
Each other room's dear personality.
The heavy scent of damp, funeral flowers,—
The very essence, hush-distilled, of Death—
Has strangled that habitual breath of home
Whose expiration leaves all houses dead;
And wheresoe'er I look is hideous change.
Save here. Here 'twas as if a weed-choked gate
Had opened at my touch, and I had stepped
Into some long-forgot, enchanted, strange,
Sweet garden of a thousand years ago
And suddenly thought, "I have been here before!"

You are not here. I know that you are gone,
And will not ever enter here again.
And yet it seems to me, if I should speak,

Your silent step must wake across the hall;
If I should turn my head, that your sweet eyes
Would kiss me from the door.—So short a time
To teach my life its transposition to
This difficult and unaccustomed key!—

The room is as you left it; your last touch—
A thoughtless pressure, knowing not itself
As saintly—hallows now each simple thing;
Hallows and glorifies, and glows between
The dust's grey fingers like a shielded light.

There is your book, just as you laid it down,
Face to the table,—I cannot believe
That you are gone!—Just then it seemed to me
You must be here. I almost laughed to think
How like reality the dream had been;
Yet knew before I laughed, and so was still.
That book, outspread, just as you laid it down!
Perhaps you thought, "I wonder what comes next,
And whether this or this will be the end";
So rose, and left it, thinking to return.

Perhaps that chair, when you arose and passed
Out of the room, rocked silently a while
Ere it again was still. When you were gone
Forever from the room, perhaps that chair,
Stirred by your movement, rocked a little while,
Silently, to and fro . . .

And here are the last words your fingers wrote,
Scrawled in broad characters across a page
In this brown book I gave you. Here your hand,
Guiding your rapid pen, moved up and down.
Here with a looping knot you crossed a "t,"
And here another like it, just beyond
These two eccentric "e's." You were so small,
And wrote so brave a hand!

How strange it seems
That of all words these are the words you chose!
And yet a simple choice; you did not know
You would not write again. If you had known—
But then, it does not matter,—and indeed
If you had known there was so little time
You would have dropped your pen and come to me

And this page would be empty, and some phrase
Other than this would hold my wonder now.
Yet, since you could not know, and it befell
That these are the last words your fingers wrote,
There is a dignity some might not see
In this, "I picked the first sweet-pea today."
Today! Was there an opening bud beside it
You left until tomorrow?—O my love,
The things that withered,—and you came not back!
That day you filled this circle of my arms
That now is empty. (O my empty life!)
That day—that day you picked the first sweet-pea,—
And brought it in to show me! I recall
With terrible distinctness how the smell
Of your cool gardens drifted in with you.
I know, you held it up for me to see
And flushed because I looked not at the flower,
But at your face; and when behind my look
You saw such unmistakable intent
You laughed and brushed your flower against my lips.
(You were the fairest thing God ever made,
I think.) And then your hands above my heart

Drew down its stem into a fastening,
And while your head was bent I kissed your hair.
I wonder if you knew.   (Belovèd hands!
Somehow I cannot seem to see them still.
Somehow I cannot seem to see the dust
In your bright hair.)   What is the need of Heaven
When earth can be so sweet?—If only God
Had let us love,—and show the world the way!
Strange cancellings must ink the eternal books
When love-crossed-out will bring the answer right!

That first sweet-pea!   I wonder where it is.
It seems to me I laid it down somewhere,
And yet,—I am not sure.   I am not sure,
Even, if it was white or pink; for then
'Twas much like any other flower to me,
Save that it was the first. I did not know,
Then, that it was the last. If I had known—
But then, it does not matter. Strange how few,
After all's said and done, the things that are
Of moment.

Few indeed! When I can make
Of ten small words a rope to hang the world!
"I had you and I have you now no more."
There, there it dangles,—where's the little truth
That can for long keep footing under that
When its slack syllables tighten to a thought?
Here, let me write it down! I wish to see
Just how a thing like that will look on paper!

   "I had you and I have you now no more."

O little words, how can you run so straight
Across the page, beneath the weight you bear?
How can you fall apart, whom such a theme
Has bound together, and hereafter aid
In trivial expression, that have been
So hideously dignified?

                    Would God
That tearing you apart would tear the thread
I strung you on! Would God—O God, my mind
Stretches asunder on this merciless rack
Of imagery! Oh, let me sleep a while!

Would I could sleep, and wake to find me back
In that sweet summer afternoon with you.
Summer? 'Tis summer still by the calendar!
How easily could God, if He so willed,
Set back the world a little turn or two!—
Correct its griefs, and brings its joys again!

We were so wholly one I had not thought
That we could die apart. I had not thought
That I could move,—and you be stiff and still!
That I could speak,—and you perforce be dumb!
I think our heart-strings were, like warp and woof
In some firm fabric, woven in and out;
Your golden filaments in fair design
Across my duller fibre. And today
The shining strip is rent; the exquisite
Fine pattern is destroyed; part of your heart
Aches in my breast; part of my heart lies chilled
In the damp earth with you.   I have been torn
In two, and suffer for the rest of me.
What is my life to me?   And what am I
To life,—a ship whose star has guttered out?

A Fear that in the deep night starts awake
Perpetually, to find its senses strained
Against the taut strings of the quivering air,
Awaiting the return of some dread chord?

Dark, Dark, is all I find for metaphor;
All else were contrast;—save that contrast's wall
Is down, and all opposed things flow together
Into a vast monotony, where night
And day, and frost and thaw, and death and life,
Are synonyms. What now—what now to me
Are all the jabbering birds and foolish flowers
That clutter up the world? You were my song!
Now, now, let discord scream! You were my flower!
Now let the world grow weeds! For I shall not
Plant things above your grave—(the common balm
Of the conventional woe for its own wound!)
Amid sensations rendered negative
By your elimination stands today,
Certain, unmixed, the element of grief;
I sorrow; and I shall not mock my truth
With travesties of suffering, nor seek

To effigy its incorporeal bulk
In little wry-faced images of woe.
I cannot call you back; and I desire
No utterance of my immaterial voice.
I cannot even turn my face this way
Or that, and say, "My face is turned to you";
I know not where you are, I do not know
If heaven hold you or if earth transmute,
Body and soul, you into earth again;
But this I know:—not for one second's space
Shall I insult my sight with visionings
Such as the credulous crowd so eager-eyed
Beholds, self-conjured in the empty air.
Let the world wail! Let drip its easy tears!
My sorrow shall be dumb!

                 —What do I say?
God! God!—God pity me! Am I gone mad
That I should spit upon a rosary?
Am I become so shrunken? Would to God
I too might feel that frenzied faith whose touch
Makes temporal the most enduring grief;

Though it must walk a while, as is its wont,
With wild lamenting! Would I too might weep
Where weeps the world and hangs its piteous wreaths
For its new dead! Not Truth, but Faith, it is
That keeps the world alive. If all at once
Faith were to slacken,—that unconscious faith
Which must, I know, yet be the corner-stone
Of all believing,—birds now flying fearless
Across, would drop in terror to the earth;
Fishes would drown; and the all-governing reins
Would tangle in the frantic hands of God
And the worlds gallop headlong to destruction!

O God, I see it now, and my sick brain
Staggers and swoons! How often over me
Flashes this breathlessness of sudden sight
In which I see the universe unrolled
Before me like a scroll and read thereon
Chaos and Doom, where helpless planets whirl
Dizzily round and round and round and round,
Like tops across a table, gathering speed
With every spin, to waver on the edge

One instant—looking over—and the next
To shudder and lurch forward out of sight!

Ah, I am worn out—I am wearied out—
It is too much—I am but flesh and blood,
And I must sleep. Though you were dead again,
I am but flesh and blood and I must sleep.

"Curse thee, Life, I will live with thee no more!
Thou hast mocked me, starved me, beat my body sore!
And all for a pledge that was not pledged by me,
I have kissed thy crust and eaten sparingly
That I might eat again, and met thy sneers
With deprecations, and thy blows with tears,—
Aye, from thy glutted lash, glad, crawled away,
As if spent passion were a holiday!
And now I go. Nor threat, nor easy vow
Of tardy kindness can avail thee now
With me, whence fear and faith alike are flown;
Lonely I came, and I depart alone,
And know not where nor unto whom I go;
But that thou canst not follow me I know."

Thus I to Life, and ceased; but through my brain
My thought ran still, until I spake again:

"Ah, but I go not as I came,—no trace
Is mine to bear away of that old grace
I brought! I have been heated in thy fires,

Bent by thy hands, fashioned to thy desires,
Thy mark is on me! I am not the same
Nor ever more shall be, as when I came.
Ashes am I of all that once I seemed.
In me all's sunk that leapt, and all that dreamed
Is wakeful for alarm,—oh, shame to thee,
For the ill change that thou hast wrought in me
Who laugh no more nor lift my throat to sing!
Ah, Life, I would have been a pleasant thing
To have about the house when I was grown
If thou hadst left my little joys alone!
I asked of thee no favour save this one:
That thou wouldst leave me playing in the sun!
And this thou didst deny, calling my name
Insistently, until I rose and came.
I saw the sun no more.—It were not well
So long on these unpleasant thoughts to dwell,
Need I arise tomorrow and renew
Again my hated tasks, but I am through
With all things save my thoughts and this one night;
So that in truth I seem already quite
Free and remote from thee,—I feel no haste
And no reluctance to depart; I taste

Merely, with thoughtful mien, an unknown draught,
That in a little while I shall have quaffed."

Thus I to Life, and ceased, and slightly smiled,
Looking at nothing; and my thin dreams filed
Before me one by one till once again
I set new words unto an old refrain:

"Treasures thou hast that never have been mine!
Warm lights in many a secret chamber shine
Of thy gaunt house, and gusts of song have blown
Like blossoms out to me that sat alone!
And I have waited well for thee to show
If any share were mine,—and now I go!
Nothing I leave, and if I naught attain
I shall but come into mine own again!"

Thus I to Life, and ceased, and spake no more,
But turning, straightway sought a certain door
In the rear wall. Heavy it was, and low
And dark,—a way by which none e'er would go

That other exit had, and never knock
Was heard thereat,—bearing a curious lock,
Some chance had shown me fashioned faultily,
Whereof Life held content the useless key;
And great coarse hinges, thick and rough with rust,
Whose sudden voice across a silence must,
I knew, be harsh and horrible to hear,—
A strange door, ugly like a dwarf.—So near
I came I felt upon my feet the chill
Of acid wind creeping across the sill.
So stood longtime, till over me at last
Came weariness, and all things other passed
To make it room; the still night drifted deep
Like snow about me, and I longed for sleep.

But, suddenly, marking the morning hour,
Bayed the deep-throated bell within the tower!
Startled, I raised my head,—and with a shout
Laid hold upon the latch,—and was without.

———————

Ah, long-forgotten, well-remembered road,
Leading me back unto my old abode,
My Father's house! There in the night I came,
And found them feasting, and all things the same
As they had been before. A splendour hung
Upon the walls, and such sweet songs were sung
As, echoing out of very long ago,
Had called me from the house of Life, I know.
So fair their raiment shone I looked in shame
On the unlovely garb in which I came;
Then straightway at my hesitancy mocked:
"It is my Father's house!" I said and knocked;
And the door opened. To the shining crowd
Tattered and dark I entered, like a cloud,
Seeing no face but His; to Him I crept,
And "Father!" I cried, and clasped His knees, and wept.

———

Ah, days of joy that followed! All alone
I wandered through the house. My own, my own,
My own to touch, my own to taste and smell,
All I had lacked so long and loved so well!

None shook me out of sleep, nor hushed my song,
Nor called me in from the sunlight all day long.

I know not when the wonder came to me
Of what my Father's business might be,
And whither fared and on what errands bent
The tall and gracious messengers He sent.
Yet one day with no song from dawn till night
Wondering, I sat, and watched them out of sight.
And the next day I called; and on the third
Asked them if I might go,—but no one heard.
Then, sick with longing, I arose at last
And went unto my Father,—in that vast
Chamber wherein He for so many years
Has sat, surrounded by His charts and spheres.
"Father," I said, "Father, I cannot play
The harp that Thou didst give me, and all day
I sit in idleness, while to and fro
About me Thy serene, grave servants go;
And I am weary of my lonely ease.
Better a perilous journey overseas
Away from Thee, than this, the life I lead,

To sit all day in the sunshine like a weed
That grows to naught,—I love Thee more than they
Who serve Thee most; yet serve Thee in no way.
Father, I beg of Thee a little task
To dignify my days,—'tis all I ask
Forever, but forever, this denied,
I perish."

        "Child," my Father's voice replied,
"All things thy fancy hath desired of me
Thou hast received. I have prepared for thee
Within my house a spacious chamber, where
Are delicate things to handle and to wear,
And all these things are thine. Dost thou love song?
My minstrels shall attend thee all day long.
Or sigh for flowers? My fairest gardens stand
Open as fields to thee on every hand.
And all thy days this word shall hold the same:
No pleasure shalt thou lack that thou shalt name.
But as for tasks—" He smiled, and shook His head;
"Thou hadst thy task, and laidst it by," He said.

God's World

O world, I cannot hold thee close enough!
　　Thy winds, thy wide grey skies!
　　Thy mists, that roll and rise!
Thy woods, this autumn day, that ache and sag
And all but cry with colour! That gaunt crag
To crush! To lift the lean of that black bluff!
World, World, I cannot get thee close enough!

Long have I known a glory in it all,
　　　　But never knew I this:
　　　　Here such a passion is
As stretcheth me apart,—Lord, I do fear
Thou'st made the world too beautiful this year;
My soul is all but out of me,—let fall
No burning leaf; prithee, let no bird call.

Afternoon on a Hill

I will be the gladdest thing
      Under the sun!
I will touch a hundred flowers
      And not pick one.

I will look at cliffs and clouds
      With quiet eyes,
Watch the wind bow down the grass,
      And the grass rise.

And when lights begin to show
      Up from the town,
I will mark which must be mine,
      And then start down!

Sorrow

Sorrow like a ceaseless rain
    Beats upon my heart.
People twist and scream in pain,—
Dawn will find them still again;
This has neither wax nor wane,
    Neither stop nor start.

People dress and go to town;
    I sit in my chair.
All my thoughts are slow and brown:
Standing up or sitting down
Little matters, or what gown
    Or what shoes I wear.

Tavern

I'll keep a little tavern
  Below the high hill's crest,
Wherein all grey-eyed people
  May sit them down and rest.

There shall be plates a-plenty,
  And mugs to melt the chill
Of all the grey-eyed people
  Who happen up the hill.

There sound will sleep the traveller,
  And dream his journey's end,
But I will rouse at midnight
  The falling fire to tend.

Aye, 'tis a curious fancy—
  But all the good I know
Was taught me out of two grey eyes
  A long time ago.

Ashes of Life

Love has gone and left me and the days are all alike;
   Eat I must, and sleep I will,—and would that night were here!
But ah!—to lie awake and hear the slow hours strike!
   Would that it were day again!—with twilight near!

Love has gone and left me and I don't know what to do;
   This or that or what you will is all the same to me;
But all the things that I begin I leave before I'm through,—
   There's little use in anything as far as I can see.

Love has gone and left me,—and the neighbours knock and
      borrow,
   And life goes on forever like the gnawing of a mouse,—
And tomorrow and tomorrow and tomorrow and tomorrow
   There's this little street and this little house.

The Little Ghost

I knew her for a little ghost
   That in my garden walked;
The wall is high—higher than most—
   And the green gate was locked.

And yet I did not think of that
   Till after she was gone—
I knew her by the broad white hat,
   All ruffled, she had on,

By the dear ruffles round her feet,
   By her small hands that hung
In their lace mitts, austere and sweet,
   Her gown's white folds among.

I watched to see if she would stay,
   What she would do—and oh!
She looked as if she liked the way
   I let my garden grow!

She bent above my favourite mint
　　With conscious garden grace,
She smiled and smiled—there was no hint
　　Of sadness in her face.

She held her gown on either side
　　To let her slippers show,
And up the walk she went with pride,
　　The way great ladies go.

And where the wall is built in new,
　　And is of ivy bare,
She paused—then opened and passed through
　　A gate that once was there.

Kin to Sorrow

Am I kin to Sorrow,
　　That so oft
Falls the knocker of my door—
　　Neither loud nor soft,
But as long accustomed—
　　Under Sorrow's hand?
Marigolds around the step
　　And rosemary stand,
And then comes Sorrow—
　　And what does Sorrow care
For the rosemary
　　Or the marigolds there?
Am I kin to Sorrow?
　　Are we kin?
That so oft upon my door—
　　Oh, come in!

I

The first rose on my rose-tree
    Budded, bloomed, and shattered,
During sad days when to me
    Nothing mattered.

Grief of grief has drained me clean;
    Still it seems a pity
No one saw,—it must have been
    Very pretty.

II

Let the little birds sing;
  Let the little lambs play;
Spring is here; and so 'tis spring;—
  But not in the old way!

I recall a place
  Where a plum-tree grew;
There you lifted up your face,
  And blossoms covered you.

If the little birds sing,
  And the little lambs play,
Spring is here; and so 'tis spring—
  But not in the old way!

III

All the dog-wood blossoms are underneath the tree!
　　Ere spring was going—ah, spring is gone!
And there comes no summer to the like of you and me,—
　　Blossom time is early, but no fruit sets on.

All the dog-wood blossoms are underneath the tree,
　　Browned at the edges, turned in a day;
And I would with all my heart they trimmed a mound for me,
　　And weeds were tall on all the paths that led that way!

The Shroud

Death, I say, my heart is bowed
　　Unto thine,—O mother!
This red gown will make a shroud
　　Good as any other!

(I, that would not wait to wear
　　My own bridal things,
In a dress dark as my hair
　　Made my answerings.

I, to-night, that till he came
　　Could not, could not wait,
In a gown as bright as flame
　　Held for them the gate.)

Death, I say, my heart is bowed
　　Unto thine,—O mother!
This red gown will make a shroud
　　Good as any other!

The Dream

Love, if I weep it will not matter,
    And if you laugh I shall not care;
Foolish am I to think about it,
    But it is good to feel you there.

Love, in my sleep I dreamed of waking,—
    White and awful the moonlight reached
Over the floor, and somewhere, somewhere
    There was a shutter loose,—it screeched!—

Swung in the wind!—and no wind blowing!—
    I was afraid, and turned to you,
Put out my hand to you for comfort,—
    And you were gone! Cold, cold as dew,

Under my hand the moonlight lay!
    Love, if you laugh I shall not care,
But if I weep it will not matter,—
    Ah, it is good to feel you there!

Indifference

I said,—for Love was laggard, oh, Love was slow to come,—
  "I'll hear his step and know his step when I am warm in bed;
But I'll never leave my pillow, though there be some
  As would let him in—and take him in with tears!" I said.

I lay,—for Love was laggard, oh, he came not until dawn,—
  I lay and listened for his step and could not get to sleep;
And he found me at my window with my big cloak on,
  All sorry with the tears some folks might weep!

Witch-Wife

She is neither pink nor pale,
    And she never will be all mine;
She learned her hands in a fairy-tale,
    And her mouth on a valentine.

She has more hair than she needs;
    In the sun 'tis a woe to me!
And her voice is a string of coloured beads,
    Or steps leading into the sea.

She loves me all that she can,
    And her ways to my ways resign;
But she was not made for any man,
    And she never will be all mine.

Blight

Hard seeds of hate I planted
    That should by now be grown,—
Rough stalks, and from thick stamens
    A poisonous pollen blown,
And odours rank, unbreathable,
    From dark corollas thrown!

At dawn from my damp garden
    I shook the chilly dew;
The thin boughs locked behind me
    That sprang to let me through;
The blossoms slept,—I sought a place
    Where nothing lovely grew.

And there, when day was breaking,
    I knelt and looked around:
The light was near, the silence .
    Was palpitant with sound;
I drew my hate from out my breast
    And thrust it in the ground.

Oh, ye so fiercely tended,
　　Ye little seeds of hate!
I bent above your growing
　　Early and noon and late,
Yet are ye drooped and pitiful,—
　　I cannot rear ye straight!

The sun seeks out my garden,
　　No nook is left in shade,
No mist nor mold nor mildew
　　Endures on any blade,
Sweet rain slants under every bough:
　　Ye falter, and ye fade.

When the Year Grows Old

I cannot but remember
    When the year grows old—
October—November—
    How she disliked the cold!

She used to watch the swallows
    Go down across the sky,
And turn from the window
    With a little sharp sigh.

And often when the brown leaves
    Were brittle on the ground,
And the wind in the chimney
    Made a melancholy sound,

She had a look about her
    That I wish I could forget—
The look of a scared thing
    Sitting in a net!

Oh, beautiful at nightfall
  The soft spitting snow!
And beautiful the bare boughs
  Rubbing to and fro!

But the roaring of the fire,
  And the warmth of fur,
And the boiling of the kettle
  Were beautiful to her!

I cannot but remember
  When the year grows old—
October—November—
  How she disliked the cold!

From *SECOND APRIL*

Υ

Spring

To what purpose, April, do you return again?
Beauty is not enough.
You can no longer quiet me with the redness
Of little leaves opening stickily.
I know what I know.
The sun is hot on my neck as I observe
The spikes of the crocus.
The smell of the earth is good.
It is apparent that there is no death.
But what does that signify?
Not only under ground are the brains of men
Eaten by maggots.
Life in itself
Is nothing,
An empty cup, a flight of uncarpeted stairs.
It is not enough that yearly, down this hill,
April
Comes like an idiot, babbling and strewing flowers.

City Trees

The trees along this city street,
  Save for the traffic and the trains,
Would make a sound as thin and sweet
  As trees in country lanes.

And people standing in their shade
  Out of a shower, undoubtedly
Would hear such music as is made
  Upon a country tree.

Oh, little leaves that are so dumb
  Against the shrieking city air,
I watch you when the wind has come,—
  I know what sound is there.

God had called us, and we came;
   Our loved Earth to ashes left;
Heaven was a neighbour's house,
   Open flung to us, bereft.

Gay the lights of Heaven showed,
   And 'twas God who walked ahead;
Yet I wept along the road,
   Wanting my own house instead.

Wept unseen, unheeded cried,
   "All you things my eyes have kissed,
Fare you well! We meet no more,
   Lovely, lovely tattered mist!

Weary wings that rise and fall
   All day long above the fire!"
(Red with heat was every wall,
   Rough with heat was every wire)

"Fare you well, you little winds
   That the flying embers chase!
Fare you well, you shuddering day,
   With your hands before your face!

And, ah, blackened by strange blight,
   Or to a false sun unfurled,
Now forevermore goodbye,
   All the gardens in the world!

On the windless hills of Heaven,
   That I have no wish to see,
White, eternal lilies stand,
   By a lake of ebony.

But the Earth forevermore
   Is a place where nothing grows,—
Dawn will come, and no bud break;
   Evening, and no blossom close.

Spring will come, and wander slow
    Over an indifferent land,
Stand beside an empty creek,
    Hold a dead seed in her hand."

————

God had called us, and we came,
    But the blessèd road I trod
Was a bitter road to me,
    And at heart I questioned God.

"Though in Heaven," I said, "be all
    That the heart would most desire,
Held Earth naught save souls of sinners
    Worth the saving from a fire?

Withered grass,—the wasted growing!
    Aimless ache of laden boughs!"
Little things God had forgotten
    Called me, from my burning house.

"Though in Heaven," I said, "be all
      That the eye could ask to see,
All the things I ever knew
      Are this blaze in back of me."

"Though in Heaven," I said, "be all
      That the ear could think to lack,
All the things I ever knew
      Are this roaring at my back."

———

It was God who walked ahead,
      Like a shepherd to the fold;
In his footsteps fared the weak,
      And the weary and the old,

Glad enough of gladness over,
      Ready for the peace to be,—
But a thing God had forgotten
      Was the growing bones of me.

And I drew a bit apart,
  And I lagged a bit behind,
And I thought on Peace Eternal,
  Lest He look into my mind:

And I gazed upon the sky,
  And I thought of Heavenly Rest,—
And I slipped away like water
  Through the fingers of the blest!

All their eyes were fixed on Glory,
  Not a glance brushed over me;
"Alleluia! Alleluia!"
  Up the road,—and I was free.

And my heart rose like a freshet,
  And it swept me on before,
Giddy as a whirling stick,
  Till I felt the earth once more.

———

All the Earth was charred and black,
    Fire had swept from pole to pole;
And the bottom of the sea
    Was as brittle as a bowl;

And the timbered mountain-top
    Was as naked as a skull,—
Nothing left, nothing left,
    Of the Earth so beautiful!

"Earth," I said, "how can I leave you?"
    "You are all I have," I said;
"What is left to take my mind up,
    Living always, and you dead?"

"Speak!" I said, "Oh, tell me something!
    Make a sign that I can see!
For a keepsake! To keep always!
    Quick!—before God misses me!"

And I listened for a voice;—
   But my heart was all I heard;
Not a screech-owl, not a loon,
   Not a tree-toad said a word.

And I waited for a sign;—
   Coals and cinders, nothing more;
And a little cloud of smoke
   Floating on a valley floor.

And I peered into the smoke
   Till it rotted, like a fog:—
There, encompassed round by fire,
   Stood a blue-flag in a bog!

Little flames came wading out,
   Straining, straining towards its stem,
But it was so blue and tall
   That it scorned to think of them!

Red and thirsty were their tongues,
    As the tongues of wolves must be,
But it was so blue and tall—
    Oh, I laughed, I cried, to see!

All my heart became a tear,
    All my soul became a tower,
Never loved I anything
    As I loved that tall blue flower!

It was all the little boats
    That had ever sailed the sea,
It was all the little books
    That had gone to school with me;

On its roots like iron claws
    Rearing up so blue and tall,—
It was all the gallant Earth
    With its back against a wall!

In a breath, ere I had breathed,—
  Oh, I laughed, I cried, to see!—
I was kneeling at its side,
  And it leaned its head on me!

———

Crumbling stones and sliding sand
  Is the road to Heaven now;
Icy at my straining knees
  Drags the awful under-tow;

Soon but stepping-stones of dust
  Will the road to Heaven be,—
Father, Son and Holy Ghost,
  Reach a hand and rescue me!

"There—there, my blue-flag flower;
  Hush—hush—go to sleep;
That is only God you hear,
  Counting up His folded sheep!

Lullabye—lullabye—
    That is only God that calls,
Missing me, seeking me,
    Ere the road to nothing falls!

He will set His mighty feet
    Firmly on the sliding sand;
Like a little frightened bird
    I will creep into His hand;

I will tell Him all my grief,
    I will tell Him all my sin;
He will give me half His robe
    For a cloak to wrap you in.

Lullabye—lullabye—"
    Rocks the burnt-out planet free!—
Father, Son and Holy Ghost,
    Reach a hand and rescue me!

————

Ah, the voice of love at last!
　　Lo, at last the face of light!
And the whole of His white robe
　　For a cloak against the night!

And upon my heart asleep
　　All the things I ever knew!—
"Holds Heaven not some cranny, Lord,
　　For a flower so tall and blue?"

All's well and all's well!
　　Gay the lights of Heaven show!
In some moist and Heavenly place
　　We will set it out to grow.

Journey

Ah, could I lay me down in this long grass
And close my eyes, and let the quiet wind
Blow over me—I am so tired, so tired
Of passing pleasant places! All my life,
Following Care along the dusty road,
Have I looked back at loveliness and sighed;
Yet at my hand an unrelenting hand
Tugged ever, and I passed. All my life long
Over my shoulder have I looked at peace;
And now I fain would lie in this long grass
And close my eyes.

          Yet onward!
                    Cat-birds call
Through the long afternoon, and creeks at dusk
Are guttural. Whip-poor-wills wake and cry,
Drawing the twilight close about their throats.
Only my heart makes answer. Eager vines
Go up the rocks and wait; flushed apple-trees

Pause in their dance and break the ring for me;
Dim, shady wood-roads, redolent of fern
And bayberry, that through sweet bevies thread
Of round-faced roses, pink and petulant,
Look back and beckon ere they disappear.
Only my heart, only my heart responds.

Yet, ah, my path is sweet on either side
All through the dragging day,—sharp underfoot
And hot, and like dead mist the dry dust hangs—
But far, oh, far as passionate eye can reach,
And long, ah, long as rapturous eye can cling,
The world is mine: blue hill, still silver lake,
Broad field, bright flower, and the long white road;
A gateless garden, and an open path;
My feet to follow, and my heart to hold.

Eel-Grass

No matter what I say,
　　All that I really love
Is the rain that flattens on the bay,
　　And the eel-grass in the cove;
The jingle-shells that lie and bleach
　　At the tide-line, and the trace
Of higher tides along the beach:
　　Nothing in this place.

There will be rose and rhododendron
    When you are dead and under ground;
Still will be heard from white syringas
    Heavy with bees, a sunny sound;

Still will the tamaracks be raining
    After the rain has ceased, and still
Will there be robins in the stubble,
    Grey sheep upon the warm green hill.

Spring will not ail nor autumn falter;
    Nothing will know that you are gone,—
Saving alone some sullen plough-land
    None but yourself sets foot upon;

Saving the may-weed and the pig-weed
    Nothing will know that you are dead,—
These, and perhaps a useless wagon
    Standing beside some tumbled shed.

Oh, there will pass with your great passing
Little of beauty not your own,—
Only the light from common water,
Only the grace from simple stone!

Ho, Giant! This is I!
I have built me a bean-stalk into your sky!
La,—but it's lovely, up so high!

This is how I came,—I put
Here my knee, there my foot,
Up and up, from shoot to shoot—
And the blessèd bean-stalk thinning
Like the mischief all the time,
Till it took me rocking, spinning,
In a dizzy, sunny circle,
Making angles with the root,
Far and out above the cackle
Of the city I was born in,
Till the little dirty city
In the light so sheer and sunny
Shone as dazzling bright and pretty
As the money that you find
In a dream of finding money—
What a wind! What a morning!—

Till the tiny, shiny city,
When I shot a glance below,
Shaken with a giddy laughter,
Sick and blissfully afraid,
Was a dew-drop on a blade,
And a pair of moments after
Was the whirling guess I made,—
And the wind was like a whip
Cracking past my icy ears,
And my hair stood out behind,
And my eyes were full of tears,
Wide-open and cold,
More tears than they could hold,
The wind was blowing so,
And my teeth were in a row,
Dry and grinning,
And I felt my foot slip,
And I scratched the wind and whined,
And I clutched the stalk and jabbered,
With my eyes shut blind,—
What a wind! What a wind!

Your broad sky, Giant,
Is the shelf of a cupboard;
I make bean-stalks, I'm
A builder, like yourself,
But bean-stalks is my trade,
I couldn't make a shelf,
Don't know how they're made,
Now, a bean-stalk is more pliant—
La, what a climb!

Weeds

White with daisies and red with sorrel
 And empty, empty under the sky!—
Life is a quest and love a quarrel—
 Here is a place for me to lie.

Daisies spring from damnèd seeds,
 And this red fire that here I see
Is a worthless crop of crimson weeds,
 Cursed by farmers thriftily.

But here, unhated for an hour,
 The sorrel runs in ragged flame,
The daisy stands, a bastard flower,
 Like flowers that bear an honest name.

And here a while, where no wind brings
 The baying of a pack athirst,
May sleep the sleep of blessèd things,
 The blood too bright, the brow accurst.

Passer Mortuus Est

Death devours all lovely things:
  Lesbia with her sparrow
Shares the darkness,—presently
  Every bed is narrow.

Unremembered as old rain
  Dries the sheer libation;
And the little petulant hand
  Is an annotation.

After all, my erstwhile dear,
  My no longer cherished,
Need we say it was not love,
  Just because it perished?

If it were only still!—
With far away the shrill
Crying of a cock;
Or the shaken bell
From a cow's throat
Moving through the bushes;
Or the soft shock
Of wizened apples falling
From an old tree
In a forgotten orchard
Upon the hilly rock!

Oh, grey hill,
Where the grazing herd
Licks the purple blossom,
Crops the spiky weed!
Oh, stony pasture,
Where the tall mullein
Stands up so sturdy
On its little seed!

Assault

I had forgotten how the frogs must sound
After a year of silence, else I think
I should not so have ventured forth alone
At dusk upon this unfrequented road.

I am waylaid by Beauty. Who will walk
Between me and the crying of the frogs?
Oh, savage Beauty, suffer me to pass,
That am a timid woman, on her way
From one house to another!

Travel

The railroad track is miles away,
  And the day is loud with voices speaking,
Yet there isn't a train goes by all day
  But I hear its whistle shrieking.

All night there isn't a train goes by,
  Though the night is still for sleep and dreaming,
But I see its cinders red on the sky,
  And hear its engine steaming.

My heart is warm with the friends I make,
  And better friends I'll not be knowing;
Yet there isn't a train I wouldn't take,
  No matter where it's going.

Low-Tide

These wet rocks where the tide has been,
    Barnacled white and weeded brown
And slimed beneath to a beautiful green,
    These wet rocks where the tide went down
Will show again when the tide is high
    Faint and perilous, far from shore,
No place to dream, but a place to die:
    The bottom of the sea once more.

There was a child that wandered through
    A giant's empty house all day,—
House full of wonderful things and new,
    But no fit place for a child to play!

Song of a Second April

April this year, not otherwise
   Than April of a year ago,
Is full of whispers, full of sighs,
   Of dazzling mud and dingy snow;
   Hepaticas that pleased you so
Are here again, and butterflies.

There rings a hammering all day,
   And shingles lie about the doors;
In orchards near and far away
   The grey wood-pecker taps and bores;
   And men are merry at their chores,
And children earnest at their play.

The larger streams run still and deep,
   Noisy and swift the small brooks run;
Among the mullein stalks the sheep
   Go up the hillside in the sun,
   Pensively,—only you are gone,
You that alone I cared to keep.

Rosemary

For the sake of some things
    That be now no more
I will strew rushes
    On my chamber-floor,
I will plant bergamot
    At my kitchen-door.

For the sake of dim things
    That were once so plain
I will set a barrel
    Out to catch the rain,
I will hang an iron pot
    On an iron crane.

Many things be dead and gone
    That were brave and gay;
For the sake of these things
    I will learn to say,
"An it please you, gentle sirs,"
    "Alack!" and "Well-a-day!"

The Poet and His Book

Down, you mongrel, Death!
  Back into your kennel!
I have stolen breath
  In a stalk of fennel!
You shall scratch and you shall whine
  Many a night, and you shall worry
  Many a bone, before you bury
One sweet bone of mine!

When shall I be dead?
  When my flesh is withered,
And above my head
  Yellow pollen gathered
All the empty afternoon?
  When sweet lovers pause and wonder
  Who am I that lie thereunder,
Hidden from the moon?

This my personal death?—
  That my lungs be failing
To inhale the breath

Others are exhaling?
This my subtle spirit's end?—
    Ah, when the thawed winter splashes
    Over these chance dust and ashes,
Weep not me, my friend!

Me, by no means dead
    In that hour, but surely
When this book, unread,
    Rots to earth obscurely,
And no more to any breast,
    Close against the clamorous swelling
    Of the thing there is no telling,
Are these pages pressed!

When this book is mould,
    And a book of many
Waiting to be sold
    For a casual penny,
In a little open case,
    In a street unclean and cluttered,
    Where a heavy mud is spattered
From the passing drays,

Stranger, pause and look;
   From the dust of ages
Lift this little book,
   Turn the tattered pages,
Read me, do not let me die!
   Search the fading letters, finding
   Steadfast in the broken binding
All that once was I!

When these veins are weeds,
   When these hollowed sockets
Watch the rooty seeds
   Bursting down like rockets,
And surmise the spring again,
   Or, remote in that black cupboard,
   Watch the pink worms writhing upward
At the smell of rain,

Boys and girls that lie
   Whispering in the hedges,
Do not let me die,
   Mix me with your pledges;
Boys and girls that slowly walk

In the woods, and weep, and quarrel,
    Staring past the pink wild laurel,
Mix me with your talk,

Do not let me die!
    Farmers at your raking,
When the sun is high,
    While the hay is making,
When, along the stubble strewn,
    Withering on their stalks uneaten,
    Strawberries turn dark and sweeten
In the lapse of noon;

Shepherds on the hills,
    In the pastures, drowsing
To the tinkling bells
    Of the brown sheep browsing;
Sailors crying through the storm;
    Scholars at your study; hunters
    Lost amid the whirling winter's
Whiteness uniform;

Men that long for sleep;
　　Men that wake and revel;—
If an old song leap
　　To your senses' level
At such moments, may it be
　　Sometimes, though a moment only,
　　Some forgotten, quaint and homely
Vehicle of me!

Women at your toil,
　　Women at your leisure
Till the kettle boil,
　　Snatch of me your pleasure,
Where the broom-straw marks the leaf;
　　Women quiet with your weeping
　　Lest you wake a workman sleeping,
Mix me with your grief!

Boys and girls that steal
　　From the shocking laughter
Of the old, to kneel
　　By a dripping rafter

Under the discoloured eaves,
    Out of trunks with hingeless covers
    Lifting tales of saints and lovers,
Travellers, goblins, thieves,

Suns that shine by night,
    Mountains made from valleys,—
Bear me to the light,
    Flat upon your bellies
By the webby window lie,
    Where the little flies are crawling,
    Read me, margin me with scrawling,
Do not let me die!

Sexton, ply your trade!
    In a shower of gravel
Stamp upon your spade!
    Many a rose shall ravel,
Many a metal wreath shall rust
    In the rain, and I go singing
    Through the lots where you are flinging
Yellow clay on dust!

Alms

My heart is what it was before,
    A house where people come and go;
But it is winter with your love,
    The sashes are beset with snow.

I light the lamp and lay the cloth,
    I blow the coals to blaze again;
But it is winter with your love,
    The frost is thick upon the pane.

I know a winter when it comes:
    The leaves are listless on the boughs;
I watched your love a little while,
    And brought my plants into the house.

I water them and turn them south,
    I snap the dead brown from the stem;
But it is winter with your love,
    I only tend and water them.

There was a time I stood and watched
    The small, ill-natured sparrows' fray;
I loved the beggar that I fed,
    I cared for what he had to say,

I stood and watched him out of sight;
    Today I reach around the door
And set a bowl upon the step;
    My heart is what it was before,

But it is winter with your love;
    I scatter crumbs upon the sill,
And close the window,—and the birds
    May take or leave them, as they will.

Inland

People that build their houses inland,
   People that buy a plot of ground
Shaped like a house, and build a house there,
   Far from the sea-board, far from the sound

Of water sucking the hollow ledges,
   Tons of water striking the shore,—
What do they long for, as I long for
   One salt smell of the sea once more?

People the waves have not awakened,
   Spanking the boats at the harbour's head,
What do they long for, as I long for,—
   Starting up in my inland bed,

Beating the narrow walls, and finding
   Neither a window nor a door,
Screaming to God for death by drowning,--
   One salt taste of the sea once more?

To a Poet that Died Young

Minstrel, what have you to do
With this man that, after you,
Sharing not your happy fate,
Sat as England's Laureate?
Vainly, in these iron days,
Strives the poet in your praise,
Minstrel, by whose singing side
Beauty walked, until you died.

Still, though none should hark again,
Drones the blue-fly in the pane,
Thickly crusts the blackest moss,
Blows the rose its musk across,
Floats the boat that is forgot
None the less to Camelot.

Many a bard's untimely death
Lends unto his verses breath;
Here's a song was never sung:
Growing old is dying young.

Minstrel, what is this to you:
That a man you never knew,
When your grave was far and green,
Sat and gossipped with a queen?

Thalia knows how rare a thing
Is it, to grow old and sing,
When the brown and tepid tide
Closes in on every side.
Who shall say if Shelley's gold
Had withstood it to grow old?

Wraith

"Thin Rain, whom are you haunting,
  That you haunt my door?"
Surely it is not I she's wanting . . .
  Someone living here before!
"Nobody's in the house but me:
You may come in if you like and see."

Thin as thread, with exquisite fingers,—
  Ever seen her, any of you?—
Grey shawl, and leaning on the wind,
  And the garden showing through?

Glimmering eyes,—and silent, mostly,
  Sort of a whisper, sort of a purr,
Asking something, asking it over,
  If you get a sound from her.—

Ever see her, any of you?—
  Strangest thing I've ever known,—
Every night since I moved in,
  And I came to be alone.

93

"Thin Rain, hush with your knocking!
    You may not come in!
This is I that you hear rocking;
    Nobody's with me, nor has been!"

Curious, how she tried the window,—
    Odd, the way she tries the door,—
Wonder just what sort of people
    Could have had this house before . . .

94

Ebb

I know what my heart is like
   Since your love died:
It is like a hollow ledge
Holding a little pool
   Left there by the tide,
   A little tepid pool,
Drying inward from the edge.

Elaine

Oh, come again to Astolat!
  I will not ask you to be kind.
And you may go when you will go,
  And I will stay behind.

I will not say how dear you are,
  Or ask you if you hold me dear,
Or trouble you with things for you,
  The way I did last year.

So still the orchard, Lancelot,
  So very still the lake shall be,
You could not guess—though you should guess—
  What is become of me.

So wide shall be the garden-walk,
  The garden-seat so very wide,
You needs must think—if you should think—
  The lily maid had died.

Save that, a little way away,
    I'd watch you for a little while,
To see you speak, the way you speak,
    And smile,—if you should smile.

Burial

Mine is a body that should die at sea!
   And have for a grave, instead of a grave
Six feet deep and the length of me,
   All the water that is under the wave!

And terrible fishes to seize my flesh,
   Such as a living man might fear,
And eat me while I am firm and fresh,—
   Not wait till I've been dead for a year!

Mariposa

Butterflies are white and blue
In this field we wander through.
Suffer me to take your hand.
Death comes in a day or two.

All the things we ever knew
Will be ashes in that hour:
Mark the transient butterfly,
How he hangs upon the flower.

Suffer me to take your hand.
Suffer me to cherish you
Till the dawn is in the sky.
Whether I be false or true,
Death comes in a day or two.

The Little Hill

Oh, here the air is sweet and still,
　　And soft's the grass to lie on;
And far away's the little hill
　　They took for Christ to die on.

And there's a hill across the brook,
　　And down the brook's another;
But, oh, the little hill they took,—
　　I think I am its mother!

The moon that saw Gethsemane,
　　I watch it rise and set;
It has so many things to see,
　　They help it to forget.

But little hills that sit at home
　　So many hundred years,
Remember Greece, remember Rome,
　　Remember Mary's tears.

And far away in Palestine,
  Sadder than any other,
Grieves still the hill that I call mine,—
  I think I am its mother.

Doubt no more that Oberon—
Never doubt that Pan
Lived, and played a reed, and ran
After nymphs in a dark forest,
In the merry, credulous days,—
Lived, and led a fairy band
Over the indulgent land!

Ah, for in this dourest, sorest
Age man's eye has looked upon,
Death to fauns and death to fays,
Still the dog-wood dares to raise—
Healthy tree, with trunk and root—
Ivory bowls that bear no fruit,
And the starlings and the jays—
Birds that cannot even sing—
Dare to come again in spring!

Lament

Listen, children:
Your father is dead.
From his old coats
I'll make you little jackets;
I'll make you little trousers
From his old pants.
There'll be in his pockets
Things he used to put there,
Keys and pennies
Covered with tobacco;
Dan shall have the pennies
To save in his bank;
Anne shall have the keys
To make a pretty noise with.
Life must go on,
And the dead be forgotten;
Life must go on,
Though good men die;

Anne, eat your breakfast;
Dan, take your medicine;
Life must go on;
I forget just why.

Exiled

Searching my heart for its true sorrow,
  This is the thing I find to be:
That I am weary of words and people,
  Sick of the city, wanting the sea;

Wanting the sticky, salty sweetness
  Of the strong wind and shattered spray;
Wanting the loud sound and the soft sound
  Of the big surf that breaks all day.

Always before about my dooryard,
  Marking the reach of the winter sea,
Rooted in sand and dragging drift-wood,
  Straggled the purple wild sweet-pea;

Always I climbed the wave at morning,
  Shook the sand from my shoes at night,
That now am caught beneath great buildings,
  Stricken with noise, confused with light.

If I could hear the green piles groaning
    Under the windy wooden piers,
See once again the bobbing barrels,
    And the black sticks that fence the weirs,

If I could see the weedy mussels
    Crusting the wrecked and rotting hulls,
Hear once again the hungry crying
    Overhead, of the wheeling gulls,

Feel once again the shanty straining
    Under the turning of the tide,
Fear once again the rising freshet,
    Dread the bell in the fog outside,

I should be happy!—that was happy
    All day long on the coast of Maine;
I have a need to hold and handle
    Shells and anchors and ships again!

I should be happy . . . that am happy
    Never at all since I came here.
I am too long away from water.
    I have a need of water near.

The Death of Autumn

When reeds are dead and a straw to thatch the marshes,
And feathered pampas-grass rides into the wind
Like agèd warriors westward, tragic, thinned
Of half their tribe; and over the flattened rushes,
Stripped of its secret, open, stark and bleak,
Blackens afar the half-forgotten creek,—
Then leans on me the weight of the year, and crushes
My heart. I know that Beauty must ail and die,
And will be born again,—but ah, to see
Beauty stiffened, staring up at the sky!
Oh, Autumn! Autumn!—What is the Spring to me?

Aye, but she?
Your other sister and my other soul,
Grave Silence, lovelier
Than the three loveliest maidens, what of her?
Clio, not you,
Not you, Calliope,
Nor all your wanton line,
Not Great Apollo's self shall comfort me
For Silence once departed,
For her the cool-tongued, her the tranquil-hearted,
Whom evermore I follow wistfully,
Wandering Heaven and Earth and Hell and the four seasons
    through;
Thalia, not you,
Not you, Melpomene,
Not your incomparable feet, O thin Terpsichore,
I seek in this great hall,
But one more pale, more pensive, most beloved of you all.

I seek her from afar.
I come from temples where her altars are;

From groves that bear her name;—
Noisy with stricken victims now and sacrificial flame,
And cymbals struck on high and strident faces
Obstreperous in her praise
They neither love nor know,
A goddess of gone days,
Departed long ago,
Abandoning the invaded shrines and fanes
Of her old sanctuary,
A deity obscure and legendary,
Of whom there now remains,
For sages to decipher and priests to garble,
Only and for a little while her letters wedged in marble;
Which even now, behold, the friendly mumbling rain erases,
And the inarticulate snow,
Leaving at last of her least signs and traces
None whatsoever, nor whither she is vanished from these places.

"She will love well," I said,
"If love be of that heart inhabiter,
The flowers of the dead:
The red anemone that with no sound

Moves in the wind; and from another wound
That sprang, the heavily-sweet blue hyacinth,
That blossoms underground;
And sallow poppies, will be dear to her.
And will not Silence know
In the black shade of what obsidian steep
Stiffens the white narcissus numb with sleep?
(Seed which Demeter's daughter bore from home,
Uptorn by desperate fingers long ago,
Reluctant even as she,
Undone Persephone,
And even as she, set out again to grow,
In twilight, in perdition's lean and inauspicious loam)
She will love well," I said,
"The flowers of the dead.
Where dark Persephone the winter round,
Uncomforted for home, uncomforted,
Lacking a sunny southern slope in northern Sicily,
With sullen pupils focussed on a dream
Stares on the stagnant stream
That moats the unequivocable battlements of Hell,
There, there will she be found,
She that is Beauty veiled from men and Music in a swound."

"I long for Silence as they long for breath
Whose helpless nostrils drink the bitter sea;
What thing can be
So stout, what so redoubtable, in Death
What fury, what considerable rage, if only she,
Upon whose icy breast,
Unquestioned, uncaressed,
One time I lay,
And whom always I lack,
Even to this day,
Being by no means from that frigid bosom weaned away,
If only she therewith be given me back?"

I sought her down that dolourous labyrinth,
Wherein no shaft of sunlight ever fell,
And in among the bloodless everywhere
I sought her; but the air,
Breathed many times and spent,
Was fretful with a whispering discontent;
And questioning me, importuning me to tell
Some slightest tidings of the light of day they know no more,
Plucking my sleeve, the eager shades were with me where I went.
I paused at every grievous door,

And harked a moment, holding up my hand,—and for a space
A hush was on them, while they watched my face;
And then they fell a-whispering as before;
So that I smiled at them and left them, seeing she was not there.

I sought her, too,
Among the upper gods, although I knew
She was not like to be where feasting is,
Nor near to Heaven's lord,
Being a thing abhorred
And shunned of him, although a child of his,
(Not yours, not yours: to you she owes not breath,
Mother of Song, being sown of Zeus upon a dream of Death).

Fearing to pass unvisited some place
And later learn, too late, how all the while,
With her still face,
She had been standing there and seen me pass, without a smile,
I sought her even to the sagging board whereat
The stout immortals sat;

But such a laughter shook the mighty hall
No one could hear me say:
Had she been seen upon the Hill that day?
And no one knew at all
How long I stood, or when at last I sighed and went away.

There is a garden lying in a lull
Between the mountains and the mountainous sea . . .
I know not where; but which a dream diurnal
Paints on my lids a moment, till the hull
Be lifted from the kernel,
And Slumber fed to me.
Your foot-print is not there, Mnemosene,
Though it would seem a ruined place and after
Your lichenous heart, being full
Of broken columns, caryatides
Thrown to the earth and fallen forward on their jointless knees;
And urns funereal altered into dust
Minuter than the ashes of the dead;
And Psyche's lamp out of the earth up-thrust,
Dripping itself in marble oil on what was once the bed
Of Love, and his young body asleep, but now is dust instead.

There twists the bitter-sweet, the white wisteria
Fastens its fingers in the strangling wall,
And the wide crannies quicken with bright weeds;
There dumbly like a worm all day the still white orchid feeds;
But never an echo of your daughters' laughter
Is there, nor any sign of you at all
Swells fungous from the rotten bough, grey mother of Pieria!

Only her shadow once upon a stone
I saw,—and, lo, the shadow and the garden, too, were gone.

I tell you, you have done her body an ill,
You chatterers, you noisy crew!
She is not anywhere!
I sought her in deep Hell;
And through the world as well;
I thought of Heaven and I sought her there:
Above nor under ground
Is Silence to be found,
That was the very warp and woof of you,
Lovely before your songs began and after they were through!
Oh, say if on this hill

114

Somewhere your sister's body lies in death,
So I may follow there, and make a wreath
Of my locked hands, that on her quiet breast
Shall lie till age has withered them!

                                (Ah, sweetly from the rest
I see
Turn and consider me
Compassionate Euterpe!)

"There is a gate beyond the gate of Death,
Beyond the gate of everlasting Life,
Beyond the gates of Heaven and Hell," she saith,
"Whereon but to believe is horror!
Whereon to meditate engendereth
Even in deathless spirits such as I
A tumult in the breath,
A chilling of the inexhaustible blood
Even in my veins that never will be dry,
And in the austere, divine monotony
That is my being, the madness of an unaccustomed mood.

This is her province whom you lack and seek:
And seek her not elsewhere.
Hell is a thoroughfare
For pilgrims,—Herakles,
And he that loved Euridice too well,
Have walked therein; and many more than these;
And witnessed the desire and the despair
Of souls that passed reluctantly and sicken for the air;
You, too, have entered Hell,
And issued thence; but thence whereof I speak
None has returned;—for thither fury brings
Only the driven ghosts of them that flee before all things.
Oblivion is the name of this abode: and she is there."

O radiant Song! O gracious Memory!
Be long upon this height
I shall not climb again!
I know the way you mean,—the little night,
And the long empty day,—never to see
Again the angry light,
Or hear the hungry noises cry my brain!

Ah, but she,
Your other sister and my other soul,
She shall again be mine.
And I shall drink her from a silver bowl,
A chilly thin green wine,
Not bitter to the taste,
Not sweet,
Not of your press, O restless, clamourous Nine,—
To foam beneath the frantic hoofs of mirth—
But savouring faintly of the acid earth
And trod by pensive feet
From perfect clusters ripened without haste
Out of the urgent heat
In some clear glimmering vaulted twilight under the odourous vine.

Lift up your lyres! Sing on!
But as for me, I seek your sister whither she *is* gone.

Memorial to D. C.
(Vassar College, 1918)

O, loveliest throat of all sweet throats,
Where now no more the music is,
With hands that wrote you little notes
I write you little elegies!

I

Epitaph

Heap not on this mound
    Roses that she loved so well;
Why bewilder her with roses,
    That she cannot see or smell?

She is happy where she lies
With the dust upon her eyes.

II

Prayer to Persephone

Be to her, Persephone,
All the things I might not be;
Take her head upon your knee.
She that was so proud and wild,
Flippant, arrogant and free,
She that had no need of me,
Is a little lonely child
Lost in Hell,—Persephone,
Take her head upon your knee;
Say to her, "My dear, my dear,
It is not so dreadful here."

III

Chorus

Give away her gowns,
Give away her shoes;
She has no more use
For her fragrant gowns;
Take them all down,
Blue, green, blue,
Lilac, pink, blue,
From their padded hangers;
She will dance no more
In her narrow shoes;
Sweep her narrow shoes
From the closet floor.

IV

Dirge

Boys and girls that held her dear,
   Do your weeping now;
All you loved of her lies here.

Brought to earth the arrogant brow,
   And the withering tongue
Chastened; do your weeping now.

Sing whatever songs are sung,
   Wind whatever wreath,
For a playmate perished young,
   For a spirit spent in death.

Boys and girls that held her dear,
All you loved of her lies here.

V

Elegy

Let them bury your big eyes
In the secret earth securely,
Your thin fingers, and your fair,
Soft, indefinite-coloured hair,—
All of these in some way, surely,
From the secret earth shall rise;
Not for these I sit and stare,
Broken and bereft completely:
Your young flesh that sat so neatly
On your little bones will sweetly
Blossom in the air.

But your voice . . . never the rushing
Of a river underground,
Not the rising of the wind
In the trees before the rain,
Not the woodcock's watery call,
Not the note the white-throat utters,
Not the feet of children pushing

Yellow leaves along the gutters
In the blue and bitter fall,
Shall content my musing mind
For the beauty of that sound
That in no new way at all
Ever will be heard again.

Sweetly through the sappy stalk
Of the vigourous weed,
Holding all it held before,
Cherished by the faithful sun,
On and on eternally
Shall your altered fluid run,
Bud and bloom and go to seed:
But your singing days are done;
But the music of your talk
Never shall the chemistry
Of the secret earth restore.
All your lovely words are spoken.
Once the ivory box is broken,
Beats the golden bird no more.

———

Wild Swans

I looked in my heart while the wild swans went over.
And what did I see I had not seen before?
Only a question less or a question more;
Nothing to match the flight of wild birds flying.
Tiresome heart, forever living and dying,
House without air, I leave you and lock your door.
Wild swans, come over the town, come over
The town again, trailing your legs and crying!

From *A FEW FIGS FROM THISTLES*

Y

First Fig

My candle burns at both ends;
    It will not last the night;
But ah, my foes, and oh, my friends—
    It gives a lovely light!

Second Fig

Safe upon the solid rock the ugly houses stand:
Come and see my shining palace built upon the sand!

Recuerdo

We were very tired, we were very merry—
We had gone back and forth all night on the ferry.
It was bare and bright, and smelled like a stable—
But we looked into a fire, we leaned across a table,
We lay on a hill-top underneath the moon;
And the whistles kept blowing, and the dawn came soon.

We were very tired, we were very merry—
We had gone back and forth all night on the ferry;
And you ate an apple, and I ate a pear,
From a dozen of each we had bought somewhere;
And the sky went wan, and the wind came cold,
And the sun rose dripping, a bucketful of gold.

We were very tired, we were very merry,
We had gone back and forth all night on the ferry.
We hailed, "Good morrow, mother!" to a shawl-covered head,
And bought a morning paper, which neither of us read;
And she wept, "God bless you!" for the apples and pears,
And we gave her all our money but our subway fares.

Thursday

And if I loved you Wednesday,
    Well, what is that to you?
I do not love you Thursday—
    So much is true.

And why you come complaining
    Is more than I can see.
I loved you Wednesday,—yes—but what
    Is that to me?

To the Not Impossible Him

How shall I know, unless I go
  To Cairo and Cathay,
Whether or not this blessèd spot
  Is blest in every way?

Now it may be, the flower for me
  Is this beneath my nose;
How shall I tell, unless I smell
  The Carthaginian rose?

The fabric of my faithful love
  No power shall dim or ravel
Whilst I stay here,—but oh, my dear,
  If I should ever travel!

Macdougal Street

As I went walking up and down to take the evening air,
  (Sweet to meet upon the street, why must I be so shy?)
I saw him lay his hand upon her torn black hair;
  ("Little dirty Latin child, let the lady by!")

The women squatting on the stoops were slovenly and fat,
  (Lay me out in organdie, lay me out in lawn!)
And everywhere I stepped there was a baby or a cat;
  (Lord God in Heaven, will it never be dawn?)

The fruit-carts and clam-carts were ribald as a fair,
  (Pink nets and wet shells trodden under heel)
She had haggled from the fruit-man of his rotting ware;
  (I shall never get to sleep, the way I feel!)

He walked like a king through the filth and the clutter,
  (Sweet to meet upon the street, why did you glance me by?)
But he caught the quaint Italian quip she flung him from the
      gutter;
  (What can there be to cry about that I should lie and cry?)

He laid his darling hand upon her little black head,
 (I wish I were a ragged child with ear-rings in my ears!)
And he said she was a baggage to have said what she had said;
 (Truly I shall be ill unless I stop these tears!)

The Singing-Woman from the Wood's Edge

What should I be but a prophet and a liar,
Whose mother was a leprechaun, whose father was a friar?
Teethed on a crucifix and cradled under water,
What should I be but the fiend's god-daughter?

And who should be my playmates but the adder and the frog,
That was got beneath a furze-bush and born in a bog?
And what should be my singing, that was christened at an altar,
But Aves and Credos and Psalms out of the Psalter?

You will see such webs on the wet grass, maybe,
As a pixie-mother weaves for her baby,
You will find such flame at the wave's weedy ebb
As flashes in the meshes of a mer-mother's web,

But there comes to birth no common spawn
From the love of a priest for a leprechaun,
And you never have seen and you never will see
Such things as the things that swaddled me!

After all's said and after all's done,
What should I be but a harlot and a nun?

In through the bushes, on any foggy day,
My Da would come a-swishing of the drops away,
With a prayer for my death and a groan for my birth,
A-mumbling of his beads for all that he was worth.

And there'd sit my Ma, with her knees beneath her chin,
A-looking in his face and a-drinking of it in,
And a-marking in the moss some funny little saying
That would mean just the opposite of all that he was praying!

He taught me the holy-talk of Vesper and of Matin,
He heard me my Greek and he heard me my Latin,
He blessed me and crossed me to keep my soul from evil,
And we watched him out of sight, and we conjured up the devil!

Oh, the things I haven't seen and the things I haven't known,
What with hedges and ditches till after I was grown,
And yanked both ways by my mother and my father,
With a "Which would you better?" and a "Which would you
        rather?"

With him for a sire and her for a dam,
What should I be but just what I am?

She Is Overheard Singing

Oh, Prue she has a patient man,
    And Joan a gentle lover,
And Agatha's Arth' is a hug-the-hearth, —
    But my true love's a rover!

Mig, her man's as good as cheese
    And honest as a briar,
Sue tells her love what he's thinking of, —
    But my dear lad's a liar!

Oh, Sue and Prue and Agatha
    Are thick with Mig and Joan!
They bite their threads and shake their heads
    And gnaw my name like a bone;

And Prue says, "Mine's a patient man,
    As never snaps me up,"
And Agatha, "Arth' is a hug-the-hearth,
    Could live content in a cup;"

Sue's man's mind is like good jell—
    All one colour, and clear—
And Mig's no call to think at all
    What's to come next year,

While Joan makes boast of a gentle lad,
    That's troubled with that and this;—
But they all would give the life they live
    For a look from the man I kiss!

Cold he slants his eyes about,
    And few enough's his choice,—
Though he'd slip me clean for a nun, or a queen,
    Or a beggar with knots in her voice,—

And Agatha will turn awake
    While her good man sleeps sound,
And Mig and Sue and Joan and Prue
    Will hear the clock strike round,

For Prue she has a patient man,
    As asks not when or why,

And Mig and Sue have naught to do
   But peep who's passing by,

Joan is paired with a putterer
   That bastes and tastes and salts,
And Agatha's Arth' is a hug-the-hearth,—
   But my true love is false!

The Unexplorer

There was a road ran past our house
Too lovely to explore.
I asked my mother once—she said
That if you followed where it led
It brought you to the milk-man's door.
(That's why I have not travelled more.)

Grown-up

Was it for this I uttered prayers,
And sobbed and cursed and kicked the stairs,
That now, domestic as a plate,
I should retire at half-past eight?

The Penitent

I had a little Sorrow,
  Born of a little Sin,
I found a room all damp with gloom
  And shut us all within;
And, "Little Sorrow, weep," said I,
"And, Little Sin, pray God to die,
And I upon the floor will lie
  And think how bad I've been!"

Alas for pious planning—
  It mattered not a whit!
As far as gloom went in that room,
  The lamp might have been lit!
My little Sorrow would not weep,
My little Sin would go to sleep—
To save my soul I could not keep
  My graceless mind on it!

So up I got in anger,
    And took a book I had,
And put a ribbon on my hair
    To please a passing lad,
And, "One thing there's no getting by—
I've been a wicked girl," said I;
"But if I can't be sorry, why,
    I might as well be glad!"

Daphne

Why do you follow me?—
Any moment I can be
Nothing but a laurel-tree.

Any moment of the chase
I can leave you in my place
A pink bough for your embrace.

Yet if over hill and hollow
Still it is your will to follow,
I am off;—to heel, Apollo!

Portrait by a Neighbour

Before she has her floor swept
   Or her dishes done,
Any day you'll find her
   A-sunning in the sun!

It's long after midnight
   Her key's in the lock,
And you never see her chimney smoke
   Till past ten o'clock!

She digs in her garden
   With a shovel and a spoon,
She weeds her lazy lettuce
   By the light of the moon,

She walks up the walk
   Like a woman in a dream,
She forgets she borrowed butter
   And pays you back cream!

Her lawn looks like a meadow,
And if she mows the place
She leaves the clover standing
And the Queen Anne's lace!

Midnight Oil

Cut if you will, with Sleep's dull knife,
    Each day to half its length, my friend,—
The years that Time takes off *my* life,
    He'll take from off the other end!

The Merry Maid

Oh, I am grown so free from care
   Since my heart broke!
I set my throat against the air,
   I laugh at simple folk!

There's little kind and little fair
   Is worth its weight in smoke
To me, that's grown so free from care
   Since my heart broke!

Lass, if to sleep you would repair
   As peaceful as you woke,
Best not besiege your lover there
   For just the words he spoke
To me, that's grown so free from care
   Since my heart broke!

To Kathleen

Still must the poet as of old,
In barren attic bleak and cold,
Starve, freeze, and fashion verses to
Such things as flowers and song and you;

Still as of old his being give
In Beauty's name, while she may live,
Beauty that may not die as long
As there are flowers and you and song.

To S. M.

(If He Should Lie A-dying)

I am not willing you should go
Into the earth, where Helen went;
She is awake by now, I know.
Where Cleopatra's anklets rust
You will not lie with my consent;
And Sappho is a roving dust;
Cressid could love again; Dido,
Rotted in state, is restless still:
You leave me much against my will.

The Philosopher

And what are you that, wanting you,
  I should be kept awake
As many nights as there are days
  With weeping for your sake?

And what are you that, missing you,
  As many days as crawl
I should be listening to the wind
  And looking at the wall?

I know a man that's a braver man
  And twenty men as kind,
And what are you, that you should be
  The one man in my mind?

Yet women's ways are witless ways,
  As any sage will tell,—
And what am I, that I should love
  So wisely and so well?

From *THE HARP-WEAVER AND OTHER POEMS*

Υ

My Heart, Being Hungry

My heart, being hungry, feeds on food
    The fat of heart despise.
Beauty where beauty never stood,
    And sweet where no sweet lies
I gather to my querulous need,
Having a growing heart to feed.

It may be, when my heart is dull,
    Having attained its girth,
I shall not find so beautiful
    The meagre shapes of earth,
Nor linger in the rain to mark
The smell of tansy through the dark.

Autumn Chant

Now the autumn shudders
    In the rose's root.
Far and wide the ladders
    Lean among the fruit.

Now the autumn clambers
    Up the trellised frame,
And the rose remembers
    The dust from which it came.

Brighter than the blossom
    On the rose's bough
Sits the wizened, orange,
    Bitter berry now;

Beauty never slumbers;
    All is in her name;
But the rose remembers
    The dust from which it came.

Nuit Blanche

I am a shepherd of those sheep
   That climb a wall by night,
One after one, until I sleep,
   Or the black pane goes white.
Because of which I cannot see
   A flock upon a hill,
But doubts come tittering up to me
   That should by day be still.
And childish griefs I have outgrown
   Into my eyes are thrust,
Till my dull tears go dropping down
   Like lead into the dust.

Three Songs from "The Lamp and the Bell"

I

Oh, little rose tree, bloom!
Summer is nearly over.
The dahlias bleed, and the phlox is seed.
Nothing's left of the clover.
And the path of the poppy no one knows.
I would blossom if I were a rose.

Summer, for all your guile,
Will brown in a week to Autumn,
And launched leaves throw a shadow below
Over the brook's clear bottom,—
And the chariest bud the year can boast
Be brought to bloom by the chastening frost.

II

Beat me a crown of bluer metal;
   Fret it with stones of a foreign style:
The heart grows weary after a little
   Of what it loved for a little while.

Weave me a robe of richer fibre;
   Pattern its web with a rare device:
Give away to the child of a neighbour
   This gold gown I was glad in twice.

But buy me a singer to sing one song—
   Song about nothing—song about sheep—
Over and over, all day long;
   Patch me again my thread-bare sleep.

III

Rain comes down
And hushes the town.
And where is the voice that I heard crying?

Snow settles
Over the nettles.
Where is the voice that I heard crying?

Sand at last
On the drifting mast.
And where is the voice that I heard crying?

Earth now
On the busy brow.
And where is the voice that I heard crying?

The Wood Road

If I were to walk this way
   Hand in hand with Grief,
I should mark that maple-spray
   Coming into leaf.
I should note how the old burrs
   Rot upon the ground.
Yes, though Grief should know me hers
   While the world goes round,
It could not in truth be said
   This was lost on me:
A rock-maple showing red,
   Burrs beneath a tree.

Feast

I drank at every vine.
　　The last was like the first.
I came upon no wine
　　So wonderful as thirst.

I gnawed at every root.
　　I ate of every plant.
I came upon no fruit
　　So wonderful as want.

Feed the grape and bean
　　To the vintner and monger;
I will lie down lean
　　With my thirst and my hunger.

Souvenir

Just a rainy day or two
In a windy tower,
That was all I had of you—
Saving half an hour

Marred by greeting passing groups
In a cinder walk,
Near some naked blackberry hoops
Dim with purple chalk.

I remember three or four
Things you said in spite,
And an ugly coat you wore,
Plaided black and white.

Just a rainy day or two
And a bitter word.
Why do I remember you
As a singing bird?

Scrub

If I grow bitterly,
Like a gnarled and stunted tree,
Bearing harshly of my youth
Puckered fruit that sears the mouth;
If I make of my drawn boughs
An inhospitable house,
Out of which I never pry
Towards the water and the sky,
Under which I stand and hide
And hear the day go by outside;
It is that a wind too strong
Bent my back when I was young,
It is that I fear the rain
Lest it blister me again.

Spring rides no horses down the hill,
But comes on foot, a goose-girl still.
And all the loveliest things there be
Come simply, so, it seems to me.
If ever I said, in grief or pride,
I tired of honest things, I lied;
And should be cursed forevermore
With Love in laces, like a whore,
And neighbours cold, and friends unsteady,
And Spring on horseback, like a lady!

The Dragonfly

I wound myself in a white cocoon of singing,
   All day long in the brook's uneven bed,
   Measuring out my soul in a mucous thread;
Dimly now to the brook's green bottom clinging,
   Men behold me, a worm spun-out and dead,
Walled in an iron house of silky singing.

Nevertheless at length, O reedy shallows,
   Not as a plodding nose to the slimy stem,
   But as a brazen wing with a spangled hem,
Over the jewel-weed and the pink marshmallows,
   Free of these and making a song of them,
I shall arise, and a song of the reedy shallows!

Departure

It's little I care what path I take,
And where it leads it's little I care;
But out of this house, lest my heart break,
I must go, and off somewhere.

It's little I know what's in my heart,
What's in my mind it's little I know,
But there's that in me must up and start,
And it's little I care where my feet go.

I wish I could walk for a day and a night,
And find me at dawn in a desolate place
With never the rut of a road in sight,
Nor the roof of a house, nor the eyes of a face.

I wish I could walk till my blood should spout,
And drop me, never to stir again,
On a shore that is wide, for the tide is out,
And the weedy rocks are bare to the rain.

But dump or dock, where the path I take
Brings up, it's little enough I care;
And it's little I'd mind the fuss they'll make,
Huddled dead in a ditch somewhere.

"Is something the matter, dear," she said,
"That you sit at your work so silently?"
"No, mother, no, 'twas a knot in my thread.
There goes the kettle, I'll make the tea."

The Return from Town

As I sat down by Saddle Stream
   To bathe my dusty feet there,
A boy was standing on the bridge
   Any girl would meet there.

As I went over Woody Knob
   And dipped into the hollow,
A youth was coming up the hill
   Any maid would follow.

Then in I turned at my own gate,—
   And nothing to be sad for—
To such a man as any wife
   Would pass a pretty lad for.

A Visit to the Asylum

Once from a big, big building,
When I was small, small,
The queer folk in the windows
Would smile at me and call.

And in the hard wee gardens
Such pleasant men would hoe:
"Sir, may we touch the little girl's hair!"—
It was so red, you know.

They cut me coloured asters
With shears so sharp and neat,
They brought me grapes and plums and pears
And pretty cakes to eat.

And out of all the windows,
No matter where we went,
The merriest eyes would follow me
And make me compliment.

There were a thousand windows,
All latticed up and down.
And up to all the windows,
When we went back to town,

The queer folk put their faces,
As gentle as could be;
"Come again, little girl!" they called, and I
Called back, "You come see me!"

The Spring and the Fall

In the spring of the year, in the spring of the year,
I walked the road beside my dear.
The trees were black where the bark was wet.
I see them yet, in the spring of the year.
He broke me a bough of the blossoming peach
That was out of the way and hard to reach.

In the fall of the year, in the fall of the year,
I walked the road beside my dear.
The rooks went up with a raucous trill.
I hear them still, in the fall of the year.
He laughed at all I dared to praise,
And broke my heart, in little ways.

Year be springing or year be falling,
The bark will drip and the birds be calling.
There's much that's fine to see and hear
In the spring of a year, in the fall of a year.
'Tis not love's going hurts my days,
But that it went in little ways.

Oh, lay my ashes on the wind
That blows across the sea.
And I shall meet a fisherman
Out of Capri,

And he will say, seeing me,
"What a strange thing!
Like a fish's scale or a
Butterfly's wing."

Oh, lay my ashes on the wind
That blows away the fog.
And I shall meet a farmer boy
Leaping through the bog,

And he will say, seeing me,
"What a strange thing!
Like a peat-ash or a
Butterfly's wing."

And I shall blow to your house
And, sucked against the pane,
See you take your sewing up
And lay it down again.

And you will say, seeing me,
"What a strange thing!
Like a plum petal or a
Butterfly's wing."

And none at all will know me
That knew me well before.
But I will settle at the root
That climbs about your door,

And fishermen and farmers
May see me and forget,
But I'll be a bitter berry
In your brewing yet.

Keen

Weep him dead and mourn as you may,
    Me, I sing as I must:
Blessèd be Death, that cuts in marble
    What would have sunk to dust!

Blessèd be Death, that took my love
    And buried him in the sea,
Where never a lie nor a bitter word
    Will out of his mouth at me.

This I have to hold to my heart,
    This to take by the hand:
Sweet we were for a summer month
    As the sun on the dry white sand;

Mild we were for a summer month
    As the wind from over the weirs.
And blessèd be Death, that hushed with salt
    The harsh and slovenly years!

Who builds her a house with love for timber
Builds her a house of foam.
And I'd liefer be bride to a lad gone down
Than widow to one safe home.

The Betrothal

Oh, come, my lad, or go, my lad,
And love me if you like.
I shall not hear the door shut
Nor the knocker strike.

Oh, bring me gifts or beg me gifts,
And wed me if you will.
I'd make a man a good wife,
Sensible and still.

And why should I be cold, my lad,
And why should you repine,
Because I love a dark head
That never will be mine?

I might as well be easing you
As lie alone in bed
And waste the night in wanting
A cruel dark head.

You might as well be calling yours
What never will be his,
And one of us be happy.
There's few enough as is.

"Heaven bless the babe!" they said.
"What queer books she must have read!"
(Love, by whom I was beguiled,
Grant I may not bear a child.)

"Little does she guess to-day
What the world may be!" they say.
(Snow, drift deep and cover
Till the spring my murdered lover.)

The Pond

In this pond of placid water,
   Half a hundred years ago,
So they say, a farmer's daughter,
   Jilted by her farmer beau,

Waded out among the rushes,
   Scattering the blue dragon-flies;
That dried stick the ripple washes
   Marks the spot, I should surmise.

Think, so near the public highway,
   Well frequented even then!
Can you not conceive the sly way,—
   Hearing wheels or seeing men

Passing on the road above,—
   With a gesture feigned and silly,
Ere she drowned herself for love,
   She would reach to pluck a lily?

"Son," said my mother,
    When I was knee-high,
"You've need of clothes to cover you,
    And not a rag have I.

"There's nothing in the house
    To make a boy breeches,
Nor shears to cut a cloth with,
    Nor thread to take stitches.

"There's nothing in the house
    But a loaf-end of rye,
And a harp with a woman's head
    Nobody will buy,"
    And she began to cry.

That was in the early fall.
    When came the late fall,

177

"Son," she said, "the sight of you
  Makes your mother's blood crawl,—

"Little skinny shoulder-blades
  Sticking through your clothes!
And where you'll get a jacket from
  God above knows.

"It's lucky for me, lad,
  Your daddy's in the ground,
And can't see the way I let
  His son go around!"
  And she made a queer sound.

That was in the late fall.
  When the winter came,
I'd not a pair of breeches
  Nor a shirt to my name.

I couldn't go to school,
  Or out of doors to play.

And all the other little boys
  Passed our way.

"Son," said my mother,
  "Come, climb into my lap,
And I'll chafe your little bones
  While you take a nap."

And, oh, but we were silly
  For half an hour or more,
Me with my long legs
  Dragging on the floor,

A-rock-rock-rocking
  To a mother-goose rhyme!
Oh, but we were happy
  For half an hour's time!

But there was I, a great boy,
  And what would folks say
To hear my mother singing me
  To sleep all day,
  In such a daft way?

Men say the winter
    Was bad that year;
Fuel was scarce,
    And food was dear.

A wind with a wolf's head
    Howled about our door,
And we burned up the chairs
    And sat upon the floor.

All that was left us
    Was a chair we couldn't break,
And the harp with a woman's head
    Nobody would take,
    For song or pity's sake.

The night before Christmas
    I cried with the cold,
I cried myself to sleep
    Like a two-year-old.

And in the deep night
   I felt my mother rise,
And stare down upon me
   With love in her eyes.

I saw my mother sitting
   On the one good chair,
A light falling on her
   From I couldn't tell where,

Looking nineteen,
   And not a day older,
And the harp with a woman's head
   Leaned against her shoulder.

Her thin fingers, moving
   In the thin, tall strings,
Were weav-weav-weaving
   Wonderful things.

Many bright threads,
   From where I couldn't see,

Were running through the harp-strings
    Rapidly,

And gold threads whistling
    Through my mother's hand.
I saw the web grow,
    And the pattern expand.

She wove a child's jacket,
    And when it was done
She laid it on the floor
    And wove another one.

She wove a red cloak
    So regal to see,
"She's made it for a king's son,"
    I said, "and not for me."
    But I knew it was for me.

She wove a pair of breeches
    Quicker than that!
She wove a pair of boots
    And a little cocked hat.

She wove a pair of mittens,
    She wove a little blouse,
She wove all night
    In the still, cold house.

She sang as she worked,
    And the harp-strings spoke;
Her voice never faltered,
    And the thread never broke.
    And when I awoke,—

There sat my mother
    With the harp against her shoulder,
Looking nineteen,
    And not a day older,

A smile about her lips,
    And a light about her head,
And her hands in the harp-strings
    Frozen dead.

And piled up beside her
And toppling to the skies,
Were the clothes of a king's son,
Just my size.

Never May the Fruit Be Plucked

Never, never may the fruit be plucked from the bough
And gathered into barrels.
He that would eat of love must eat it where it hangs.
Though the branches bend like reeds,
Though the ripe fruit splash in the grass or wrinkle on the tree,
He that would eat of love may bear away with him
Only what his belly can hold,
Nothing in the apron,
Nothing in the pockets.
Never, never may the fruit be gathered from the bough
And harvested in barrels.
The winter of love is a cellar of empty bins,
In an orchard soft with rot.

No, I will go alone.
I will come back when it's over.
Yes, of course I love you.
No, it will not be long.
Why may you not come with me?—
You are too much my lover.
You would put yourself
Between me and song.

If I go alone,
Quiet and suavely clothed,
My body will die in its chair,
And over my head a flame,
A mind that is twice my own,
Will mark with icy mirth
The wise advance and retreat
Of armies without a country,
Storming a nameless gate,
Hurling terrible javelins down
From the shouting walls of a singing town

Where no women wait!
Armies clean of love and hate,
Marching lines of pitiless sound
Climbing hills to the sun and hurling
Golden spears to the ground!
Up the lines a silver runner
Bearing a banner whereon is scored
The milk and steel of a bloodless wound
Healed at length by the sword!

You and I have nothing to do with music.
We may not make of music a filigree frame,
Within which you and I,
Tenderly glad we came,
Sit smiling, hand in hand.

Come now, be content.
I will come back to you, I swear I will;
And you will know me still.
I shall be only a little taller
Than when I went.

Hyacinth

I am in love with him to whom a hyacinth is dearer
Than I shall ever be dear.
On nights when the field-mice are abroad he cannot sleep:
He hears their narrow teeth at the bulbs of his hyacinths.
But the gnawing at my heart he does not hear.

To One Who Might Have Borne a Message

Had I known that you were going
I would have given you messages for her,
Now two years dead,
Whom I shall always love.

As it is, should she entreat you how it goes with me,
You must reply: as well as with most, you fancy;
That I love easily, and pass the time.

And she will not know how all day long between
My life and me her shadow intervenes,
A young thin girl,
Wearing a white skirt and a purple sweater
And a narrow pale blue ribbon about her hair.

I used to say to her, "I love you
Because your face is such a pretty colour,
No other reason."

But it was not true.

Oh, had I only known that you were going,
I could have given you messages for her!

Siege

This I do, being mad:
Gather baubles about me,
Sit in a circle of toys, and all the time
Death beating the door in.

White jade and an orange pitcher,
Hindu idol, Chinese god,—
Maybe next year, when I'm richer—
Carved beads and a lotus pod. . . .

And all this time
Death beating the door in.

The Cairn

When I think of the little children learning
In all the schools of the world,
Learning in Danish, learning in Japanese
That two and two are four, and where the rivers of the world
Rise, and the names of the mountains and the principal cities,
My heart breaks.
Come up, children! Toss your little stones gaily
On the great cairn of Knowledge!
(Where lies what Euclid knew, a little grey stone,
What Plato, what Pascal, what Galileo:
Little grey stones, little grey stones on a cairn.)
Tell me, what is the name of the highest mountain?
Name me a crater of fire! a peak of snow!
Name me the mountains on the moon!
But the name of the mountain that you climb all day,
Ask not your teacher that.

Spring Song

I know why the yellow forsythia
Holds its breath and will not bloom,
And the robin thrusts his beak in his wing.

Want me to tell you? Think you can bear it?
Cover your eyes with your hand and hear it.
You know how cold the days are still?
And everybody saying how late the Spring is?
Well—cover your eyes with your hand—the thing is,
There isn't going to be any Spring.

No parking here! No parking here!
They said to Spring: No parking here!

Spring came on as she always does,
Laid her hand on the yellow forsythia,—
Little boys turned in their sleep and smiled,
Dreaming of marbles, dreaming of agates;
Little girls leapt from their beds to see
Spring come by with her painted wagons,
Coloured wagons creaking with wonder—

193

Laid her hand on the robin's throat;
When up comes you-know-who, my dear,
You-know-who in a fine blue coat,
And says to Spring: No parking here!

No parking here! No parking here!
Move on! Move on! No parking here!

Come walk with me in the city gardens.
(Better keep an eye out for you-know-who)
Did ever you see such a sickly showing?—
Middle of June, and nothing growing;
The gardeners peer and scratch their heads
And drop their sweat on the tulip-beds,
But not a blade thrusts through.

Come, move on! Don't you know how to walk?
No parking here! And no back-talk!

Oh, well,—hell, it's all for the best.
She certainly made a lot of clutter,
Dropping petals under the trees,
Taking your mind off your bread and butter.

Anyhow, it's nothing to me.
I can remember, and so can you.
(Though we'd better watch out for you-know-who,
When we sit around remembering Spring).

We shall hardly notice in a year or two.
You can get accustomed to anything.

The wind in the ash-tree sounds like surf on the shore at Truro.
I will shut my eyes . . . hush, be still with your silly bleating,
    sheep on Shillingstone Hill . . .

They said: Come along! They said: Leave your pebbles on the sand and come
    along, it's long after sunset!
The mosquitoes will be thick in the pine-woods along by Long Nook, the wind's
    died down!
They said: Leave your pebbles on the sand, and your shells, too, and come along,
    we'll find you another beach like the beach at Truro.

Let me listen to wind in the ash . . . it sounds like surf on the
    shore.

From *THE BUCK IN THE SNOW*

Y

Moriturus

If I could have
   Two things in one:
The peace of the grave,
   And the light of the sun;

My hands across
   My thin breast-bone,
But aware of the moss
   Invading the stone,

Aware of the flight
   Of the golden flicker
With his wing to the light;
   To hear him nicker

And drum with his bill
   On the rotted willow;
Snug and still
   On a grey pillow

Deep in the clay
   Where digging is hard,
Out of the way,—
   The blue shard

Of a broken platter—
   If I might be
Insensate matter
   With sensate me

Sitting within,
   Harking and prying,
I might begin
   To dicker with dying.

For the body at best
   Is a bundle of aches,
Longing for rest;
   It cries when it wakes

"Alas, 'tis light!"
   At set of sun

"Alas, 'tis night,
    And nothing done!"

Death, however,
    Is a spongy wall,
Is a sticky river,
    Is nothing at all.

Summon the weeper,
    Wail and sing;
Call him Reaper,
    Angel, King;

Call him Evil
    Drunk to the lees,
Monster, Devil,—
    He is less than these.

Call him Thief,
    The Maggot in the Cheese,
The Canker in the Leaf,—
    He is less than these.

Dusk without sound,
    Where the spirit by pain
Uncoiled, is wound
    To spring again;

The mind enmeshed
    Laid straight in repose,
And the body refreshed
    By feeding the rose,—

These are but visions;
    These would be
The grave's derisions,
    Could the grave see.

Here is the wish
    Of one that died
Like a beached fish
    On the ebb of the tide:

That he might wait
    Till the tide came back,

To see if a crate,
   Or a bottle, or a black

Boot, or an oar,
   Or an orange peel
Be washed ashore. . . .
   About his heel

The sand slips;
   The last he hears
From the world's lips
   Is the sand in his ears.

What thing is little?—
   The aphis hid
In a house of spittle?
   The hinge of the lid

Of the spider's eye
   At the spider's birth?
"Greater am I
   By the earth's girth

Than Mighty Death!"
　　All creatures cry
That can summon breath;—
　　And speak no lie.

For He is nothing;
　　He is less
Than Echo answering
　　"Nothingness!"—

Less than the heat
　　Of the furthest star
To the ripening wheat;
　　Less by far,

When all the lipping
　　Is said and sung,
Than the sweat dripping
　　From a dog's tongue.

This being so,
　　And I being such,

I would liever go
   On a cripple's crutch,

Lopped and felled;
   Liever be dependent
On a chair propelled
   By a surly attendant

With a foul breath,
   And be spooned my food,
Than go with Death
   Where nothing good,

Not even the thrust
   Of the summer gnat,
Consoles the dust
   For being that.

Needy, lonely,
   Stitched by pain,
Left with only
   The drip of the rain

Out of all I had;
    The books of the wise,
Badly read
    By other eyes,

Lewdly bawled
    At my closing ear;
Hated, called
    A lingerer here;—

Withstanding Death
    Till Life be gone,
I shall treasure my breath,
    I shall linger on.

I shall bolt my door
    With a bolt and a cable;
I shall block my door
    With a bureau and a table;

With all my might
    My door shall be barred.

I shall put up a fight,
   I shall take it hard.

With his hand on my mouth
   He shall drag me forth,
Shrieking to the south
   And clutching at the north.

Song

Gone, gone again is Summer the lovely.
  She that knew not where to hide,
Is gone again like a jeweled fish from the hand,
  Is lost on every side.

Mute, mute, I make my way to the garden,
  Thither where she last was seen;
The heavy foot of the frost is on the flags there,
  Where her light step has been.

Gone, gone again is Summer the lovely,
  Gone again on every side,
Lost again like a shining fish from the hand
  Into the shadowy tide.

Shelter this candle from the wind.
Hold it steady. In its light
The cave wherein we wander lost
Glitters with frosty stalactite,
Blossoms with mineral rose and lotus,
Sparkles with crystal moon and star,
Till a man would rather be lost than found:
We have forgotten where we are.

Shelter this candle. Shrewdly blowing
Down the cave from a secret door
Enters our only foe, the wind.
Hold it steady. Lest we stand,
Each in a sudden, separate dark,
The hot wax spattered upon your hand,
The smoking wick in my nostrils strong,
The inner eyelid red and green
For a moment yet with moons and roses,—
Then the unmitigated dark.

Alone, alone, in a terrible place,
In utter dark without a face,
With only the dripping of the water on the stone,
And the sound of your tears, and the taste of my own.

The Bobolink

Black bird scudding
Under the rainy sky,
How wet your wings must be!
And your small head how sleek and cold with water.

Oh, Bobolink, 'tis you!
Over the buffeted orchard in the summer draught,
Chuckling and singing, charging the rainy cloud,
A little bird gone daft,
A little bird with a secret.

Only the bobolink on the rainy
Rhubarb blossom,
Knows my heart. . . .
For whom adversity has not a word to say that can be heard
Above the din of summer.
The rain has taught us nothing. And the hooves of cattle, and
      the cat in the grass
Have taught us nothing.

The hawk that motionless above the hill
In the pure sky
Stands like a blackened planet
Has taught us nothing,—seeing him shut his wings and fall
Has taught us nothing at all.
In the shadow of the hawk we feather our nests.

Bobolink, you and I, an airy fool and an earthy,
Chuckling under the rain!

I shall never be sad again.
I shall never be sad again.

Ah, sweet, absurd,
Belovèd, bedraggled bird!

The Hawkweed

Between the red-top and the rye,
  Between the buckwheat and the corn,
The ploughman sees with sullen eye
The hawkweed licking at the sky:

  Three level acres all forlorn,
  Unfertile, sour, outrun, outworn,
  Free as the day that they were born.

Southward and northward, west and east,
  The sulphate and the lime are spread;
Harrowed and sweetened, urged, increased,
The furrow sprouts for man and beast:

  While of the hawkweed's radiant head
  No stanchion reeks, no stock is fed.

Triumphant up the taken field
  The tractor and the plough advance;
Blest be the healthy germ concealed
In the rich earth, and blest the yield:

And blest be Beauty, that enchants
The frail, the solitary lance.

To a Friend Estranged from Me

Now goes under, and I watch it go under, the sun
That will not rise again.
Today has seen the setting, in your eyes cold and senseless as the sea,
Of friendship better than bread, and of bright charity
That lifts a man a little above the beasts that run.

That this could be!
That I should live to see
Most vulgar Pride, that stale obstreperous clown,
So fitted out with purple robe and crown
To stand among his betters! Face to face
With outraged me in this once holy place,
Where Wisdom was a favoured guest and hunted
Truth was harboured out of danger,
He bulks enthroned, a lewd, an insupportable stranger!

I would have sworn, indeed I swore it:
The hills may shift, the waters may decline,
Winter may twist the stem from the twig that bore it,
But never your love from me, your hand from mine.

Now goes under the sun, and I watch it go under.

Farewell, sweet light, great wonder!

You, too, farewell,—but fare not well enough to dream

You have done wisely to invite the night before the darkness
came.

The Road to Avrillé

April again in Avrillé,
    And the brown lark in air.
And you and I a world apart,
    That walked together there.

The cuckoo spoke from out the wood,
    The lark from out the sky.
Embraced upon the highway stood
    Love-sick you and I.

The rosy peasant left his bees,
    The carrier slowed his cart,
To shout us blithe obscenities,
    And bless us from the heart,

Who long before the year was out,
    Under the autumn rain,
Far from the road to Avrillé,
    Parted with little pain.

For Pao-Chin, a Boatman on the Yellow Sea

Where is he now, in his soiled shirt reeking of garlic,
Sculling his sampan home, and night approaching fast—
The red sail hanging wrinkled on the bamboo mast;

Where is he now, I shall remember my whole life long
With love and praise, for the sake of a small song
Played on a Chinese flute?
       I have been sad;
I have been in cities where the song was all I had,—
A treasure never to be bartered by the hungry days.

Where is he now, for whom I carry in my heart
This love, this praise?

Northern April

O mind, beset by music never for a moment quiet,—
The wind at the flue, the wind strumming the shutter;
The soft, antiphonal speech of the doubled brook, never for a
    moment quiet;
The rush of the rain against the glass, his voice in the eaves-
    gutter!

Where shall I lay you to sleep, and the robins be quiet?
Lay you to sleep—and the frogs be silent in the marsh?
Crashes the sleet from the bough and the bough sighs upward,
    never for a moment quiet.
April is upon us, pitiless and young and harsh.

O April, full of blood, full of breath, have pity upon us!
Pale, where the winter like a stone has been lifted away, we
    emerge like yellow grass.
Be for a moment quiet, buffet us not, have pity upon us,
Till the green come back into the vein, till the giddiness pass.

There at Dusk I Found You

There at dusk I found you, walking and weeping
Upon the broken flags,
Where at dusk the dumb white nicotine awakes and utters her
    fragrance
In a garden sleeping.

Looking askance you said:
Love is dead.

Under our eyes without warning softly the summer afternoon
    let fall
The rose upon the wall,
And it lay there splintered.
Terribly then into my heart the forgotten anguish entered.

I saw the dark stone on the smallest finger of your hand,
And the clean cuff above.
No more, no more the dark stone on the smallest finger
Of your brown and naked arm,
Lifting my body in love!

Worse than dead is he of the wounded wing,
Who walks between us, weeping upon the cold flags,
Bleeding and weeping, dragging his broken wing.
He has gathered the rose into his hand and chafed her with his
    breath.
But the rose is quiet and pale. She has forgotten us all.
Even spring.
Even death.

As for me, I have forgotten nothing,—nor shall I ever forget—
But this one thing:
I have forgotten which of us it was
That hurt his wing.
I only know his limping flight above us in the blue air
Toward the sunset cloud
Is more than I can bear.

You, you there,
Stiff-necked and angry, holding up your head so proud,
Have you not seen how pitiful lame he flies, and none to befriend
    him?
Speak! Are you blind? Are you dead?
Shall we call him back? Shall we mend him?

Being Young and Green

Being young and green, I said in love's despite:
Never in the world will I to living wight
Give over, air my mind
To anyone,
Hang out its ancient secrets in the strong wind
To be shredded and faded. . . .

Oh, me, invaded
And sacked by the wind and the sun!

Mist in the Valley

These hills, to hurt me more,
That am hurt already enough,—
Having left the sea behind,
Having turned suddenly and left the shore
That I had loved beyond all words, even a song's words, to convey,

And built me a house on upland acres,
Sweet with the pinxter, bright and rough
With the rusty blackbird long before the winter's done,
But smelling never of bayberry hot in the sun,
Nor ever loud with the pounding of the long white breakers,—

These hills, beneath the October moon,
Sit in the valley white with mist
Like islands in a quiet bay,

Jut out from shore into the mist,
Wooded with poplar dark as pine,
Like points of land into a quiet bay.

(Just in that way
The harbour met the bay)

Stricken too sore for tears,
I stand, remembering the islands and the sea's lost sound. . . .
Life at its best no longer than the sand-peep's cry,
And I two years, two years,
Tilling an upland ground!

The Hardy Garden

Now let forever the phlox and the rose be tended
Here where the rain has darkened and the sun has dried
So many times the terrace, yet is love unended,
    Love has not died.

Let here no seed of a season, that the winter
But once assails, take root and for a time endure;
But only such as harbour at the frozen centre
    The germ secure.

Set here the phlox and the iris, and establish
Pink and valerian, and the great and lesser bells;
But suffer not the sisters of the year, to publish
    That frost prevails.

How far from home in a world of mortal burdens
Is Love, that may not die, and is forever young!
Set roses here: surround her only with such maidens
    As speak her tongue.

The Pigeons

Well I remember the pigeons in the sunny arbour
Beyond your open door;
How they conversed throughout the afternoon in their mo-
notonous voices never for a moment still;
Always of yesterday they spoke, and of the days before,
Rustling the vine-leaves, twitching the dark shadows of the
leaves on the bright sill.

You said, the soft curring and droning of the pigeons in the vine
Was a pretty thing enough to the passer-by,
But a maddening thing to a man with his head in his hands,—
"Like mine! Like mine!"
You said, and ran to the door and waved them off into the sky.

They did not come back. The arbour was empty of their cooing.
The shadows of the leaves were still. "Whither have they
flown, then?"
I said, and waited for their wings, but they did not come back.
If I had known then
What I know now, I never would have left your door.

Tall in your faded smock, with steady hand
Mingling the brilliant pigments, painting your intersecting
    planes you stand,
In a quiet room, empty of the past, of its droning and cooing,
Thinking I know not what, but thinking of me no more,
That left you with a light word, that loving and rueing
Walk in the streets of a city you have never seen,
Walk in a noise of yesterday and of the days before,
Walk in a cloud of wings intolerable, shutting out the sun as if
    it never had been.

White sky, over the hemlocks bowed with snow,
Saw you not at the beginning of evening the antlered buck and
    his doe
Standing in the apple-orchard? I saw them. I saw them suddenly
    go,
Tails up, with long leaps lovely and slow,
Over the stone-wall into the wood of hemlocks bowed with snow.

Now lies he here, his wild blood scalding the snow.

How strange a thing is death, bringing to his knees, bringing to
    his antlers
The buck in the snow.
How strange a thing,—a mile away by now, it may be,
Under the heavy hemlocks that as the moments pass
Shift their loads a little, letting fall a feather of snow—
Life, looking out attentive from the eyes of the doe.

The Anguish

I would to God I were quenched and fed
As in my youth
From the flask of song, and the good bread
Of beauty richer than truth.

The anguish of the world is on my tongue.
My bowl is filled to the brim with it; there is more than I can eat.
Happy are the toothless old and the toothless young,
That cannot rend this meat.

Let us abandon then our gardens and go home
And sit in the sitting-room.
Shall the larkspur blossom or the corn grow under this cloud?
Sour to the fruitful seed
Is the cold earth under this cloud,
Fostering quack and weed, we have marched upon but cannot
    conquer;
We have bent the blades of our hoes against the stalks of them.

Let us go home, and sit in the sitting-room.
Not in our day
Shall the cloud go over and the sun rise as before,
Beneficent upon us
Out of the glittering bay,
And the warm winds be blown inward from the sea
Moving the blades of corn
With a peaceful sound.
Forlorn, forlorn,
Stands the blue hay-rack by the empty mow.
And the petals drop to the ground,

Leaving the tree unfruited.
The sun that warmed our stooping backs and withered the weed
     uprooted—
We shall not feel it again.
We shall die in darkness, and be buried in the rain.

What from the splendid dead
We have inherited—
Furrows sweet to the grain, and the weed subdued—
See now the slug and the mildew plunder.
Evil does overwhelm
The larkspur and the corn;
We have seen them go under.

Let us sit here, sit still,
Here in the sitting-room until we die;
At the step of Death on the walk, rise and go;
Leaving to our children's children this beautiful doorway,
And this elm,
And a blighted earth to till
With a broken hoe.

Before the cock in the barnyard spoke,
    Before it well was day,
Horror like a serpent from about the Hangman's Oak
    Uncoiled and slid away.

Pity and Peace were on the limb
    That bore such bitter fruit.
Deep he lies, and the desperate blood of him
    Befriends the innocent root.

Brother, I said to the air beneath the bough
    Whence he had swung,
It will not be long for any of us now;
    We do not grow young.

It will not be long for the knotter of ropes, not long
    For the sheriff or for me,
Or for any of them that came five hundred strong
    To see you swing from a tree.

Side by side together in the belly of Death
   We sit without hope,
You, and I, and the mother that gave you breath,
   And the tree, and the rope.

Wine from These Grapes

Wine from these grapes I shall be treading surely
Morning and noon and night until I die.
Stained with these grapes I shall lie down to die.

If you would speak with me on any matter,
At any time, come where these grapes are grown;
And you will find me treading them to must.
Lean then above me sagely, lest I spatter
Drops of the wine I tread from grapes and dust.

Stained with these grapes I shall lie down to die.
Three women come to wash me clean
Shall not erase this stain.
Nor leave me lying purely,
Awaiting the black lover.
Death, fumbling to uncover
My body in his bed,
Shall know
There has been one
Before him.

To Those Without Pity

Cruel of heart, lay down my song.
Your reading eyes have done me wrong.
Not for you was the pen bitten,
And the mind wrung, and the song written.

Dawn

All men are lonely now.
This is the hour when no man has a friend.
Memory and Faith suspend
From their spread wings above a cool abyss.
All friendships end.

He that lay awake
All night
For sweet love's unregenerate sake,
Sleeps in the grey light.

The lover, if he dream at all,
Dreams not of her whose languid hand sleeps open at his side;
He is gone to another bride.
And she he leaves behind
Sighs not in sleep "Unkind . . . unkind . . .";
She walks in a garden of yellow quinces;
Smiling, she gathers yellow quinces in a basket
Of willow and laurel combined.

Should I return to your door,
Fresh and haggard out of the morning air,
There would be darkness on the stair,
And a dead close odour painfully sad,
That was not there before.
There would be silence. There would be heavy steps across the
    floor.
And you would let me in, frowning with sleep
Under your rumpled hair.

Beautiful now upon the ear unshut by slumber
The rich and varied voices of the waking day!—
The mighty, mournful whistles without number
Of tugs and ferries, mingling, confounding, failing,
Thinning to separate notes of wailing,
Making stupendous music on the misty bay.

Now through the echoing street in the growing light,
Intent on errands that the sun approves,
Clatter unashamed the heavy wheels and hooves
Before the silent houses; briskly they say:
"Marshal not me among the enterprises of the night.
I am the beginning of the day."

To a Young Girl

Shall I despise you that your colourless tears
Made rainbows in your lashes, and you forgot to weep?
Would we were half so wise, that eke a grief out
By sitting in the dark, until we fall asleep.

I only fear lest, being by nature sunny,
By and by you will weep no more at all,
And fall asleep in the light, having lost with the tears
The colour in the lashes that comes as the tears fall.

I would not have you darken your lids with weeping,
Beautiful eyes, but I would have you weep enough
To wet the fingers of the hand held over the eye-lids,
And stain a little the light frock's delicate stuff.

For there came into my mind, as I watched you winking the tears
        down,
Laughing faces, blown from the west and the east,
Faces lovely and proud that I have prized and cherished;
Nor were the loveliest among them those that had wept the least.

Evening on Lesbos

Twice having seen your shingled heads adorable
Side by side, the onyx and the gold,
I know that I have had what I could not hold.

Twice have I entered the room, not knowing she was here.
Two agate eyes, two eyes of malachite,
Twice have been turned upon me, hard and bright.

Whereby I know my loss.

                    Oh, not restorable
Sweet incense, mounting in the windless night!

Dirge Without Music

I am not resigned to the shutting away of loving hearts in the
    hard ground.
So it is, and so it will be, for so it has been, time out of mind:
Into the darkness they go, the wise and the lovely.   Crowned
With lilies and with laurel they go; but I am not resigned.

Lovers and thinkers, into the earth with you.
Be one with the dull, the indiscriminate dust.
A fragment of what you felt, of what you knew,
A formula, a phrase remains,—but the best is lost.

The answers quick and keen, the honest look, the laughter, the
    love,—
They are gone. They are gone to feed the roses. Elegant and
    curled
Is the blossom. Fragrant is the blossom. I know. But I do not
    approve.
More precious was the light in your eyes than all the roses in the
    world.

Down, down, down into the darkness of the grave
Gently they go, the beautiful, the tender, the kind;
Quietly they go, the intelligent, the witty, the brave.
I know. But I do not approve. And I am not resigned.

Memory of Cassis

Do you recall how we sat by the smokily-burning
Twisted odourous trunk of the olive-tree,
In the inn on the cliff, and skinned the ripe green figs,
And heard the white sirocco driving in the sea?

The thunder and the smother there where like a ship's prow
The light-house breasted the wave? how wanly through the wild
    spray
Under our peering eyes the eye of the light looked out,
Disheveled, but without dismay?

Do you recall the sweet-alyssum over the ledges
Crawling and the tall heather and the mushrooms under the pines,
And the deep white dust of the broad road leading outward
To a world forgotten, between the dusty almonds and the dusty
    vines?

Portrait

Over and over I have heard,
As now I hear it,
Your voice harsh and light as the scratching of dry leaves over
    the hard ground,
Your voice forever assailed and shaken by the wind from the
    island
Of illustrious living and dead, that never dies down,
And bending at moments under the terrible weight of the perfect
    word,
Here in this room without fire, without comfort of any kind,
Reading aloud to me immortal page after page conceived in a
    mortal mind.
Beauty at such moments before me like a wild bright bird
Has been in the room, and eyed me, and let me come near it.

I could not ever nor can I to this day
Acquaint you with the triumph and the sweet rest
These hours have brought to me and always bring, —
Rapture, coloured like the wild bird's neck and wing,
Comfort, softer than the feathers of its breast.

Always, and even now, when I rise to go,

Your eyes blaze out from a face gone wickedly pale;

I try to tell you what I would have you know,—

What peace it was; you cry me down; you scourge me with a
     salty flail;

You will not have it so.

Winter Night

Pile high the hickory and the light
Log of chestnut struck by the blight.
Welcome-in the winter night.

The day has gone in hewing and felling,
Sawing and drawing wood to the dwelling
For the night of talk and story-telling.

These are the hours that give the edge
To the blunted axe and the bent wedge,
Straighten the saw and lighten the sledge.

Here are question and reply,
And the fire reflected in the thinking eye.
So peace, and let the bob-cat cry.

The Cameo

Forever over now, forever, forever gone
That day. Clear and diminished like a scene
Carven in cameo, the lighthouse, and the cove between
The sandy cliffs, and the boat drawn up on the beach;
And the long skirt of a lady innocent and young,
Her hand resting on her bosom, her head hung;
And the figure of a man in earnest speech.

Clear and diminished like a scene cut in cameo
The lighthouse, and the boat on the beach, and the two shapes
Of the woman and the man; lost like the lost day
Are the words that passed, and the pain,—discarded, cut away
From the stone, as from the memory the heat of the tears escapes.

O troubled forms, O early love unfortunate and hard,
Time has estranged you into a jewel cold and pure;
From the action of the waves and from the action of sorrow for-
        ever secure,
White against a ruddy cliff you stand, chalcedony on sard.

Silver bark of beech, and sallow
Bark of yellow birch and yellow
　Twig of willow.

Stripe of green in moosewood maple,
Colour seen in leaf of apple,
　Bark of popple.

Wood of popple pale as moonbeam,
Wood of oak for yoke and barn-beam,
　Wood of hornbeam.

Silver bark of beech, and hollow
Stem of elder, tall and yellow
　Twig of willow.

The Plum Gatherer

The angry nettle and the mild
  Grew together under the blue-plum trees.
I could not tell as a child
  Which was my friend of these.

Always the angry nettle in the skirt of his sister
  Caught my wrist that reached over the ground,
Where alike I gathered,—for the one was sweet and the other
    wore a frosty dust—
  The broken plum and the sound.

The plum-trees are barren now and the black knot is upon them,
  That stood so white in the spring.
I would give, to recall the sweetness and the frost of the lost blue
    plums,
  Anything, anything.
I thrust my arm among the grey ambiguous nettles, and wait.
  But they do not sting.

West Country Song

Sun came up, bigger than all my sorrow;
Lark in air so high, and his song clean through me.
Now comes night, hushing the lark in's furrow,
   And the rain falls fine.
What have I done with what was dearest to me?

Thatch and wick, fagot, and tea on trivet,—
These and more it was; it was all my cheer.
Now comes night, smelling of box and privet,
   And the rain falls fine.
Have I left it out in the rain?—It is not here.

Pueblo Pot

There as I bent above the broken pot from the mesa pueblo,
Mournfully many times its patterned shards piecing together and
    laying aside,
Appeared upon the house-top, two Navajos enchanted, the red-
    shafted flicker and his bride,
And stepped with lovely stride
To the pergola, flashing the wonder of their underwings;
There stood, mysterious and harsh and sleek,
Wrenching the indigo berry from the shedding woodbine with
    strong ebony beak.

His head without a crest
Wore the red full moon for crown;
The black new moon was crescent on the breast of each;
From the bodies of both a visible heat beat down,
And from the motion of their necks a shadow would fly and fall,
Skimming the court and in the yellow adobe wall
Cleaving a blue breach.

Powerful was the beauty of these birds.
It boomed like a struck bell in the silence deep and hot.
I stooped above the shattered clay; passionately I cried to the
     beauty of these birds,
"Solace the broken pot!"

The beauty of these birds
Opened its lips to speak;
Colours were its words,
The scarlet shaft on the grey cheek,
The purple berry in the ebony beak.
It said, "I cannot console
The broken thing; I can only make it whole."

Wisdom, heretic flower, I was ever afraid
Of your large, cool petals without scent!
Shocked, betrayed,
I turned to the comfort of grief, I bent
Above the lovely shards.
But their colours had faded in the fierce light of the birds.
And as for the birds, they were gone. As suddenly as they had
     come, they went.

When Caesar fell, where yellow Tiber rolls
    Its heavy waters muddy,
Life, that was ebbing from a hundred holes
    In Caesar's body,
Cried with a hundred voices to the common air,
    The unimperial day,
"Gather me up, oh, pour me into the veins of even a gilder of
      hair!
    Let me not vanish away!"

The teeth of Caesar at the ignoble word
    Were ground together in pride;
No sound came from his lips: the world has heard
    How Caesar died.
In the Roman dust the cry of Caesar's blood
    Was heard and heard without wonder
Only by the fly that swam in the red flood
    Till his head went under.

Lethe

Ah, drink again
This river that is the taker-away of pain,
And the giver-back of beauty!

In these cool waves
What can be lost?—
Only the sorry cost
Of the lovely thing, ah, never the thing itself!

The level flood that laves
The hot brow
And the stiff shoulder
Is at our temples now.

Gone is the fever,
But not into the river;
Melted the frozen pride,
But the tranquil tide
Runs never the warmer for this,
Never the colder.

Immerse the dream.
Drench the kiss.
Dip the song in the stream.

On First Having Heard the Skylark

Not knowing he rose from earth, not having seen him rise,
Not knowing the fallow furrow was his home,
And that high wing, untouchable, untainted,
A wing of earth, with the warm loam
Closely acquainted,
I shuddered at his cry and caught my heart.
Relentless out of heaven his sweet crying like a crystal dart
Was launched against me. Scanning the empty sky
I stood with thrown-back head until the world reeled.
Still, still he sped his unappeasable shafts against my breast with-
    out a shield.
He cried forever from his unseen throat
Between me and the sun.
He would not end his singing, he would not have done.
"Serene and pitiless note, whence, whence are you?"
I cried. "Alas, these arrows, how fast they fall!
Ay, me, beset by angels in unequal fight,
Alone high on the shaven down surprised, and not a tree in sight!"

Even as I spoke he was revealed
Above me in the bright air,
A dark articulate atom in the mute enormous blue,
A mortal bird, flying and singing in the morning there.
Even as I spoke I spied him, and I knew,
And called him by his name;
"Blithe Spirit!" I cried. Transfixed by more than mortal spears
I fell; I lay among the foreign daisies pink and small,
And wept, staining their innocent faces with fast-flowing tears.

To a Musician

Who, now, when evening darkens the water and the stream is dull,
Slowly, in a delicate frock, with her leghorn hat in her hand,
At your side from under the golden osiers moves,
Faintly smiling, shattered by the charm of your voice?

There, today, as in the days when I knew you well,
The willow sheds upon the stream its narrow leaves,
And the quiet flowing of the water and its faint smell
Are balm to the heart that grieves.

Together with the sharp discomfort of loving you,
Ineffable you, so lovely and so aloof,
There is laid upon the spirit the calmness of the river view:
Together they fall, the pain and its reproof.

Who, now, under the yellow willows at the water's edge
Closes defeated lips upon the trivial word unspoken,
And lifts her soft eyes freighted with a heavy pledge
To your eyes empty of pledges, even of pledges broken?

From *POEMS SELECTED FOR YOUNG PEOPLE*

Υ

I

Come along in then, little girl!
Or else stay out!
But in the open door she stands,
And bites her lip and twists her hands,
And stares upon me, trouble-eyed:
"Mother," she says, "I can't decide!
I can't decide!"

II

Oh, burdock, and you other dock,
That have ground coffee for your seeds,
And lovely long thin daisies, dear—
She said that you are weeds!
She said, "Oh, what a fine bouquet!"
But afterwards I heard her say,
"She's always dragging in those weeds."

III

Everybody but just me
Despises burdocks. Mother, she
Despises 'em the most because
They stick so to my socks and drawers.
But father, when he sits on some,
Can't speak a decent word for 'em.

IV

I know a hundred ways to die.
I've often thought I'd try one:
Lie down beneath a motor truck
Some day when standing by one.

Or throw myself from off a bridge—
Except such things must be
So hard upon the scavengers
And men that clean the sea.

I know some poison I could drink.
I've often thought I'd taste it.
But mother bought it for the sink,
And drinking it would waste it.

V

Look, Edwin! Do you see that boy
Talking to the other boy?
No, over there by those two men—
Wait, don't look now—now look again.
No, not the one in navy-blue;
That's the one he's talking to.
Sure you see him? Stripèd pants?
Well, *he was born in Paris, France.*

VI

All the grown-up people say,
"What, those ugly thistles?
Mustn't touch them! Keep away!
Prickly! Full of bristles!"

Yet they never make me bleed
Half so much as roses!
Must be purple is a weed,
And pink and white is posies.

VII

Wonder where this horseshoe went.
Up and down, up and down,
Up and past the monument,
Maybe into town.

Wait a minute. "Horseshoe,
How far have you been?"
Says it's been to Salem
And halfway to Lynn.

Wonder who was in the team.
Wonder what they saw.
Wonder if they passed a bridge—
Bridge with a draw.

Says it went from one bridge
Straight upon another.
Says it took a little girl
Driving with her mother.

267

From *WINE FROM THESE GRAPES*

Y

The Return

Earth does not understand her child,
    Who from the loud gregarious town
Returns, depleted and defiled,
    To the still woods, to fling him down.

Earth can not count the sons she bore:
    The wounded lynx, the wounded man
Come trailing blood unto her door;
    She shelters both as best she can.

But she is early up and out,
    To trim the year or strip its bones;
She has no time to stand about
    Talking of him in undertones

Who has no aim but to forget,
    Be left in peace, be lying thus
For days, for years, for centuries yet,
    Unshaven and anonymous;

Who, marked for failure, dulled by grief,
Has traded in his wife and friend
For this warm ledge, this alder leaf:
Comfort that does not comprehend.

October—An Etching

There where the woodcock his long bill among the alders
Forward in level flight propels,
Tussocks of faded grass are islands in the pasture swamp
Where the small foot, if it be light as well, can pass
Dry-shod to rising ground.

Not so the boot of the hunter.
Chilly and black and halfway to the knee
Is the thick water there, heavy wading,
Uneven to the step; there the more cautious ones,
Pausing for a moment, break their guns.
There the white setter ticked with black
Sets forth with silky feathers on the bird's track
And wet to his pink skin and half his size comes back.

Cows are pastured there; they have made a path among the alders.
By now the keeper's boy has found
The chalk of the woodcock on the trampled ground.

Autumn Daybreak

Cold wind of autumn, blowing loud
At dawn, a fortnight overdue,
Jostling the doors, and tearing through
My bedroom to rejoin the cloud,

I know—for I can hear the hiss
And scrape of leaves along the floor—
How many boughs, lashed bare by this,
Will rake the cluttered sky once more.

Tardy, and somewhat south of east,
The sun will rise at length, made known
More by the meagre light increased
Than by a disk in splendour shown;

When, having but to turn my head,
Through the stripped maple I shall see,
Bleak and remembered, patched with red,
The hill all summer hid from me.

Yet in the end, defeated too, worn out and ready to fall,
Hangs from the drowsy tree with cramped and desperate stem
    above the ditch the last leaf of all.

There is something to be learned, I guess, from looking at the
    dead leaves under the living tree;
Something to be set to a lusty tune and learned and sung, it well
    might be;
Something to be learned—though I was ever a ten-o'clock scholar
    at this school—
Even perhaps by me.

But my heart goes out to the oak-leaves that are the last to sigh
"Enough," and loose their hold;
They have boasted to the nudging frost and to the two-and-thirty
    winds that they would never die,
Never even grow old.
(These are those russet leaves that cling
All winter, even into the spring,
To the dormant bough, in the wood knee-deep in snow the only
    coloured thing.)

The Fledgling

So, art thou feathered, art thou flown,
Thou naked thing?—and canst alone
Upon the unsolid summer air
Sustain thyself, and prosper there?

Shall I no more with anxious note
Advise thee through the happy day,
Thrusting the worm into thy throat,
Bearing thine excrement away?

Alas, I think I see thee yet,
Perched on the windy parapet,
Defer thy flight a moment still
To clean thy wing with careful bill.

And thou art feathered, thou art flown;
And hast a project of thine own.

The Hedge of Hemlocks

Somebody long ago
Set out this hedge of hemlocks; brought from the woods, I'd say,
Saplings ten inches tall, curving and delicate, not shaped like trees,
And set them out, to shut the marshes from the lawn,
A hedge of ferns.

Four feet apart he set them, far apart, leaving them room to
    grow . . .
Whose crowded lower boughs these fifty years at least
Are spiky stumps outthrust in all directions, dry, dropping scaly
    bark, in the deep shade making a thick
Dust which here and there floats in a short dazzling beam.

Green tops, delicate and curving yet, above this fence of brush,
    like ferns,
You have done well: more than the marshes now is shut away
    from his protected dooryard;
The mountain, too, is shut away; not even the wind
May trespass here to stir the purple phlox in the tall grass.

And yet how easily one afternoon between
Your stems, unheard, snapping no twig, dislodging
    no shell of loosened bark, unseen
Even by the spider through whose finished web he walked, and
    left it as he found it,
A neighbour entered.

Cap D'Antibes

The storm is over, and the land has forgotten the storm; the trees
    are still.
Under this sun the rain dries quickly.
Cones from the sea-pines cover the ground again
Where yesterday for my fire I gathered all in sight;
But the leaves are meek. The smell of the small alyssum that
    grows wild here
Is in the air. It is a childish morning.

More sea than land am I; my sulky mind, whipped high by tem-
    pest in the night, is not so soon appeased.
Into my occupations with dull roar
It washes,
It recedes.
Even as at my side in the calm day the disturbed Mediterranean
Lurches with heavy swell against the bird-twittering shore.

From a Train Window

Precious in the light of the early sun the Housatonic
Between its not unscalable mountains flows.
Precious in the January morning the shabby fur of the cat-tails
    by the stream.
The farmer driving his horse to the feed-store for a sack of cracked
    corn
Is not in haste; there is no whip in the socket.

Pleasant enough, gay even, by no means sad
Is the rickety graveyard on the hill. Those are not cypress trees
Perpendicular among the lurching slabs, but cedars from the
    neighbourhood,
Native to this rocky land, self-sown. Precious
In the early light, reassuring
Is the grave-scarred hillside.
As if after all, the earth might know what it is about.

The Fawn

There it was I saw what I shall never forget
And never retrieve.
Monstrous and beautiful to human eyes, hard to believe,
He lay, yet there he lay,
Asleep on the moss, his head on his polished cleft small ebony
    hooves,
The child of the doe, the dappled child of the deer.

Surely his mother had never said, "Lie here
Till I return," so spotty and plain to see
On the green moss lay he.
His eyes had opened; he considered me.

I would have given more than I care to say
To thrifty ears, might I have had him for my friend
One moment only of that forest day:

Might I have had the acceptance, not the love
Of those clear eyes;

Might I have been for him the bough above
Or the root beneath his forest bed,
A part of the forest, seen without surprise.

Was it alarm, or was it the wind of my fear lest he depart
That jerked him to his jointy knees,
And sent him crashing off, leaping and stumbling
On his new legs, between the stems of the white trees?

I

Valentine

Oh, what a shining town were Death
Woke you therein, and drew your breath,
My buried love; and all you were,
Caught up and cherished, even there.
Those evil windows loved of none
Would blaze as if they caught the sun.

Woke you in Heaven, Death's kinder name,
And downward in sweet gesture came
From your cold breast your rigid hand,
Then Heaven would be my native land.

But you are nowhere: you are gone
All roads into Oblivion.
Whither I would disperse, till then
From home a banished citizen.

In the Grave No Flower

Here dock and tare.
But there
No flower.

Here beggar-ticks, 'tis true;
Here the rank-smelling
Thorn-apple,—and who
Would plant this by his dwelling?
Here every manner of weed
To mock the faithful harrow:
Thistles, that feed
None but the finches; yarrow,
Blue vervain, yellow charlock; here
Bindweed, that chokes the struggling year;
Broad plantain and narrow.

But there no flower.

The rye is vexed and thinned,
The wheat comes limping home,
By vetch and whiteweed harried, and the sandy bloom
Of the sour-grass; here
Dandelions,—and the wind
Will blow them everywhere.

Save there.
There
No flower.

III

Childhood Is the Kingdom Where Nobody Dies

Childhood is not from birth to a certain age and at a certain age
The child is grown, and puts away childish things.
Childhood is the kingdom where nobody dies.

Nobody that matters, that is. Distant relatives of course
Die, whom one never has seen or has seen for an hour,
And they gave one candy in a pink-and-green stripèd bag, or a
     jack-knife,
And went away, and cannot really be said to have lived at all.

And cats die. They lie on the floor and lash their tails,
And their reticent fur is suddenly all in motion
With fleas that one never knew were there,
Polished and brown, knowing all there is to know,
Trekking off into the living world.
You fetch a shoe-box, but it's much too small, because she won't
     curl up now:
So you find a bigger box, and bury her in the yard, and weep.

But you do not wake up a month from then, two months,
A year from then, two years, in the middle of the night
And weep, with your knuckles in your mouth, and say Oh, God!
      Oh, God!
Childhood is the kingdom where nobody dies that matters,—
      mothers and fathers don't die.

And if you have said, "For heaven's sake, must you always be
      kissing a person?"
Or, "I do wish to gracious you'd stop tapping on the window
      with your thimble!"
Tomorrow, or even the day after tomorrow if you're busy having
      fun,
Is plenty of time to say, "I'm sorry, mother."

To be grown up is to sit at the table with people who have died,
      who neither listen nor speak;
Who do not drink their tea, though they always said
Tea was such a comfort.

Run down into the cellar and bring up the last jar of raspberries;
      they are not tempted.

Flatter them, ask them what was it they said exactly
That time, to the bishop, or to the overseer, or to Mrs. Mason;
They are not taken in.
Shout at them, get red in the face, rise,
Drag them up out of their chairs by their stiff shoulders and shake
    them and yell at them;
They are not startled, they are not even embarrassed; they slide
    back into their chairs.

Your tea is cold now.
You drink it standing up,
And leave the house.

IV

The Solid Sprite Who Stands Alone

The solid sprite who stands alone,
　　And walks the world with equal stride,
Grieve though he may, is not undone
　　Because a friend has died.

He knows that man is born to care,
　　And ten and threescore's all his span;
And this is comfort and to spare
　　For such a level man.

He is not made like crooked me,
　　Who cannot rise nor lift my head,
And all because what had to be
　　Has been, what lived is dead;

Who lie among my tears and rust,
　　And all because a mortal brain
That loved to think, is clogged with dust,
　　And will not think again.

V

Spring in the Garden

Ah, cannot the curled shoots of the larkspur that you loved so,
Cannot the spiny poppy that no winter kills
Instruct you how to return through the thawing ground and the
    thin snow
Into this April sun that is driving the mist between the hills?

A good friend to the monkshood in a time of need
You were, and the lupine's friend as well;
But I see the lupine lift the ground like a tough weed
And the earth over the monkshood swell,

And I fear that not a root in all this heaving sea
Of land, has nudged you where you lie, has found
Patience and time to direct you, numb and stupid as you still
    must be
From your first winter underground.

290

VI

Sonnet

Time, that renews the tissues of this frame,
That built the child and hardened the soft bone,
Taught him to wail, to blink, to walk alone,
Stare, question, wonder, give the world a name,
Forget the watery darkness whence he came,
Attends no less the boy to manhood grown,
Brings him new raiment, strips him of his own:
All skins are shed at length, remorse, even shame.
Such hope is mine, if this indeed be true,
I dread no more the first white in my hair,
Or even age itself, the easy shoe,
The cane, the wrinkled hands, the special chair:
Time, doing this to me, may alter too
My anguish, into something I can bear.

Aubade

Cool and beautiful as the blossom of the wild carrot
With its crimson central eye,
Round and beautiful as the globe of the onion blossom
Were her pale breasts whereon I laid me down to die.

From the wound of my enemy that thrust me through in the
    dark wood
I arose; with sweat on my lip and the wild woodgrasses in my
    spur
I arose and stood.
But never did I arise from loving her.

Charon, indeed, your dreaded oar,
With what a peaceful sound it dips
Into the stream; how gently, too,
From the wet blade the water drips.

I knew a ferryman before.
But he was not so old as you.
He spoke from unembittered lips,
With careless eyes on the bright sea
One day, such bitter words to me
As age and wisdom never knew.

This was a man of meagre fame;
He ferried merchants from the shore
To Mitylene (whence I came)
On Lesbos; Phaon is his name.

I hope that he will never die,
As I have done, and come to dwell
In this pale city we approach.

Not that, indeed, I wish him well,
(Though never have I wished him harm)
But rather that I hope to find
In some unechoing street of Hell
The peace I long have had in mind:
A peace whereon may not encroach
That supple back, the strong brown arm,
That curving mouth, the sunburned curls;
But rather that I would rely,
Having come so far, at such expense,
Upon some quiet lodging whence
I need not hear his voice go by
In scraps of talk with boys and girls.

Epitaph

Grieve not for happy Claudius, he is dead;
And empty is his skull.
Pity no longer, arm-in-arm with Dread,
Walks in that polished hall.

Joy, too, is fled.
But no man can have all.

On Thought in Harness

My falcon to my wrist
Returns
From no high air.
I sent her toward the sun that burns
Above the mist;
But she has not been there.

Her talons are not cold; her beak
Is closed upon no wonder;
Her head stinks of its hood, her feathers reek
Of me, that quake at the thunder.

Degraded bird, I give you back your eyes forever, ascend now
      whither you are tossed;
Forsake this wrist, forsake this rhyme;
Soar, eat ether, see what has never been seen; depart, be lost,
But climb.

Desolation Dreamed Of

Desolation dreamed of, though not accomplished,
Set my heart to rocking like a boat in a swell.
To every face I met, I said farewell.

Green rollers breaking white along a clean beach . . . when shall I reach that
    island?
Gladly, O painted nails and shaven arm-pits, would I see less of you!
Gladly, gladly would I be far from you for a long time, O noise and stench of
    man!

I said farewell. Nevertheless,
Whom have I quitted?—which of my possessions do I propose
    to leave?
Not one. This feigning to be asleep when wide awake is all the
    loneliness
I shall ever achieve.

The Leaf and the Tree

When will you learn, my self, to be
A dying leaf on a living tree?
Budding, swelling, growing strong,
Wearing green, but not for long,
Drawing sustenance from air,
That other leaves, and you not there,
May bud, and at the autumn's call
Wearing russet, ready to fall?

Has not this trunk a deed to do
Unguessed by small and tremulous you?
Shall not these branches in the end
To wisdom and the truth ascend?
And the great lightning plunging by
Look sidewise with a golden eye
To glimpse a tree so tall and proud
It sheds its leaves upon a cloud?

Here, I think, is the heart's grief:
The tree, no mightier than the leaf,
Makes firm its root and spreads its crown
And stands; but in the end comes down.
That airy top no boy could climb
Is trodden in a little time
By cattle on their way to drink.
The fluttering thoughts a leaf can think,
That hears the wind and waits its turn,
Have taught it all a tree can learn.

Time can make soft that iron wood.
The tallest trunk that ever stood,
In time, without a dream to keep,
Crawls in beside the root to sleep.

On the wide heath at evening overtaken,
    When the fast-reddening sun
Drops, and against the sky the looming bracken
    Waves, and the day is done,

Though no unfriendly nostril snuffs his bone,
    Though English wolves be dead,
The fox abroad on errands of his own,
    The adder gone to bed,

The weary traveler from his aching hip
    Lengthens his long stride;
Though Home be but a humming on his lip,
    No happiness, no pride,

He does not drop him under the yellow whin
    To sleep the darkness through;
Home to the yellow light that shines within
    The kitchen of a loud shrew,

Home over stones and sand, through stagnant water
  He goes, mile after mile
Home to a wordless poaching son and a daughter
  With a disdainful smile,

Home to the worn reproach, the disagreeing,
  The shelter, the stale air; content to be
Pecked at, confined, encroached upon,—it being
  Too lonely, to be free.

Apostrophe to Man

(on reflecting that the world is ready to go to war again)

Detestable race, continue to expunge yourself, die out.

Breed faster, crowd, encroach, sing hymns, build bombing air-
   planes;

Make speeches, unveil statues, issue bonds, parade;

Convert again into explosives the bewildered ammonia and the
   distracted cellulose;

Convert again into putrescent matter drawing flies

The hopeful bodies of the young; exhort,

Pray, pull long faces, be earnest, be all but overcome, be photo-
   graphed;

Confer, perfect your formulae, commercialize

Bacteria harmful to human tissue,

Put death on the market;

Breed, crowd, encroach, expand, expunge yourself, die out,

Homo called *sapiens.*

My Spirit, Sore from Marching

My spirit, sore from marching
  Toward that receding west
Where Pity shall be governor,
  With Wisdom for his guest:

Lie down beside these waters
  That bubble from the spring;
Hear in the desert silence
  The desert sparrow sing;

Draw from the shapeless moment
  Such pattern as you can;
And cleave henceforth to Beauty;
  Expect no more from man.

Man, with his ready answer,
  His sad and hearty word,
For every cause in limbo,
  For every debt deferred,

For every pledge forgotten,
   His eloquent and grim
Deep empty gaze upon you,—
   Expect no more from him.

From cool and aimless Beauty
   Your bread and comfort take,
Beauty, that made no promise,
   And has no word to break;

Have eyes for Beauty only,
   That has no eyes for you;
Follow her struck pavilion,
   Halt with her retinue;

Catch from the board of Beauty
   Such careless crumbs as fall.
Here's hope for priest and layman;
   Here's heresy for all.

I shall die, but that is all that I shall do for Death.

I hear him leading his horse out of the stall; I hear the clatter on
    the barn-floor.
He is in haste; he has business in Cuba, business in the Balkans,
    many calls to make this morning.
But I will not hold the bridle while he cinches the girth.
And he may mount by himself: I will not give him a leg up.

Though he flick my shoulders with his whip, I will not tell him
    which way the fox ran.
With his hoof on my breast, I will not tell him where the black
    boy hides in the swamp.
I shall die, but that is all that I shall do for Death; I am not on
    his pay-roll.

I will not tell him the whereabouts of my friends nor of my ene-
    mies either.
Though he promise me much, I will not map him the route to
    any man's door.

Am I a spy in the land of the living, that I should deliver men to
    Death?
Brother, the password and the plans of our city are safe with me;
    never through me
Shall you be overcome.

Above These Cares

Above these cares my spirit in calm abiding
Floats like a swimmer at sunrise, facing the pale sky;
Peaceful, heaved by the light infrequent lurch of the heavy wave
    serenely sliding
Under his weightless body, aware of the wide morning, aware of
    the gull on the red buoy bedaubed with guano, aware of his
    sharp cry;
Idly athirst for the sea, as who should say:
In a moment I will roll upon my mouth and drink it dry.

Painfully, under the pressure that obtains
At the sea's bottom, crushing my lungs and my brains
(For the body makes shift to breathe and after a fashion flourish
Ten fathoms deep in care,
Ten fathoms down in an element denser than air
Wherein the soul must perish)
I trap and harvest, stilling my stomach's needs;
I crawl forever, hoping never to see
Above my head the limbs of my spirit no longer free
Kicking in frenzy, a swimmer enmeshed in weeds.

If Still Your Orchards Bear

Brother, that breathe the August air
    Ten thousand years from now,
And smell—if still your orchards bear
    Tart apples on the bough—

The early windfall under the tree,
    And see the red fruit shine,
I cannot think your thoughts will be
    Much different from mine.

Should at that moment the full moon
    Step forth upon the hill,
And memories hard to bear at noon,
    By moonlight harder still,

Form in the shadows of the trees,—
    Things that you could not spare
And live, or so you thought, yet these
    All gone, and you still there,

A man no longer what he was,
  Nor yet the thing he'd planned,
The chilly apple from the grass
  Warmed by your living hand—

I think you will have need of tears;
  I think they will not flow;
Supposing in ten thousand years
  Men ache, as they do now.

Lines for a Grave-Stone

Man alive, that mournst thy lot,
Desiring what thou hast not got,
Money, beauty, love, what not;

Deeming it blesseder to be
A rotted man, than live to see
So rude a sky as covers thee;

Deeming thyself of all unblest
And wretched souls the wretchedest,
Longing to die and be at rest;

Know: that however grim the fate
Which sent thee forth to meditate
Upon my enviable state,

Here lieth one who would resign
Gladly his lot, to shoulder thine.
Give me thy coat; get into mine.

How Naked, How Without a Wall

How naked, how without a wall
    Against the wind and the sharp sleet,
He fares at night, who fares at all
    Forth from the stove's heat.

Or if the moon be in the sky,
    Or if the stars, and the late moon
Not rising till an hour goes by,
    And Libra setting soon,

How naked, how without a stitch
    To shut him from the earnest air,
He goes, who by the whispering ditch
    Alone at night will fare.

Nor is it but the rising chill
    From the warm weeds, that strikes him cold;
Nor that the stridulant hedge grows still,
    Like what has breath to hold,

Until his tiny foot go past
    At length, with its enormous sound;
Nor yet his helpless shadow cast
    To any wolf around.

Bare to the moon and her cold rays
    He takes the road, who by and by
Goes bare beneath the moony gaze
    Of his own awful eye.

He sees his motive, like a fox
    Hid in a badger's hole; he sees
His honour, strangled, in a box,
    Her neck lashed to her knees.

The man who ventures forth alone
    When other men are snug within,
Walks on his marrow, not his bone,
    And lacks his outer skin.

The draughty caverns of his breath
    Grow visible, his heart shines through:
Surely a thing which only death
    Can have the right to do.

From *HUNTSMAN, WHAT QUARRY?*

Y

In April, when the yellow whin
Was out of doors, and I within,—
And magpies nested in the thorn
Where not a man of woman born
Might spy upon them, save he be
Content to bide indefinitely
On Chaldon Heath, hung from a pin,
A great man in a small thorn tree—

In April, when, as I have said,
The golden gorse was all in bloom,
And I confinèd to my room,
And there confined to my bed,
As sick as mortal man could be,
A lady came from over the sea,
All for to say good-day to me.

All in a green and silver gown,
With half its flounces in her hand,
She came across the windy down,

She came, and pricked the furrowed land
With heels of slippers built for town,
All for to say good-day to me.

The Channel fog was in her hair,
Her cheek was cool with Channel fog;
Pale cowslips from the sloping hedge,
And samphire from the salty ledge,
And the sweet myrtle of the bog
She brought me as I languished there;
But of the blackthorn, the blue sloe,
No branch to lay a body low.

She came to me by ditch and stile,
She came to me through heather and brake,
And many and many a flinty mile
She walked in April for my sake,
All for to say good-day to me.

She came by way of Lulworth Cove,
She came by way of Diffey's Farm;
All in a green and silver frock,
With half its flounces over her arm,

By the Bat's Head at dusk she came,
Where inland from the Channel drove
The fog, and from the Shambles heard
The horn above the hidden rock;

And startled many a wild sea-bird
To fly unseen from Durdle Door
Into the fog; and left the shore,
And found a track without a name
That led to Chaldon, and so came
Over the downs to Chydyok,
All for to say good-day to me.

All for to ask me only this—
As she shook out her skirts to dry,
And laughed, and looked me in the eye,
And gave me two cold hands to kiss:
That I be steadfast, that I lie
And strengthen and forbear to die.
All for to say that I must be
Son of my sires, who lived to see
The gorse in bloom at ninety-three,
All for to say good-day to me.

Hard is my pillow
Of down from the duck's breast,
Harsh the linen cover;
I cannot rest.

Fall down, my tears,
Upon the fine hem,
Upon the lonely letters
Of my long name;
Drown the sigh of them.

We stood by the lake
And we neither kissed nor spoke;
We heard how the small waves
Lurched and broke,
And chuckled in the rock.

We spoke and turned away.
We never kissed at all.
Fall down, my tears.

I wish that you might fall
On the road by the lake,
Where my cob went lame,
And I stood with the groom
Till the carriage came.

Short Story

In a fine country, in a sunny country,
Among the hills I knew,
I built a house for the wren that lives in the orchard,
And a house for you.

The house I built for the wren had a round entrance,
Neat and very small;
But the house I built for you had a great doorway,
For a lady proud and tall.

You came from a country where the shrubby sweet lavender
Lives the mild winter through;
The lavender died each winter in the garden
Of the house I built for you.

You were troubled and came to me because the farmer
Called the autumn "the fall";
You thought that a country where the lavender died in the winter
Was not a country at all.

320

The wrens return each year to the house in the orchard;
They have lived, they have seen the world, they know what's best
For a wren and his wife; in the handsome house I gave them
They build their twiggy nest.

But you, you foolish girl, you have gone home
To a leaky castle across the sea,—
To lie awake in linen smelling of lavender,
And hear the nightingale, and long for me.

Pretty Love, I must outlive you;
And my little dog Llewelyn,
Dreaming here with treble whimpers,
Jerking paws and twitching nostrils
On the hearth-rug, will outlive you,
If no trap or shot-gun gets him.

Parrots, tortoises and redwoods
Live a longer life than men do,
Men a longer life than dogs do,
Dogs a longer life than love does.

What a fool I was to take you,
Pretty Love, into my household,
Shape my days and nights to charm you,
Center all my hopes about you,
Knowing well I must outlive you,
If no trap or shot-gun gets me.

English Sparrows

(Washington Square)

How sweet the sound in the city an hour before sunrise,
When the park is empty and grey and the light clear and so lovely
I must sit on the floor before my open window for an hour with
    my arms on the sill
And my cheek on my arm, watching the spring sky's
Soft suffusion from the roofed horizon upward with palest rose,
Doting on the charming sight with eyes
Open, eyes closed;
Breathing with quiet pleasure the cool air cleansed by the night,
    lacking all will
To let such happiness go, nor thinking the least thing ill
In me for such indulgence, pleased with the day and with myself.
    How sweet
The noisy chirping of the urchin sparrows from crevice and shelf
Under my window, and from down there in the street,
Announcing the advance of the roaring competitive day with city
    bird-song.

A bumbling bus
Goes under the arch. A man bareheaded and alone
Walks to a bench and sits down.
He breathes the morning with me; his thoughts are his own.
Together we watch the first magnanimous
Rays of the sun on the tops of greening trees and on houses of
     red brick and of stone.

Impression: Fog Off the Coast of Dorset

As day was born, as night was dying,
The seagulls woke me with their crying;
And from the reef the mooing horn
Spoke to the waker: Day is born
And night is dying, but still the fog
On dimly looming deck and spar
Is dewy, and on the vessel's log,
And cold the first-mate's fingers are,
And wet the pen wherewith they write
"Off Portland. Fog. No land in sight."
—As night was dying, and glad to die,
And day, with dull and gloomy eye,
Lifting the sun, a smoky lamp,
Peered into fog, that swaddled sky
And wave alike: a shifty damp
Unwieldy province, loosely ruled,
Turned over to a prince unschooled,
That he must govern with sure hand
Straightway, not knowing sea from land.

The Rabbit

Hearing the hawk squeal in the high sky
I and the rabbit trembled.
Only the dark small rabbits newly kittled in their neatly dis-
    sembled
Hollowed nest in the thicket thatched with straw
Did not respect his cry.
At least, not that I saw.

But I have said to the rabbit with rage and a hundred times,
    "Hop!
Streak it for the bushes! Why do you sit so still?
You are bigger than a house, I tell you, you are bigger than a
    hill, you are a beacon for air-planes!
O indiscreet!
And the hawk and all my friends are out to kill!
Get under cover!" But the rabbit never stirred; she never will.

And I shall see again and again the large eye blaze
With death, and gently glaze;
The leap into the air I shall see again and again, and the kicking
    feet;
And the sudden quiet everlasting, and the blade of grass green in
    the strange mouth of the interrupted grazer.

Song for Young Lovers in a City

Though less for love than for the deep
Though transient death that follows it
These childish mouths grown soft in sleep
Here in a rented bed have met,

They have not met in love's despite . . .
Such tiny loves will leap and flare
Lurid as coke-fires in the night,
Against a background of despair.

To treeless grove, to grey retreat
Descend in flocks from corniced eaves
The pigeons now on sooty feet,
To cover them with linden leaves.

To a Calvinist in Bali

You that are sprung of northern stock,
And nothing lavish,—born and bred
With tablets at your foot and head,
And CULPA carven in the rock,

Sense with delight but not with ease
The fragrance of the quinine trees,
The *kembang-spatu's* lolling flame
With solemn envy kin to shame.

Ah, be content!—the scorpion's tail
Atones for much; without avail
Under the sizzling solar pan
Our sleeping servant pulls the fan.

Even in this island richly blest,
Where Beauty walks with naked breast,
Earth is too harsh for Heaven to be
One little hour in jeopardy.

Thanksgiving Dinner

Ah, broken garden, frost on the melons and on the beans!
Frozen are the ripe tomatoes, the red fruit and the hairy golden
    stem;
Frozen are the grapes, and the vine above them frozen, and the
    peppers are frozen!
And I walk among them smiling,—for what of them?

I can live on the woody fibres of the overgrown
Kohl-rabi, on the spongy radish coarse and hot,
I can live on what the squirrels may have left of the beechnuts
    and the acorns . . .
For pride in my love, who might well have died, and did not.

I will cook for my love a banquet of beets and cabbages,
Leeks, potatoes, turnips, all such fruits . . .
For my clever love, who has returned from further than the far
    east;
We will laugh like spring above the steaming, stolid winter roots.

The Snow Storm

No hawk hangs over in this air:
The urgent snow is everywhere.
The wing adroiter than a sail
Must lean away from such a gale,
Abandoning its straight intent,
Or else expose tough ligament
And tender flesh to what before
Meant dampened feathers, nothing more.

Forceless upon our backs there fall
Infrequent flakes hexagonal,
Devised in many a curious style
To charm our safety for a while,
Where close to earth like mice we go
Under the horizontal snow.

Huntsman, What Quarry?

"Huntsman, what quarry
On the dry hill
Do your hounds harry?

When the red oak is bare
And the white oak still
Rattles its leaves
In the cold air:
What fox runs there?"

"Girl, gathering acorns
In the cold autumn,
I hunt the hot pads
That ever run before,
I hunt the pointed mask
That makes no reply,
I hunt the red brush
Of remembered joy."

"To tame or to destroy?"

"To destroy."

"Huntsman, hard by
In a wood of grey beeches
Whose leaves are on the ground,
Is a house with a fire;
You can see the smoke from here.
There's supper and a soft bed
And not a soul around.
Come with me there;
Bide there with me;
And let the fox run free."

The horse that he rode on
Reached down its neck,
Blew upon the acorns,
Nuzzled them aside;
The sun was near setting;
He thought, "Shall I heed her?"
He thought, "Shall I take her
For a one-night's bride?"

He smelled the sweet smoke,
He looked the lady over;
Her hand was on his knee;
But like a flame from cover
The red fox broke—
And "Hoick! Hoick!" cried he.

Not So Far as the Forest

I

That chill is in the air
Which the wise know well, and even have learned to bear.
This joy, I know,
Will soon be under snow.

The sun sets in a cloud
And is not seen.
Beauty, that spoke aloud,
Addresses now only the remembering ear.
The heart begins here
To feed on what has been.

Night falls fast.
Today is in the past.

Blown from the dark hill hither to my door
Three flakes, then four
Arrive, then many more.

II

Branch by branch
This tree has died. Green only
Is one last bough, moving its leaves in the sun.

What evil ate its root, what blight,
What ugly thing,
Let the mole say, the bird sing;
Or the white worm behind the shedding bark
Tick in the dark.

You and I have only one thing to do:
Saw the trunk through.

III

Distressèd mind, forbear
To tease the hooded Why;
That shape will not reply.

From the warm chair
To the wind's welter
Flee, if storm's your shelter.

But no, you needs must part,
Fling him his release—
On whose ungenerous heart
Alone you are at peace.

IV

Not dead of wounds, not borne
Home to the village on a litter of branches, torn
By splendid claws and the talk all night of the villagers,
But stung to death by gnats
Lies Love.

What swamp I sweated through for all these years
Is at length plain to me.

V

Poor passionate thing,
Even with this clipped wing how well you flew!—though not so
  far as the forest.

Unwounded and unspent, serene but for the eye's bright trouble,
Was it the lurching flight, the unequal wind under the lopped
  feathers that brought you down,
To sit in folded colours on the level empty field,
Visible as a ship, paling the yellow stubble?

Rebellious bird, warm body foreign and bright,
Has no one told you?—Hopeless is your flight
Towards the high branches. Here is your home,
Between the barnyard strewn with grain and the forest tree.
Though Time refeather the wing,
Ankle slip the ring,
The once-confined thing
Is never again free.

Not for these lovely blooms that prank your chambers did I
        come. Indeed,
I could have loved you better in the dark;
That is to say, in rooms less bright with roses, rooms more
        casual, less aware
Of History in the wings about to enter with benevolent air
On ponderous tiptoe, at the cue "Proceed."
Not that I like the ash-trays over-crowded and the place in a
        mess,
Or the monastic cubicle too unctuously austere and stark,
But partly that these formal garlands for our Eighth Street
        Aphrodite are a bit too Greek,
And partly that to make the poor walls rich with our unaided
        loveliness
Would have been more *chic*.

Yet here I am, having told you of my quarrel with the taxi-driver
        over a line of Milton, and you laugh; and you are you,
        none other.
Your laughter pelts my skin with small delicious blows.

But I am perverse: I wish you had not scrubbed—with pumice,
   I suppose—
The tobacco stains from your beautiful fingers. And I wish I did
   not feel like your mother.

The Fitting

The fitter said, *"Madame, vous avez maigri,"*
And pinched together a handful of skirt at my hip.
"Tant mieux," I said, and looked away slowly, and took my
　　under-lip
Softly between my teeth.

Rip—rip!
Out came the seam, and was pinned together in another place.
She knelt before me, a hardworking woman with a familiar and
　　unknown face,
Dressed in linty black, very tight in the arm's-eye and smelling
　　of sweat.
She rose, lifting my arm, and set her cold shears against me,—
　　snip-snip;
Her knuckles gouged my breast. My drooped eyes lifted to my
　　guarded eyes in the glass, and glanced away as from some-
　　one they had never met.

"*Ah, que madame a maigri!*" cried the *vendeuse*, coming in with
dresses over her arm.

"*C'est la chaleur*," I said, looking out into the sunny tops of
the horse-chestnuts—and indeed it was very warm.

I stood for a long time so, looking out into the afternoon, think-
ing of the evening and you. . . .

While they murmured busily in the distance, turning me, touch-
ing my secret body, doing what they were paid to do.

What Savage Blossom

Do I not know what savage blossom only under the pitting hail
Of your inclement climate could have prospered? Here lie
Green leaves to wade in, and of the many roads not one road
    leading outward from this place
But is blocked by boughs that will hiss and simmer when they
    burn—green autumn, lady, green autumn on this land!

Do I not know what inward pressure only could inflate its petals
    to withstand
(No, no, not hate, not hate) the onslaught of a little time with
    you?

No, no, not love, not love. Call it by name,
Now that it's over, now that it is gone and cannot hear us.

It was an honest thing. Not noble. Yet no shame.

Menses

(He speaks, but to himself, being aware how it is with her)

Think not I have not heard.
Well-fanged the double word
And well-directed flew.

I felt it. Down my side
Innocent as oil I see the ugly venom slide:
Poison enough to stiffen us both, and all our friends;
But I am not pierced, so there the mischief ends.

There is more to be said; I see it coiling;
The impact will be pain.
Yet coil; yet strike again.
You cannot riddle the stout mail I wove
Long since, of wit and love.

As for my answer . . . stupid in the sun
He lies, his fangs drawn:
I will not war with you.

345

You know how wild you are. You are willing to be turned
To other matters; you would be grateful, even.
You watch me shyly. I (for I have learned
More things than one in our few years together)
Chafe at the churlish wind, the unseasonable weather.

"Unseasonable?" you cry, with harsher scorn
Than the theme warrants; "Every year it is the same!
'Unseasonable!' they whine, these stupid peasants!—and never
    since they were born
Have they known a spring less wintry! Lord, the shame,
The crying shame of seeing a man no wiser than the beasts he
    feeds—
His skull as empty as a shell!"

("Go to. You are unwell.")

Such is my thought, but such are not my words.

"What is the name," I ask, "of those big birds
With yellow breast and low and heavy flight,
That make such mournful whistling?"

                          "Meadowlarks,"
You answer primly, not a little cheered.
"Some people shoot them." Suddenly your eyes are wet
And your chin trembles. On my breast you lean,
And sob most pitifully for all the lovely things that are not and
      have been.

"How silly I am!—and I *know* how silly I am!"
You say; "You are very patient. You are very kind.
I shall be better soon. Just Heaven consign and damn
To tedious Hell this body with its muddy feet in my mind!"

The Plaid Dress

Strong sun, that bleach
The curtains of my room, can you not render
Colourless this dress I wear?—
This violent plaid
Of purple angers and red shames; the yellow stripe
Of thin but valid treacheries; the flashy green of kind deeds done
Through indolence, high judgments given in haste;
The recurring checker of the serious breach of taste?

No more uncoloured than unmade,
I fear, can be this garment that I may not doff;
Confession does not strip it off,
To send me homeward eased and bare;

All through the formal, unoffending evening, under the clean
Bright hair,
Lining the subtle gown . . . it is not seen,
But it is there.

"Fontaine, Je Ne Boirai Pas De Ton Eau!"

I know I might have lived in such a way
As to have suffered only pain:
Loving not man nor dog;
Not money, even; feeling
Toothache perhaps, but never more than an hour away
From skill and novocaine;
Making no contacts, dealing with life through agents, drinking
    one cocktail, betting two dollars, wearing raincoats in the
    rain;
Betrayed at length by no one but the fog
Whispering to the wing of the plane.

"Fountain," I have cried to that unbubbling well, "I will not
    drink of thy water!" Yet I thirst
For a mouthful of—not to swallow, only to rinse my mouth in
    —peace. And while the eyes of the past condemn,
The eyes of the present narrow into assignation. And . . .
    worst . . .
The young are so old, they are born with their fingers crossed;
    I shall get no help from them.

I think I will learn some beautiful language, useless for commercial
Purposes, work hard at that.
I think I will learn the Latin name of every songbird, not only in
America but wherever they sing.
(Shun meditation, though; invite the controversial:
Is the world flat? Do bats eat cats?) By digging hard I might
deflect that river, my mind, that uncontrollable thing,
Turgid and yellow, strong to overflow its banks in spring, carry-
ing away bridges;
A bed of pebbles now, through which there trickles one clear
narrow stream, following a course henceforth nefast—

Dig, dig; and if I come to ledges, blast.

To a Young Poet

Time cannot break the bird's wing from the bird.
Bird and wing together
Go down, one feather.

No thing that ever flew,
Not the lark, not you,
Can die as others do.

Modern Declaration

I, having loved ever since I was a child a few things, never having
    wavered
In these affections; never through shyness in the houses of the
    rich or in the presence of clergymen having denied these
    loves;
Never when worked upon by cynics like chiropractors having
    grunted or clicked a vertebra to the discredit of these loves;
Never when anxious to land a job having diminished them by a
    conniving smile; or when befuddled by drink
Jeered at them through heartache or lazily fondled the fingers of
    their alert enemies; declare

That I shall love you always.
No matter what party is in power;
No matter what temporarily expedient combination of allied
    interests wins the war;
Shall love you always.

The Road to the Past

It is this that you get for being so far-sighted. Not so many years
For the myopic, as for me,
The delightful shape, implored and hard of heart, proceeding
Into the past unheeding,
(No wave of the hand, no backward look to see
If I still stand there) clear and precise along that road appears.

The trees that edge that road run parallel
For eyes like mine past many towns, past hell seen plainly;
All that has happened shades that street;
Children all day, even the awkward, the ungainly
Of mind, work out on paper problems more abstruse;
Demonstrably these eyes will close
Before those hedges meet.

"Wolf!" cried my cunning heart
　　At every sheep it spied,
　　And roused the countryside.

"Wolf! Wolf!"—and up would start
　　Good neighbours, bringing spade
　　And pitchfork to my aid.

At length my cry was known:
　　Therein lay my release.
I met the wolf alone
　　And was devoured in peace.

Theme and Variations

I

Not even my pride will suffer much;
Not even my pride at all, maybe,
If this ill-timed, intemperate clutch
Be loosed by you and not by me,
Will suffer; I have been so true
A vestal to that only pride
Wet wood cannot extinguish, nor
Sand, nor its embers scattered, for,
See all these years, it has not died.

And if indeed, as I dare think,
You cannot push this patient flame,
By any breath your lungs could store,
Even for a moment to the floor
To crawl there, even for a moment crawl,
What can you mix for me to drink
That shall deflect me? What you do
Is either malice, crude defense
Of ego, or indifference:

355

I know these things as well as you;
You do not dazzle me at all.

Some love, and some simplicity,
Might well have been the death of me.

II

Heart, do not bruise the breast
That sheltered you so long;
Beat quietly, strange guest.

Or have I done you wrong
To feed you life so fast?
Why, no; digest this food
And thrive. You could outlast
Discomfort if you would.

You do not know for whom
These tears drip through my hands.
You thud in the bright room
Darkly. This pain demands
No action on your part,
Who never saw that face.

357

These eyes, that let him in,
(Not you, my guiltless heart)
These eyes, let them erase
His image, blot him out
With weeping, and go blind.

Heart, do not stain my skin
With bruises; go about
Your simple function. Mind,
Sleep now; do not intrude;
And do not spy; be kind.

Sweet blindness, now begin.

III

Rolled in the trough of thick desire,
No oars, and no sea-anchor out
To bring my bow into the pyre
Of sunset, suddenly chilling out
To shadow over sky and sea,
And the boat helpless in the trough;
No oil to pour; no power in me
To breast these waves, to shake them off:

I feel such pity for the poor,
Who take the fracas on the beam—
Being ill-equipped, being insecure—
Daily; and caulk the opening seam
With strips of shirt and scribbled rhyme;
Who bail disaster from the boat
With a pint can; and have no time,
Being so engrossed to keep afloat,
Even for quarrelling (that chagrined
And lavish comfort of the heart),
Who never came into the wind,
Who took life beam-on from the start.

IV

And do you think that love itself,
Living in such an ugly house,
Can prosper long?

         We meet and part;
Our talk is all of heres and nows,
Our conduct likewise; in no act
Is any future, any past;
Under our sly, unspoken pact,
I know with whom I saw you last,
But I say nothing; and you know
At six-fifteen to whom I go.

Can even love be treated so?

I know, but I do not insist,
Having stealth and tact, though not enough,
What hour your eye is on your wrist.

No wild appeal, no mild rebuff
Deflates the hour, leaves the wine flat.

Yet if you drop the picked-up book
To intercept my clockward look—
Tell me, can love go on like that?

Even the bored, insulted heart,
That signed so long and tight a lease,
Can break its contract, slump in peace.

V

I had not thought so tame a thing
Could deal me this bold suffering.

I have loved badly, loved the great
Too soon, withdrawn my words too late;
And eaten in an echoing hall
Alone and from a chipped plate
The words that I withdrew too late.
Yet even so, when I recall
How ardently, ah! and to whom
Such praise was given, I am not sad:
The very rafters of this room
Are honoured by the guests it had.

You only, being unworthy quite
And specious,—never, as I think,
Having noticed how the gentry drink
Their poison, how administer
Silence to those they would inter—
Have brought me to dementia's brink.

Not that this blow be dealt to *me*:
But by thick hands, and clumsily.

VI

Leap now into this quiet grave.
How cool it is. Can you endure
Packed men and their hot rivalries—
The plodding rich, the shiftless poor,
The bold inept, the weak secure—
Having smelt this grave, how cool it is?

Why, here's a house, why, here's a bed
For every lust that drops its head
In sleep, for vengeance gone to seed,
For the slashed vein that will not bleed,
The jibe unheard, the whip unfelt,
The mind confused, the smooth pelt
Of the breast, compassionate and brave.
Pour them into this quiet grave.

VII

Now from a stout and more imperious day
Let dead impatience arm me for the act.
We bear too much. Let the proud past gainsay
This tolerance. Now, upon the sleepy pact
That bound us two as lovers, now in the night
And ebb of love, let me with stealth proceed,
Catch the vow nodding, harden, feel no fright,
Bring forth the weapon sleekly, do the deed.

I know—and having seen, shall not deny—
This flag inverted keeps its colour still;
This moon in wane and scooped against the sky
Blazes in stern reproach. Stare back, my Will—
We can out-gaze it; can do better yet:
We can expunge it. I will not watch it set.

VIII

The time of year ennobles you.
The death of autumn draws you in.

The death of those delights I drew
From such a cramped and troubled source
Ennobles all, including you,
Involves you as a matter of course.

You are not, you have never been
(Nor did I ever hold you such),
Between your banks, that all but touch,
Fit subject for heroic song. . . .
The busy stream not over-strong,
The flood that any leaf could dam. . . .

Yet more than half of all I am
Lies drowned in shallow water here:
And you assume the time of year.

I do not say this love will last:
Yet Time's perverse, eccentric power
Has bound the hound and stag so fast
That strange companions mount the tower
Where Lockhart's fate with Keats is cast,
And Booth with Lincoln shares the hour.

That which has quelled me, lives with me,
Accomplice in catastrophe.

To Elinor Wylie

(Died 1928)

I

Song for a Lute

(1927)

Seeing how I love you utterly,
And your disdain is my despair,
Alter this dulcet eye, forbear
To wear those looks that latterly
You wore, and won me wholly, wear
A brow more dark, and bitterly
Berate my dulness and my care,
Seeing how your smile is my despair,
Seeing how I love you utterly.

Seeing how I love you utterly,
And your distress is my despair,
Alter this brimming eye, nor wear
The trembling lip that latterly

Under a more auspicious air
You wore, and thrust me through, forbear
To drop your head so bitterly
Into your hands, seeing how I dare
No tender touch upon your hair,
Knowing as I do how fitterly
You do reproach me than forbear,
Seeing how your tears are my despair,
Seeing how I love you utterly.

II
(1928)

For you there is no song . . .
   Only the shaking
Of the voice that meant to sing; the sound of the
    strong
   Voice breaking.

Strange in my hand appears
   The pen, and yours broken.
There are ink and tears on the page; only the tears
   Have spoken.

III

Sonnet in Answer to a Question
(1938)

Oh, she was beautiful in every part!—
The auburn hair that bound the subtle brain;
The lovely mouth cut clear by wit and pain,
Uttering oaths and nonsense, uttering art
In casual speech and curving at the smart
On startled ears of excellence too plain
For early morning!—*Obit*. Death from strain;
The soaring mind outstripped the tethered heart.

Yet here was one who had no need to die
To be remembered. Every word she said
The lively malice of the hazel eye
Scanning the thumb-nail close—oh, dazzling dead,
How like a comet through the darkening sky
You raced! . . . would your return were heralded.

IV

Nobody now throughout the pleasant day,
The flowers well tended and the friends not few,
Teases my mind as only you could do
To mortal combat erudite and gay . . .
"So Mr. S. was kind to Mr. K.!
Whilst Mr. K.—wait, I've a word or two!"
(I think that Keats and Shelley died with you—
They live on paper now, another way.)

You left in time, too soon; to leave too soon
Was tragic and in order—had the great
Not taught us how to die?—My simple blood,
Loving you early, lives to mourn you late . . .
As Mr. K., it may be, would have done;
As Mr. S. (*oh, answer!*) never would.

V

Gone over to the enemy now and marshalled against me
Is my best friend.
What hope have I to hold with my narrow back
This town, whence all surrender?

Someone within these walls has been in love with Death
     longer than I care to say;
It was not you! . . . but he gets in that way.

Gone under cover of darkness, leaving a running track,
And the mark of a dusty paw on all our splendour,
Are they that smote the table with the loudest blow,
Saying, "I will not have it so!"

No, no.
This is the end.
What hope have I?
You, too, led captive and without a cry!

VI

Over the Hollow Land

Over the hollow land the nightingale
Sang out in the full moonlight.
"Immortal bird,"
We said, who heard;
"What rapture, what serene despair";
And paused between a question and reply
To hear his varied song across the tulip-scented air.

But I thought of the small brown bird among the rhodo-
    dendrons at the garden's end,
Crouching, close to the bough,
Pale cheek wherefrom the black magnificent eye obliquely
    stared,
The great song boiling in the narrow throat
And the beak near splitting,
A small bird hunched and frail,
Whom the divine uncompromising note that brought the
    world to its window
Shook from head to tail.

Close to the branch, I thought, he cowers now,
Lest his own passion shake him from the bough.

Thinking of him, I thought of you . . .
Shaken from the bough, and the pure song half-way through.

"Inert Perfection, let me chip your shell.
You cannot break it through with that soft beak.
What if you broke it never, and it befell
You should not issue thence, should never speak?"

Perfection in the egg, a fluid thing,
Grows solid in due course, and there exists;
Knowing no urge to struggle forth and sing;
Complete, though shell-bound. But the mind insists

It shall be hatched . . . to this ulterior end:
That it be bound by Function, that it be
Less than Perfection, having to expend
Some force on a nostalgia to be free.

Say that We Saw Spain Die

Say that we saw Spain die. O splendid bull, how well you fought!
Lost from the first.

                   . . . the tossed, the replaced, the
      watchful *torero* with gesture elegant and spry,
Before the dark, the tiring but the unglazed eye deploying the
      bright cape,
Which hid for once not air, but the enemy indeed, the authentic
      shape,
A thousand of him, interminably into the ring released . . .
      the turning beast at length between converging colours
      caught.

Save for the weapons of its skull, a bull
Unarmed, considering, weighing, charging
Almost a world, itself without ally.

Say that we saw the shoulders more than the mind confused, so
      profusely
Bleeding from so many more than the accustomed barbs, the
      game gone vulgar, the rules abused.

Say that we saw Spain die from loss of blood, a rustic reason, in
    a reinforced
And proud punctilious land, no *espada*—
A hundred men unhorsed,
A hundred horses gored, and the afternoon aging, and the crowd
    growing restless (all, all so much later than planned),
And the big head heavy, sliding forward in the sand, and the
    tongue dry with sand,—no *espada*
Toward that hot neck, for the delicate and final thrust, having
    dared trust forth his hand.

Set the foot down with distrust upon the crust of the world—it
    is thin.
Moles are at work beneath us; they have tunnelled the sub-soil
With separate chambers, which at an appointed knock
Could be as one, could intersect and interlock. We walk on the
    skin
Of life. No toil
Of rake or hoe, no lime, no phosphate, no rotation of crops, no
    irrigation of the land,
Will coax the limp and flattened grain to stand
On that bad day, or feed to strength the nibbled roots of our
    nation.

Ease has demoralized us, nearly so; we know
Nothing of the rigours of winter: the house has a roof against—
    the car a top against—the snow.
All will be well, we say; it is a habit, like the rising of the sun,
For our country to prosper; who can prevail against us? No one.

The house has a roof; but the boards of its floor are rotting, and
   hall upon hall
The moles have built their palace beneath us: we have not far to
   fall.

Two Voices

FIRST VOICE

Let us be circumspect, surrounded as we are
By every foe but one, and he from the woods watching.
Let us be courteous, since we cannot be wise, guilty of no neglect,
    pallid with seemly terror, yet regarding with indulgent eyes
Violence, and compromise.

SECOND VOICE

We shall learn nothing; or we shall learn it too late. Why should
    we wait
For Death, who knows the road so well? Need we sit hatching—
Such quiet fowl as we, meek to the touch,—a clutch of adder's
    eggs? Let us not turn them; let us not keep them warm;
    let us leave our nests and flock and tell
All that we know, all that we can piece together, of a time when
    all went, or seemed to go, well.

Mortal Flesh, Is Not Your Place in the Ground?

Mortal flesh, is not your place in the ground?—Why do you
    stare so
At the bright planet serene in the clear green evening sky above
    the many-coloured streakèd clouds?—
Your brows drawn together as if to chide, your mouth set as if
    in anger.

Learn to love blackness while there is yet time, blackness
Unpatterned, blackness without horizons.

Beautiful are the trees in autumn, the emerald pines
Dark among the light-red leaves of the maple and the dark-red
Leaves of the white oak and the indigo long
Leaves of the white ash.
But why do you stand so, staring with stern face of ecstasy at the
    autumn leaves,
At the boughs hung with banners along the road as if a proces-
    sion were about to pass?

Learn to love roots instead, that soon above your head shall be
    as branches.

No Earthly Enterprise

No earthly enterprise
Will cloud this vision; so beware,
You whom I love, when you are weak, of seeking comfort stair
    by stair
Up here: which leads nowhere.

I am at home—oh, I am safe in bed and well tucked in—Despair
Put out the light beside my bed.
I smiled, and closed my eyes.
"Goodnight—goodnight," she said.

But you, you do not like this frosty air.

Cold of the sun's eclipse,
When cocks crow for the first time hopeless, and dogs in kennel
    howl,
Abandoning the richly-stinking bone,
And the star at the edge of the shamed and altered sun shivers
    alone,
And over the pond the bat but not the swallow dips,
And out comes the owl.

I could not bring this splendid world nor any trading beast
In charge of it, to defer, no, not to give ear, not in the least
Appearance, to my handsome prophecies, which here I ponder
    and put by.

I am left simpler, less encumbered, by the consciousness that I
    shall by no pebble in my dirty sling avail
To slay one purple giant four feet high and distribute arms
    among his tall attendants, who spit at his name when spit-
    ting on the ground:
They will be found one day
Prone where they fell, or dead sitting—and a pockmarked wall
Supporting the beautiful back straight as an oak before it is old.

I have learned to fail. And I have had my say.
Yet shall I sing until my voice crack (this being my leisure, this
    my holiday)
That man was a special thing and no commodity, a thing im-
    proper to be sold.

This Dusky Faith

Why, then, weep not,
Since naught's to weep.

Too wild, too hot
For a dead thing,
Altered and cold,
Are these long tears:
Relinquishing
To the sovereign force
Of the pulling past
What you cannot hold
Is reason's course.

Wherefore, sleep.

Or sleep to the rocking
Rather, of this:
The silver knocking
Of the moon's knuckles
At the door of the night;

385

Death here becomes
Being, nor truckles
To the sun, assumes
Light as its right.

So, too, this dusky faith
In Man, transcends its death,
Shines out, gains emphasis;
Shorn of the tangled past,
Shows its fine skull at last,
Cold, lovely satellite.

Truce for a moment between Earth and Ether
Slackens the mind's allegiance to despair:
Shyly confer earth, water, fire and air
With the fifth essence.

For the duration, if the mind require it,
Trigged is the wheel of Time against the slope;
Infinite Space lies curved within the scope
Of the hand's cradle.

Thus between day and evening in the autumn,
High in the west alone and burning bright,
Venus has hung, the earliest riding-light
In the calm harbour.

From *MAKE BRIGHT THE ARROWS*

Y

To the Maid of Orleans

Joan, Joan, can you be
Tending sheep in Domrémy?
Have no voices spoken plain:
France has need of you again?—

You, so many years ago
Welcomed into Heaven, we know
Maiden without spot or taint,
First as foundling, then as saint.

Or do faggot, stake and torch
In your memory roar and scorch
Till no sound of voice comes through
Saying France has need of you?

Joan, Joan, hearken still,
Hearken, child, against your will:
Saint thou art, but at the price
Of recurring sacrifice;

Martyred many times must be
Who would keep his country free.

Memory of England
(October 1940)

I am glad, I think, my happy mother died
Before the German airplanes over the English countryside
Dropped bombs into the peaceful hamlets that we used to
    know—
Sturminster-Newton, and the road that used to run
Past bridge, past cows in meadow,
Warm in the sun,
Cool in the elm-tree's shadow,
To the thatched cottage roofs of Shillingstone;
Dropped bombs on Romsey Abbey, where the aging records
    show ·
(Or did a little while ago)
In faded ink and elegant fine hand
The name of a boy baby christened there
In 15—(I forget the year)
Later to sail away to this free land

And build in what is now named Massachusetts a new Romsey
    here.
(My ancestor,—I still can see the page,
Our sentimental journey, our quaint pilgrimage!)

Dorset and Hampshire were our home in England: the tall
    holly trees, the chestnuts that we found
Glossy within their shaggy burrs on the cold autumn ground
In the New Forest, new in the Norman's day, where we walked
    alone,
Easing at times our joyful weary backs
By shifting to a stump the weight of our small shoulder-packs,
Meeting no living creature all one lovely day
But trees and ferns and bracken and, directly in our way
Or grazing near at hand,
From time to time a herd of small wild ponies; well aware
Of imminent sunset—and we two alone long miles from
    anywhere.

All that we moved among, heath, bracken, hollies with round
    berries red

Bright for an English Christmas, beech and oak,
Chestnut, with its sweet mealy food
On the leaves thick about us in the autumn air
Plentiful, gleaming from its rough burrs everywhere—
All this was good,
And all had speech, and spoke,
And all the magic unfamiliar land
Was ours by distant heritage and ours by deep love close at hand.
How many miles we walked I now forget, dog-tired at night
Spying an inn's warm light
Through small-paned windows thrown,—
To Romsey, and then back to Shillingstone.

So gravely threatened now
That lovely village under the Barrow's brow,
Where peering from my window at dawn under the shelving
    thatch
With cold bare feet and neck scratched by the straw
I saw the hounds go by;
So gravely threatened the kind people there,
She in her neat front flower plot,

He like as not
Up in the 'lotment hoeing,
Or coming home to his supper of beer and cheese,
Bread and shallots,
These thoughts . . .
And thoughts like these . . .
Make me content that she, not I,
Went first, went without knowing.

Poems Which Have Not Appeared

in Any of the Previous Volumes

Υ

(In the following pages, poems not titled are headed by an ornament.)

The Pear Tree

In this squalid, dirty dooryard
    Where the chickens squawk and run,
White, incredible, the pear tree
    Stands apart, and takes the sun;

Mindful of the eyes upon it,
    Vain of its new holiness,—
Like the waste-man's little daughter
    In her First Communion dress.

Tree Ceremonies

(Vassar College, 1915)

Druids' Chant

Great voice that calls us in the wind of dawn,
Strange voice that stills us in the heat of noon,
    Heard in the sunset,
    Heard in the moonrise
And in the stirring of the wakeful night,
    Speak now in blessing,
    Chide us no longer,
Great voice of love, we will not grieve thee more.

Song of the Nations

    Out of
    Night and alarm,
    Out of
    Darkness and dread,
    Out of old hate,
    Grudge and distrust,
    Sin and remorse,

Passion and blindness;
Shall come
Dawn and the birds,
Shall come
Slacking of greed,
Snapping of fear—
Love shall fold warm like a cloak
Round the shuddering earth
Till the sound of its woe cease.

After
Terrible dreams,
After
Crying in sleep,
Grief beyond thought,
Twisting of hands,
Tears from shut lids
Wetting the pillow;
Shall come
Sun on the wall,
Shall come
Sounds from the street,

Children at play—
Bubbles too big blown, and dreams
Filled too heavy with horror
Will burst and in mist fall.

Sing then,
You who were dumb,
Shout then
Into the dark;
Are we not one?
Are not our hearts
Hot from one fire,
And in one mold cast?
Out of
Night and alarm,
Out of
Terrible dreams,
Reach me your hand,
This is the meaning of all that we
Suffered in sleep,—the white peace
Of the waking.

Baccalaureate Hymn

(*Vassar College, 1917*)

Thou great offended God of love and kindness,
　We have denied, we have forgotten Thee!
With deafer sense endow, enlighten us with blindness,
　Who, having ears and eyes, nor hear nor see.

Bright are the banners on the tents of laughter;
　Shunned is Thy temple, weeds are on the path;
Yet if Thou leave us, Lord, what help is ours thereafter?—
　Be with us still,—Light not today Thy wrath!

Dark were the ways where of ourselves we sought Thee,
　Anguish, Derision, Doubt, Desire and Mirth;
Twisted, obscure, unlovely, Lord, the gifts we brought Thee,
　Teach us what ways have light, what gifts have worth.

Since we are dust, how shall we not betray Thee?
　Still blows about the world the ancient wind—
Nor yet for lives untried and tearless would we pray Thee:
　Lord let us suffer that we may grow kind!

"Lord, Lord!" we cried of old, who now before Thee,
　Stricken with prayer, shaken with praise, are dumb;
Father accept our worship when we least adore Thee,
　And when we call Thee not, oh, hear and come!

Facsimile of original broadside of Baccalaureate Hymn

Tune:—"St. Vincent."

Words and music by EDNA ST. VINCENT MILLAY, '17.

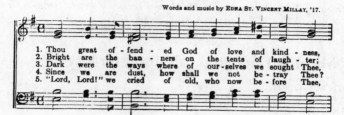

1. Thou great of-fend - ed God of love and kind - ness,
2. Bright are the ban - ners on the tents of laugh - ter;
3. Dark were the ways where of our-selves we sought Thee,
4. Since we are dust, how shall we not be - tray Thee?
5. "Lord, Lord!" we cried of old, who now be - fore Thee,

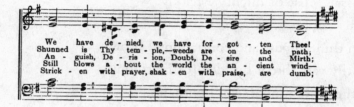

We have de - nied, we have for - got - ten Thee!
Shunned is Thy tem - ple,—weeds are on the path;
An - guish, De - ri - sion, Doubt, De - sire and Mirth;
Still blows a - bout the world the an - cient wind—
Strick - en with prayer, shak - en with praise, are dumb;

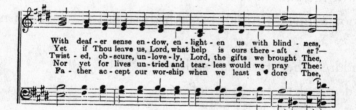

With deaf - er sense en - dow, en - light - en us with blind - ness,
Yet if Thou leave us, Lord, what help is ours there - aft - er?—
Twist - ed, ob - scure, un - love - ly, Lord, the gifts we brought Thee,
Nor yet for lives un - tried and tear - less would we pray Thee:
Fa - ther ac - cept our wor-ship when we least a - dore Thee,

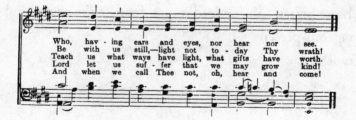

Who, hav - ing ears and eyes, nor hear nor see.
Be with us still,—light not to - day Thy wrath!
Teach us what ways have light, what gifts have worth.
Lord let us suf - fer that we may grow kind!
And when we call Thee not, oh, hear and come!

Invocation to the Muses

Read by the poet at The Public Ceremonial of The National Institute of Arts and Letters at Carnegie Hall, New York, January 18th, 1941.

Great Muse, that from this hall absent for long
Hast never been,
Great Muse of Song,
Colossal Muse of mighty Melody,
Vocal Calliope,
With thine august and contrapuntal brow
And thy vast throat builded for Harmony,
For the strict monumental pure design,
And the melodic line:
Be thou tonight with all beneath these rafters—be with me.

If I address thee in archaic style—
Words obsolete, words obsolescent,
It is that for a little while
The heart must, oh, indeed must from this angry and out-
    rageous present
Itself withdraw

Into some past in which most crooked Evil,
Although quite certainly conceived and born, was not as yet the
　　Law.

Archaic, or obsolescent at the least,
Be thy grave speaking and the careful words of thy clear song,
For the time wrongs us, and the words most common to our
　　speech today
Salute and welcome to the feast
Conspicuous Evil—or against him all day long
Cry out, telling of ugly deeds and most uncommon wrong.

Be thou tonight with all beneath these rafters—be with me;
But oh, be more with those who are not free.
Who, herded into prison camps all shame must suffer and all
　　outrage see.
Where music is not played nor sung,
Though the great voice be there, no sound from the dry throat
　　across the thickened tongue
Comes forth; nor has he heart for it.
Beauty in all things—no, we cannot hope for that; but some
　　place set apart for it.

Here it may dwell;
And with your aid, Melpomene
And all thy sister-muses (for ye are, I think, daughters of
    Memory)
Within the tortured mind as well.

Reaped are those fields with dragon's-teeth so lately sown;
Many the heaped men dying there—so close, hip touches
    thigh; yet each man dies alone.
Music, what overtone
For the soft ultimate sigh or the unheeded groan
Hast thou—to make death decent, where men slip
Down blood to death, no service of grieved heart or ritual lip
Transferring what was recently a man and still is warm—
Transferring his obedient limbs into the shallow grave where
    not again a friend shall greet him,
Nor hatred do him harm . . .
Nor true love run to meet him?

In the last hours of him who lies untended
On a cold field at night, and sees the hard bright stars

Above his upturned face, and says aloud, "How strange . . . my
    life is ended."—
If in the past he loved great music much, and knew it well,
Let not his lapsing mind be teased by well-beloved but ill-
    remembered bars—
Let the full symphony across the blood-soaked field
By him be heard, most pure in every part,
The lonely horror of whose painful death is thus repealed,
Who dies with quiet tears upon his upturned face, making to
    glow with softness the hard stars.

And bring to those who knew great poetry well
Page after page that they have loved but have not learned by
    heart!
We who in comfort to well-lighted shelves
Can turn for all the poets ever wrote,
Beseech you: Bear to those
Who love high art no less than we ourselves,
Those who lie wounded, those who in prison cast
Strive to recall, to ease them, some great ode, and every stanza
    save the last

Recall—oh, in the dark, restore them
The unremembered lines; make bright the page before them!
Page after page present to these,
In prison concentrated, watched by barbs of bayonet and wire,
Give ye to them their hearts' intense desire—
The words of Shelley, Virgil, Sophocles.

And thou, O lovely and not sad,
Euterpe, be thou in this hall tonight!
Bid us remember all we ever had
Of sweet and gay delight—
We who are free,
But cannot quite be glad,
Thinking of huge, abrupt disaster brought
Upon so many of our kind
Who treasure as do we the vivid look on the unfrightened face,
The careless happy stride from place to place,
And the unbounded regions of untrammelled thought
Open as interstellar space
To the exploring and excited mind.

O Muses, O immortal Nine!—
Or do ye languish? *Can* ye die?
Must all go under?—
How shall we heal without your help a world
By these wild horses torn asunder?
How shall we build anew?—how start again?
How cure, how even moderate this pain
Without you, and you strong?
And if ye sleep, then waken!
And if ye sicken and do plan to die,
Do not that now!

Hear us, in what sharp need we cry!
For we have help nowhere
If not in you!
Pity can much, and so a mighty mind, but cannot all things
    do!—
By you forsaken,
We shall be scattered, we shall be overtaken!
Oh, come! Renew in us the ancient wonder,
The grace of life, its courage, and its joy!
Weave us those garlands nothing can destroy!
Come! with your radiant eyes!—with your throats of thunder!

To S. V. B.—June 15, 1940

You will not haunt the *rue Vavin*
Behind the old *Rotonde* we knew,—
Whose waiters called *"les quat' copains"*
Henry and Stan and me and you.

You, with your merry wit, will not,
You, with your slouched and awkward grace,
O owlish infant polyglot!—
You will not haunt so sad a place.

The opal city in the mist
Of dusk, before the evening rain,
When topaz, rose and amethyst
The arch was echoed in the Seine;

The drives by moonlight through the *Bois;*
The thinned-out wood, the cared-for tree;
The elegance, the *"Quant à moi,"*
The "Now, old son, you listen to me!"

A story sold, a cheque from home—
All four of us would dine that day:
Apéritifs before the *Dôme;*
Then dinner at some smart café;

Where I would dance with Stan, while you
And Henry talked, or watched the floor;
Or bought pink drinks for girls we knew
A little, from the cheque before.

All of us knew our guarded truth:
We called, *"L'addition!"* not, "The cheque!"
I always ordered French vermouth,
So I could say, *"Un export sec!"*

And Henry would have much preferred
His brandy straight; but, ordered so,
What waiter ever would have heard
His *"Bien—et moi, une fine à l'eau"?*

———

Sad, sad, to call a place "so sad",
That once was heaven and hell-on-wheels
To four hard-working, Paris-mad,
Eager, blasé, young imbeciles!

———

Yet, should you come in ghostly guise,
You will not haunt the *rue Vavin:*
Connecticut and her allies
You still will champion if you can;

But whence your soaring spirit flew,
You will not circle down to see
A Paris, lost no more to you,
Than lost to Henry, Stan, and me.

If, in the Foggy Aleutians

Not ever, now, any more, upon this mildewed planet
Shines the sweet, wholesome sun: we live in fog.
Our leaves grow large and green, but we bear no blossom;
No coloured hope unfolds, no poem speaks out
In Dutch, Korean, English or Tagalog.

Yet, if, in the foggy Aleutians, if on the misty
Island of Kiska, island of Attu, any
Flower, however weak and bleak, appears
In spring, between the cloudy craters, why then, although
It should take us a thousand years,
We can stare into the fog until it shines, we can force it to
     unfold us.
We must ask the men who have been there; they will know.

Poem and Prayer for an Invading Army

*(Written to be broadcast over the NBC Network on D-Day, June 6, 1944.
Read by Ronald Colman.)*

They must not go alone
into that burning building!—which today
is all of Europe!
        Say
that you go with them, spirit and heart and mind!
Although the body, grown
too old to fight a young man's war; or wounded
too deeply under the healed and whitened scars
of earlier battles, must remain behind.

You, too, may not be with them, save in spirit, you
so greatly needed here, here in the very van
and front of Duty,
to fashion tools and engines, and to engineer
their transport; build the ships and mine the coal
without which all their efforts would be worse than vain!

You men and women working in the workshops,
      working on the farms;
makers of tanks and of tractors, fitters of wings

to metal birds which have not left the nest
as yet, which yet must try their flight;
sowers of seed in season, planters of little plants
at intervals, on acres newly plowed
and disked and harrowed,
to feed a starving world;

You workers in the shipyards, building ships
which crowd each other down the ways;
you miners of coal in dark and dangerous corridors,
    who see the sun's
total eclipse
each morning, disappearing as you do under the earth's rim,
not to emerge into the daylight till the day's
over, and the light dim;

All you
without whose constant effort and whose skill—
without whose loyal and unfailing aid—
our men would stand
stranded upon a foreign and a hostile shore

417

without so much as a stout stick to beat away
Death or Pain:
bullets like angry hornets buzzing 'round the ears and the
    bewildered brain,
and from the sky again and yet again
the downpour of the heavy, evil, accurate, murderous rain;

You who have stood behind them to this hour,
move strong behind them now: let still
the weary bones encase the indefatigable Will.

But how can men draw near
so fierce a conflagration?—even here,
across a gray and cold and foggy sea
its heat is felt!—Why,
touch your cheek—is it not hot and tight and dry?

And look what light climbs up the eastern sky, and sinks
and climbs again!
like to the bright Aurora of the North
it floods and flushes, pulses, pales—then glows,

lighting the entire East majestically;
as if it were the sun that rose.

I wish it were!

Have patience, friend; it yet may be.

Surely our fibre and our sinews, the backbone
and brain of us, are made of some less common stuff
than clay?—Surely the blood which warms the veins
of heroes at the front, our brothers and our sons,
runs also in our own!
And are we not then capable perhaps of something
        more courageous than we yet have shown?

Surely some talisman, some token of
our lofty pride in them, our heavy gratitude,
and so much, so much love,
will find its way to them!
Some messenger, the vicar and the angel
of what we feel,
will fly before them where they fly, before them and above,
like patron goddesses in wars of old,

cleaving with level lovely brows the hard air
before the eager prows,
lighting their way with incandescent wings and wingèd heel.

This is the hour, this the appointed time.
The sound of the clock falls awful on our ears,
and the sound of the bells, their metal clang and chime,
tolling, tolling,
for those about to die.
For we know well they will not all come home, to lie
in summer on the beaches.

And yet weep not, you mothers of young men, their wives,
their sweethearts, all who love them well—
fear not the tolling of the solemn bell:
it does not prophesy,
and it cannot foretell;
it only can record;
and it records today the passing of a most uncivil age,
which had its elegance, but lived too well,
and far, oh, far too long;

and which, on History's page,
will be found guilty of injustice and grave wrong.

———————

O Thou, Thou Prince of Peace, this is a prayer for War!
Yet not a war of man against his fellowman.
Say, rather, Lord, we do beseech
Thy guidance and Thy help:
In exorcising from the mind of Man, where she has made her
      nest,
a hideous and most fertile beast—
and this to bring about with all dispatch, for look, where
          even now she would lie down again to whelp!

Lord God of Hosts! Thou Lord of Hosts not only, not alone
of battling armies Lord and King;
but of the child-like heart as well, which longs
to put away—oh, not the childish, but the adult
circuitous and adroit, antique and violent thing
called War;
and sing
the beauties of this late-to-come but oh-so-lovely Spring!
For see

where our young men go forth in mighty numbers, to set free
from torture and from every jeopardy
things that are dear to Thee.

Keep in Thy loving care, we pray, those of our fighting men
whose happy fortune it may be to come back home again
after the War is over; and all those who must perforce remain,
the mourned, the valiant slain.
This we beseech Thee, Lord. And now, before
we rise from kneeling, one thing more:
Soften our hard and angry hearts; make us ashamed
of doing what we do, beneath Thy very eyes, knowing it does
    displease Thee.
Make us more humble, Lord, for we are proud
without sufficient reason; let our necks be bowed
more often to Thy will;
for well we know what deeds find favour in Thy sight; and still
we do not do them.

Oh Lord, all through the night, all through the day,
keep watch over our brave and dear, so far away.

Make us more worthy of
their valour; and Thy love.

"Let them come home! Oh, let the battle, Lord, be brief,
and let our boys come home!"
So cries the heart, sick for relief
from its anxiety, and seeking to forestall
a greater grief.

So cries the heart aloud. But the thoughtful mind
has something of its own to say:
"On that day—
when they come home—from very far away—
and further than you think—
(for each of them has stood upon the very brink
or sat and waited in the anteroom
of Death, expecting every moment to be called by name)

Now look you to this matter well: that they
upon returning shall not find
seated at their own tables,—at the head,

perhaps, of the long festive board prinked out in prodigal array,
the very monster which they sallied forth to conquer and to
  quell;
and left behind for dead."

Let us forget such words, and all they mean,
as Hatred, Bitterness and Rancor, Greed,
Intolerance, Bigotry; let us renew
our faith and pledge to Man, his right to be
Himself, and free.

Say that the Victory is ours—then say—
and each man search his heart in true humility—
"Lord! Father! Who are we,
that we should wield so great a weapon for the rights
and rehabilitation of Thy creature Man?
Lo, from all corners of the Earth we ask
all great and noble to come forth—converge
upon this errand and this task with generous and gigantic plan:

Hold high this Torch, who will.
Lift up this Sword, who can!"

Christmas Canticle

The Angel:

Thou sinful Soul, how wilt thou feel,
On Christmas Eve when the oxen kneel,
For all thy vows to Christ so dear,
Which thou didst break in this bad year?

Man:

Full of fear— oh, full of fear!
I will fall to my knees in yellow straw;
I will clasp my hands in terror and awe!
I will lift my tears and to Mary appeal—
On Christmas Eve when the oxen kneel!

The Angel:

And dost thou think that Mary will hear,
And wash thee clean of the dirty year?—
Wherein thou didst lie and slay and steal?

Man:

Aye, for the sake of Christ so dear!
She will cool my brow. She will cleanse and heal,—
On Christmas Eve, when the oxen kneel!

The Angel:

And what wilt thou do for Mary, then,
In daylight, out in the world of men?

Man:

I will try hard not to be bad again.
I will try hard not to be bad again.

The Angel:

And when thou art tempted—wilt thou go wrong?

Man:

Jesus will help me, and make me strong;
And see that by me no evil is done.

The Angel:

Then Hail Mary and Her Little Son!

The Angel and Man:

Then Hail Mary and Her Little Son!

Υ

We have gone too far; we do not know how to stop: impetus
Is all we have. And we share it with the pushed Inert.

We are clever,—we are as clever as monkeys; and some of us
Have intellect, which is our danger, for we lack intelligence
And have forgotten instinct.

Progress—progress is the dirtiest word in the language—who
 ever told us—
And made us believe it—that to take a step forward was
 necessarily, was always
A good idea?
In this unlighted cave, one step forward
That step can be the down-step into the Abyss.
But we, we have no sense of direction; impetus
Is all we have; we do not proceed, we only
Roll down the mountain,
Like disbalanced boulders, crushing before us many
Delicate springing things, whose plan it was to grow.

427

Clever, we are, and inventive,—but not creative:
For, to create, one must decide—the cells must decide—what
    form,
What colour, what sex, how many petals, five, or more than
    five,
Or less than five.

But we, we decide nothing: the bland Opportunity
Presents itself, and we embrace it,—we are so grateful
When something happens which is not directly War;
For we think—although of course, now, we very seldom
Clearly think—
That the other side of War is Peace.

We have no sense; we only roll downhill. Peace
Is the temporary beautiful ignorance that War
Somewhere progresses.

Υ

Deep in the muck of unregarded doom,
Where none can make a conquest, none have room
To stretch an aching muscle,—there might be
Interstices where impulse could go free . . .
There, where accomplishment cannot achieve,
Valour defend, religion quite believe,
Or vengeance plot behavior,—there may still
Be cracks, uneasy instinct well might fill
And even worm its way along, until
All might begin again; and Man receive
In prospect, what he never can retrieve.

The Animal Ball

Let us go to the Animal Ball, disguised as bipeds!
And the first man down on all fours, pays for the drinks!
Stan has a cocker that can walk on his hind legs, too:
We'll take him along, to support us when the spirit sinks.

We've walked on our hind-legs now so many ages,
We're hoof to the knee, and hock to the hip, but still—
How hot the feet get when you've only two to hit the ground
    with!
It takes real nerve to walk erect, and a pretty strong will.

We went too far when we put on the fur of lynxes,
Of weasels trapped in winter when they've lost their tan;
We went too far when we let the fox assist us
To warm the hide that houses the soul of Man.

The reek of the leopard and the stink of the inky cat
Striped handsomely with white, are in the concert hall;
We sleekly writhe from under them, and are above all that:
But, the concert over, back into our pelts we crawl.

"It is bad to let the dog taste leather."

Through the green forest softly without a sound,
Wrapped in a still mood
As in a cloak and hood
I went, and cast no shadow in the shadow of the wood.

There grew beeches taller than a ship's mast
That rocks from wave to wave
On the great seas of the world.
I looked into their tops;
Their tops were in another world;
Tossed in a sunny air as far from me
As the foam on waves that follow each other fast,
All day, unseen by man, over the sunny sea.

Naked birches, whiter than a god's thigh,
I saw, and stared, between the stems of the black pines;
Boulders whiter than a dream remembered by day
Stood in the brook's way,
Damp with mosses greener than an emerald's eye.

And ferns where the water sloped from stone to stone in the
    clear dark
Without ripple or speech
Curved motionless, rooted in rotted bark
And leaves laid together and the rifled husks of the beech.

Y

As sharp as in my childhood, still
Ecstasy shocks me fixed. The will
Cannot entice it, never could,
So never tries. But from the wood
The wind will hurl the clashing sleet;
Or a small fawn with lovely feet,
Uncertain in its gait, will walk
Among the ferns, not breaking back
One frond, not bruising one fern black,
Into the clearing, and appraise
With mild, attracted, wondering gaze,
And lifted head unhurt and new,
This world that he was born into.

Such marvels as, one time, I feared
Might go, and leave me unprepared
For hardship. But they never did.
They blaze before me still, as wild
And clear, as when I was a child.

They never went away at all.
I need not, though I do, recall
Such moments in my childhood, when
Wonder sprang out at me again,
And took me by the heels, and whirled
Me round and round above the world.

For wonder leaps upon me still,
And makes me dizzy, makes me ill,
But never frightened—for I know—
Not where—but in whose hands I go:
The lovely fingers of Delight
Have hold of me and hold me tight.

Y

By goodness and by evil so surrounded, how can the heart
Maintain a quiet beat?
It races like an idling engine, shaking the whole machine;
And the skin of the inner wrist is blue and green
And yellow, where it has been pounded.

Or else, reluctant to repeat
Bright battles ending always in defeat,
From sadness and discouragement it all but fails;
And the warm blood welling slowly from the weary heart
Before it reaches wrist or temple cools,
Collects in little pools
Along its way, and wishes to remain there, while the face pales,
And diastole and systole meet.

Y

At least, my dear,
You did not have to live to see me die.

Considering now how many things I did that must have
        caused you pain,
Sweating at certain memories, blushing dark blood, unable
To gather home my scattered thoughts that graze the forbidden
        hills, cropping the mind-bane,
I cut from the hedge for crook the one disservice
I never did you,—you never saw me die.

I find in my disorderly files among unfinished
Poems, and photographs of picnics on the rocks, letters from
        you in your bold hand.
I find in the pocket of a coat I could not bring myself to give
        away
A knotted handkerchief, containing columbine-seeds.
A few more moments such as these and I shall have paid all.

Not that you ever—
O, love inflexible, O militant forgiveness, I know

You kept no books against me! In my own hand
Are written down the sum and the crude items of my
        inadequacy.

It is only that there are moments when for the sake of a
        little quiet in the brawling mind I must search out,
Recorded in my favour,
One princely gift.
The most I ever did for you was to outlive you.
But that is much.

437

From *MINE THE HARVEST*

Y

Small hands, relinquish all :
Nothing the fist can hold,—
Not power, not love, not gold—
But suffers from the cold,
And is about to fall.

The mind, at length bereft
Of thinking, and its pain,
Will soon disperse again,
And nothing will remain :
No, not a thought be left.

Exhort the closing eye,
Urge the resisting ear,
To say, "The thrush is here" ;
To say, "His song is clear" ;
To live, before it die.

Small hands, relinquish all:
Nothing the fist can hold,
Not power, not love, not gold,
But suffers from the cold,
And is about to fall.

The mind, at length bereft
Of thinking and its pain,
Will soon disperse again,
And nothing will remain:
No, not a thing be left.

Only the ardent eye,
Only the listening ear
Can say, "The thrush was here!"
Can say, "His song was clear!"
Can live, before it die.

Ragged Island

There, there where those black spruces crowd
To the edge of the precipitous cliff,
Above your boat, under the eastern wall of the island;
And no wave breaks; as if
All had been done, and long ago, that needed
Doing; and the cold tide, unimpeded
By shoal or shelving ledge, moves up and down,
Instead of in and out;
And there is no driftwood there, because there is no beach;
Clean cliff going down as deep as clear water can reach;

No driftwood, such as abounds on the roaring shingle,
To be hefted home, for fires in the kitchen stove;
Barrels, banged ashore about the boiling outer harbour;
Lobster-buoys, on the eel-grass of the sheltered cove:

There, thought unbraids itself, and the mind becomes
    single.

There you row with tranquil oars, and the ocean
Shows no scar from the cutting of your placid keel;
Care becomes senseless there; pride and promotion
Remote; you only look; you scarcely feel.

Even adventure, with its vital uses,
Is aimless ardour now; and thrift is waste.

Oh, to be there, under the silent spruces,
Where the wide, quiet evening darkens without haste
Over a sea with death acquainted, yet forever chaste.

To whom the house of Montagu
Was neighbour, and that orchard near
Wherein all pleasant fruit-trees grew
Whose tops were silvered by the clear
Light of the blessèd, sworn-by moon,
(Or all-but-sworn-by—save that She,
Knowing the moon's inconstancy,
Dreaded that Love might change as soon. . .
Which changèd never; or did change
Into something rich and strange);
To whom in infancy the sight
Of Sancho Panza and his Knight,
In noble, sad and awkward state
Approaching through the picket-gate,
Was warmer with the flesh of life
Than visits from the vicar's wife;
For whom from earliest days the lips
Of Her who launched the thousand ships
Curved in entrancing speech, and Troy

Was hurt by no historic boy,
But one more close and less a fool
Than boys who yanked your curls at school
(Far less a fool than he who lay
With willing Venus on a bed
Of anise, parsley, dill and rue,
A bank whereon the wild thyme grew,
And longed but to be gone from thence,—
Whom vainly Venus did implore
To do her that sweet violence
All boys and girls with any sense
Would die to do; but where she lay
Left her, and rose and rushed away
To stalk the tusky, small-eyed boar
He might have stalked another day),
And naked long Leander swam
The Thames, the Avon and the Cam,
And wet and chattering, white and cold
Appeared upon the pure threshold
Of Hero, whom the sight did move
To fear, to pity, and to love;

For such a child the peopled time,
When any man in any wood
Was shaggy like a goat, and stood
On hooves, and used his lusty strength
To blow through straws of different length
Bound all together; or could ride
A horse he never need bestride—
For such a child, that distant time
Was close as apple-trees to climb,
And apples crashed among the trees
Half Baldwin, half Hesperides.

This
Is mine, and I can hold it;
Lying here
In the hour before dawn, knowing that the cruel June
Frost has made the green lawn
White and brittle, smelling that the night was very cold,
Wondering if the lush, well-loved, well-tended,
Hoed and rowed and watched with pride
And with anxiety
So long,—oh, cruel, cruel,
Unseasonable June—
Whether all that green will be black long before noon—

This
I know: that what I hear
Is a thrush; and very near,
Almost on the sill of my open window, close to my ear.
I was startled, but I made no motion, I knew
What I had to do—stop breathing, not be

Here at all, and I have accomplished this. He has not yet known
Anything about me; he is singing very loud
And with leisure: he is all alone.

Oh, beautiful, oh, beautiful,
Oh, the most beautiful that I ever have heard,
Anywhere, including the nightingale.
It is not so much the tune
Although the tune is lovely, going suddenly higher
Than you expect, and neat, and something like the nightingale
    dropping
And throbbing very low.
It is not so much the notes, it is the quality of the voice,
Something to do perhaps with over-tone
And under-tone, and implication
Felt, but not quite heard—

Oh, this is much to ask
Of two delicate ear-drums and of some other perception
Which I do not understand, a little oversensitive

Perhaps to certain sounds.
All my senses
Have broken their dikes and flooded into one, the sense of
    hearing.

I have no choice,
I think, if I wish to continue to live: I am beginning to shiver
Already: I may be shattered
Like a vessel too thin
For certain vibrations.
Go away now, I think; go down to the damp hemlocks near
    the brook in the hollow,
Where I cannot quite follow
Your deepest notes, through the dissipating air.
But return soon.

Not so soon, though,
Quite, perhaps,
As tomorrow.

Υ

Of what importance, O my lovely girls, my dancers, O my
    lovely boys,
My lovers and my dancers, and my lovely girls, my lovers and
    my dancers,
In a world so loud
Is our sweet noise?

Who is so proud
Of deftness in the ordered dance or on the ever-listening strings
Or of skill about the ankles with no rudeness the fine Tyrian
    folds
Arranging with such art that none beholds, or when she sings
Her songs by Aphrodite not unheard, so proud as I?—
(Who on this day, not unequipped with garlands pleasing to
    the gods, my lyre and my stylus, my stylus and my life
    put by!)

Go now to Gorgo, you, and learn from her
What dancing is and how 'tis done;

But cut for me. if ever you loved me, and you did, from your
    sweet-smelling curls
One each, from each one one,—
For I have a death to die which I may not defer—

And lay on the grave of what I may not live with and sleep well
Your pretty ringlets, O my pretty girls!—

How long my song must slumber, we shall see, or may not
    ever see—
No one can tell,
This is, I think, the serious death of me.

I die, that the sweet tongue of bound Aeolia never from
    her throat be torn, that Mitylene may be free
To sing, long after me.

Phaon, I shall not die for you again.
There are few poets. And my own child tells me there are other
    men.

Such poets as henceforth of their own will die, must die for
        more than you.

This I propose to do.

But die to no purpose? in full waste of body's brawn and skill
        and brain's instructed, rich and devious plot

To live?—not.

Death must be fertile, from this moment on, fertile, at least, as
        life.

For Man has all to lose: ordered and organized from this day
        on, must be his nightly

Watch, the locking of his shrine against defilers:

Skillful now indeed must be the thumbers of the record, the
        compilers:

Sharpened at all hours is the knife.

Y

Few come this way; not that the darkness
Deters them, but they come
Reluctant here who fear to find,
Thickening the darkness, what they left behind
Sucking its cheeks before the fire at home,
The palsied Indecision from whose dancing head
Precipitately they fled, only to come again
Upon him here,
Clutching at the wrist of Venture with a cold
Hand, aiming to fall in with him, companion
Of the new as of the old.

The Strawberry Shrub

Strawberry Shrub, old-fashioned, quaint as quinces,
Hard to find in a world where neon and noise
Have flattened the ends of the three more subtle senses;
And blare and magenta are all that a child enjoys.

More brown than red the bloom—it is a dense colour;
Colour of dried blood; colour of the key of F.
Tie it in your handkerchief, Dorcas, take it to school
To smell. But no, as I said, it is browner than red; it is duller
Than history, tinnier than algebra; and you are colour-deaf.

Purple, a little, the bloom, like musty chocolate;
Purpler than the purple avens of the wet fields;
But brown and red and hard and hiding its fragrance;
More like an herb it is: it is not exuberant.
You must bruise it a bit: it does not exude; it yields.

Clinker-built, the bloom, over-lapped its petals
Like clapboards; like a boat I had; like the feathers of a wing;
Not graceful, not at all Grecian, something from the provinces:
A chunky, ruddy, beautiful Boeotian thing.

Take it to school, knotted in your handkerchief, Dorcas,
Corner of your handkerchief, take it to school, and see
What your teacher says; show your pretty teacher the curious
Strawberry Shrub you took to school for me.

When it is over—for it will be over,
Though we who watched it be gone, watched it and with it
    died—
Will there be none the less the yellow melilot, the white, the
    high sweet clover,
Close to the dusty, fragrant, hot roadside?
Oh, yes, there will!—
Escaped from fields of fodder, for there must be fodder still. . . .

Ah, yes, but nothing will escape . . .

Yet sweet, perhaps, in fields of fodder still.

When it is over—for it will be over—
Will there be none the less, will there be still
In April on the southern slope of an orchard, apple orchard hill,
Red-and-white buds already fragrant, intent upon blossom-
    ing?—
There will; I know there will.

But for whom will they blossom?—
                    They will blossom for what, not whom,
I think—the streakèd bloom
Red-and-white, and the hardy fragrance, strong, all but visible,
    almost but not quite in sight,
Long, long before its pretty petals in a May wind fall,
Will be the finished apple in the eyes of all beholding it;

I see him well: the human creature studying the only good
A tree can be—stout wood
For building or for pulp whereon to print the expedient thing,
Or, if not that, food.
He walks through the apple orchard just now blossoming,
Dismissing to the necessary, the developing, past
The present beauty and the fragrance enfolding it.

Y

The courage that my mother had
Went with her, and is with her still:
Rock from New England quarried;
Now granite in a granite hill.

The golden brooch my mother wore
She left behind for me to wear;
I have no thing I treasure more:
Yet, it is something I could spare.

Oh, if instead she'd left to me
The thing she took into the grave!—
That courage like a rock, which she
Has no more need of, and I have.

Ⅴ

Wild-cat, gnat and I
Go our ways under a grey sky.
Little that Himself has made
Ever finds me quite afraid . . .
Though if cat clawed me,
Gnat gnawed me,
I should shriek, or roll in grass,
Asking that this trouble pass.

Things that hunt in hunger
I stroke, across my fear:
Only anger
Brings the crashing tear.

This should be simple; if one's power were great,
If one were God, for instance,—and the world
Not yet created; Lucifer not hurled
Yet out of Heaven, to plot and instigate
Most thoughtful mischief: simple, in a state
Of non-existence, to manipulate
And mould unwieldy, heavy, obstinate
But thoughtless matter, into some bright world:—
Make something out of nothing, and create
As many planets, and as various men
And other mortal creatures as might seem
Consistent with the structure and the theme
Of one's proposed achievement; not from dream,
No, not from aspiration, not from hope,
But out of art and wisdom, and those powers
Such as must qualify a god, create
A world at least as beautiful and brave
And terrified and sorrowful as ours.

For nothingness is plastic, has no trend;
Is stubborn but in this: it is inert;
Wills not to render justice, nor do hurt;
And should be, in strong hands, easy to bend.

But evil upon evil laminate
Through layers uncountable as leaves in coal—
To strip that into strata—perpetrate
Such outrage upon evil; and create
Good out of wickedness at this late date--
There, there's a trick to tame the gamiest soul.

Sweet earth, you might from birth—oh beaming sight:—
With gentle glow have lighted all the night;
And Man, a star upon a planet, see,
Radiant beyond the furthest nebulae.

But earth, though grown to green and lush estate,
Her blossom, Man, has never yet unfurled:
Observe how bawdy, botched and profligate,
Except in greed, proceeds this pretty world.

We move in darkness solemn and extreme;
We falter forward, hesitate, decide
To turn about, pause, fumble, plunge, collide,—
Beg pardon, and then bob and bob about
From left to right,
Bump foreheads, then burst out
In nervous, merry laughter, and plunge forth
Into the forest suddenly, you running east by north,
Gasping and stumbling over stumps, and I
East by south,
Slashing through bogs, tripped by submerged logs and
  with muddy water in my mouth,
Till every sound subsides
And all is lost in darkness and in fog,
And neither of us has thought to say goodnight.

Such blindness does not intercept the sight
Of the efficient: they have learned by heart
By daylight, from a most meticulous chart
Just where to go; they know . . .
And can as well through darkness as by day

Find their direct, discreet, expedient way:
Know where to go to muster, or to hide;
They move among us all throughout the night;
They pass close by your side;
You do not hear their step, they step so light.

. . . why cannot we as well as they
Scout, reconnoiter, photograph, survey,
Make maps and study them, and learn our way?—
Or must we lie and sleep, "because 'tis night"?
Then it is true, that in this world today
Lucifer, alone, can bring men light.

Must double-dealing, like a snake's forked tongue,
Flick red at us from under every stone?
Must Honour be self-conscious, being alone?—
And Aspiration, an infected lung?

Must Justice always dawdle, don its wig,
And wipe its spectacles before it speaks?
And Government keep flapping to and fro

Like a loose shutter on a hinge that squeaks?—
Kindness of heart be such a whirligig?
Courtesy mince and bow with pointed toe?
Piety smirk?—and Scholarship repose
In camphor, saving on Commencement Day?

Evil alone has oil for every wheel;
Rolls without friction and arrives on time;
Looks forward and sees far; does not reveal
Itself in conversation; is sublime
In logic; is not wasteful; does not feel
Compunction; buries the dead past in lime.

I think, perhaps, the gods, who may not die,
May not achieve unconsciousness, forget
Even their errors or their sins, are set
On making daily pieties comply
With nightly assignations—and are shy
Of mortal things, like laughter, say, or tears,—
Things which they might regret an eon of years—
Fervour, devotion, fright, audacity.

But we are singled out,—oh, we have doom
To comfort us,—sweet peril, imminent death—
So we have leisure, we have time, have room
For wide despair and all its leagues beneath,
Lethal delights the gods dare not assume,
And, not possessing them, cannot bequeath.
And, out of haughty, smooth, serene despair,
We might envisage, and we might fulfill
Appointments and arrangements, which the fair
Soft gods have never made, and never will.

From so much energy, so little hope,
So vast a consolation in the end,
We could erect a thing of poise and scope,
Which future generations might defend,
And put to their own use; and what we grope
To get a glimpse of, they might comprehend.

To build a house would be, it seems to me,
An easy task, if you had solid, good,
Simple material, clean of history:
Honest, unbiased brick, cement, and wood—

If you had sense, authority, and time,
And need not quibble, shift, cajole, subdue,
Break down partitions, breathe old hair and lime,
And tease the out-of-plumb into the true—
If you need not, for instance, for one thing,
Lure ancient chimneys to be lined with tile,
Oh, what a joy! Oh, hear the hammers ring!
A house!—and building houses is worth while.

We, we, the living, we, the still-alive,—
Why, what a triumph, what a task is here!
But how to go about it?—how connive
To outwit Evil in his proper sphere
And element?—Evil, conservative,
Established, disciplined, adroit, severe.
And yet, in some way, yet, we may contrive
To build our world; if not this year, next year.

Song

Beautiful Dove, come back to us in April:
You could not over-winter on our world.
Fly to some milder planet until springtime;
Return with olive in your claws upcurled.

Leave us to shrikes and ravens until springtime:
We let them find their food as best they may;
But you, we do not grow the grain you feed on
And you will starve among us, if you stay.

But oh, in April, from some balmier climate
Come back to us, be with us in the spring!
If we can learn to grow the grain you feed on,
You might be happy here; might even sing.

New England Spring, 1942

The rush of rain against the glass
Is louder than my noisy mind
Crying, "Alas!"

The rain shouts: "Hear me, how I melt the ice that clamps the
      bent and frozen grass!
Winter cannot come twice
Even this year!
I break it up; I make it water the roots of spring!
I am the harsh beginning, poured in torrents down the hills,
And dripping from the trees and soaking, later, and when the
      wind is still,
Into the roots of flowers, which your eyes, incredulous, soon
      will suddenly find!
Comfort is almost here."

The sap goes up the maple; it drips fast
From the tapped maple into the tin pail
Through tubes of hollow elder; the pails brim;

Birds with scarlet throats and yellow bellies sip from the pail's
rim.
Snow falls thick; it is sifted
Through cracks about windows and under doors;
It is drifted through hedges into country roads. It cannot last.
Winter is past.
It is hurling back at us boasts of no avail.

But Spring is wise. Pale and with gentle eyes, one day somewhat
she advances;
The next, with a flurry of snow into flake-filled skies retreats
before the heat in our eyes, and the thing designed
By the sick and longing mind in its lonely fancies—
The sally which would force her and take her.
And Spring is kind.
Should she come running headlong in a wind-whipped acre
Of daffodil skirts down the mountain into this dark valley we
would go blind.

Here in a rocky cup of earth
The simple acorn brought to birth
What has in ages grown to be
A very oak, a mighty tree.
The granite of the rock is split
And crumbled by the girth of it.

Incautious was the rock to feed
The acorn's mouth; unwise indeed
Am I, upon whose stony heart
Fell softly down, sits quietly,
The seed of love's imperial tree
That soon may force my breast apart.

"I fear you not. I have no doubt
My meagre soil shall starve you out!"

Unless indeed you prove to be
The kernel of a kingly tree;

Which if you be I am content
To go the way the granite went,
And be myself no more at all,
So you but prosper and grow tall.

Y

How innocent we lie among
The righteous!—Lord, how sweet we smell,
Doing this wicked thing, this love,
Bought up by bishops!—doing well,
With all our leisure, all our pride,
What's illy done and done in haste
By licensed folk on every side,
Spitting out fruit before they taste.

(That stalk must thrust a clubby bud;
Push an abortive flower to birth.)

Under the moon and the lit scud
Of the clouds, the cool conniving earth
Pillows my head, where your head lies;

Weep, if you must, into my hair
Tomorrow's trouble: the cold eyes
That know you gone and wonder where.

473

But tell the bishops with their sons,
Shout to the City Hall how we
Under a thick barrage of guns
Filched their divine commodity.

Armenonville

By the lake at Armenonville in the Bois de Boulogne
Small begonias had been set in the embankment, both
    pink and red;
With polished leaf and brittle, juicy stem;
They covered the embankment; there were wagon-loads
    of them,
Charming and neat, gay colours in the warm shade.

We had preferred a table near the lake, half out of view,
Well out of hearing, for a voice not raised above
A low, impassioned question and its low reply.
We both leaned forward with our elbows on the table,
    and you
Watched my mouth while I answered, and it made me
    shy.
I looked about, but the waiters knew we were in love,
And matter-of-factly left us blissfully alone.

There swam across the lake, as I looked aside, avoiding
Your eyes for a moment, there swam from under the
    pink and red begonias

A small creature; I thought it was a water-rat; it swam
    very well,
In complete silence, and making no ripples at all
Hardly; and when suddenly I turned again to you,
Aware that you were speaking, and perhaps had been
    speaking for some time,
I was aghast at my absence, for truly I did not know
Whether you had been asking or telling.

Tristan

I

Put it down! I say; put it down,—here, give it to me, I know
    what is in it, you Irish believer in fairies! Here, let me
    smash it
Once and for all,
Against the corner of the wall!
Do we need philtres?

Look at me! Look at me! Then come here.
This fearful thing is pure
That is between us. I want to be sure that nothing drowses it.
    Look at me!
This torture and this rapture will endure.

I still can see
How you hastily and abstractedly flung down
To the floor,
Having raked it, arm after arm,
Over your head,
Your lustrous gown;
And how, before
Its silken susurration had subsided,
We were as close together as it is possible for two people to be.

It was your maid, I think,
Who picked it up in the morning, while we lay
Still abed, exhausted by inexhaustible love;
I saw her, I saw her through half-closed eyes, kneel above it,
And smooth it, with a concerned hand, and a face full of
    thoughtfulness.
Not that the dress
Was fragile,
Or had suffered harm,

But that you had planned
To walk in it, when you walked ashore:
And our ship was getting minute by minute, more and more
Close to Tintagel.

III

There were herbs strown
Over the bed-room floor, alkanet,
Perhaps, and several of the mints, and costmary,
Too, I think; they were fresh and brash and fragrant, but a man
    can forget
All names but one. I was not alone in the room.
Even in the morning they were fresh, they had not died.
We had meant to have tied
Some of them into garlands, but we had no time.
They were fragrant even without being touched, there was so
    much
Pressure against them from the passion that beat against that
    room
Enough to wrench its rafters down.
I was late getting down
To the shore. Women there,
With sea-wind slashing their hair into their eyes, were drying
Long net and long net and long net.

IV

Heavily on the faithful bulk of Kurvenal,

My servant for a long time, leaning,

With footsteps less from weakness than for pleasure in the
green grass, lagging, I came here,

Out of the house, to lie, propped up on pillows, under this
fine tree—

Oak older than I, but still, not being ill, growing,

Granted to feel, I think, barring lightning, year after year,—and
barring the axe—

For a long time yet, the green sap flowing.

Dream of Saba

Calm was Half-Moon Bay; we lay at anchor there
Just off Tortola; when the hurricane,
Leaving its charted path, leapt full upon us,
And we were bruised and sobbing from the blows of the rain
Before we knew by what we were attacked or could in any way
      prepare.

"How dark it is tonight!" someone had said.
The lantern in the rigging burned serene
Through its glass chimney without crack and polished clean;
The wick well trimmed; plenty of kerosene.
We went to bed.

Following a fearful night I do not quite remember came a kind
      of dawn, not light,
But something we could see by. And we saw
What we had missed by inches: what we were headed for.

Astern, in an empty sea,
Suddenly, and before a man could cry, "Look there!"

Appeared what for an instant seemed to be
Black backs of half a hundred porpoises.
Before the eyes could blink at these,
They were black reefs, which rose into the air
With awful speed till they were mountains; these, one moment
    there,
Streaming sea-water stood against the sky;
Then all together and with awful speed diminished and like
    porpoises were gone,
Leaving the sea bare.

We turned from staring aft, and dead ahead, a mile away,
It seemed, through the thick steam of a white boiling surf and
    through smashed spray,
Saw the tall naked grooved precipitous sides and concave top
Of a volcanic island—its volcano now extinct,
It seemed; but it was hard to say.
From its high crater no red flame
Was seen to pulse and pour
But was it indeed or was it alone the steam from the burning
    breakers that kept us from seeing more?

There was no harbour. Those steep sides without a strand
Went down.
Yet even as from eye to brain this swift perception flashed,
 there seemed to reach
Even more swiftly toward us from that island now mirac-
 ulously in height and size increased
A broadening sandless beach
Humped with round boulders mossed with brightest green,
And purple with prostrate sea-ferns and stiff upright purple
 fans;
Red with anemones, and brilliant blue, and yellow dotted with
 black
From many fishes, lashing in the draining pools
Or sliding down the narrow sluices from the encroaching land
 to the receding sea.

The water thinned; we saw beneath us now
The bottom clearly; and from the vessel's bow
Saw close ahead, in shallow pool or dripping crevice caught,
The lovely fishes, rosy with azure fins or cobalt blue or yellow
 striped with black,

Curve their bright bodies double and lash forth and leap and
     then fall back with heavy splash
Or from the crevice leap and on the slippery weeds slide down
     once more into the narrow crack.

The thump and scrape of our keel upon the shore
Shook us from horror to a friendly sound!
Danger, maybe death, but decent, and the cause known.
Yet neither hook nor oar
Was overside before a Wave like a giant's palm
Was under us and raising us, gently, straight into the sky.
We rose beside the cliffs; we passed them so close by
We saw some little plants with reddish-purple flowers
Growing in a rock; and lying on a narrow ledge
Some birds' eggs; and some birds screamed at us as we passed.

The Wave did not break against the cliff; with utmost calm
It lifted us. The cliff had niches now where green grass grew.
And on a foot-high bush in a cleft some raspberries were ripe.
    And then at last

We saw the crater's edge.
The Wave curved over the rim and set us down in a cradle of
    branches, and withdrew.

It has not returned. Far down, the roaring of the sea abates
From hour to hour. The sky above our bowl is blue.

Υ

Who hurt you so,
My dear?
Who, long ago
When you were very young,
Did, said, became, was . . . something that you did not know
Beauty could ever do, say, be, become?—
So that your brown eyes filled
With tears they never, not to this day, have shed . . .
Not because one more boy stood hurt by life,
No: because something deathless had dropped dead—
An ugly, an indecent thing to do—
So that you stood and stared, with open mouth in which the
        tongue
Froze slowly backward toward its root,
As if it would not speak again, too badly stung
By memories thick as wasps about a nest invaded
To know if or if not you suffered pain.

Y

When the tree-sparrows with no sound through the pearl-pale
     air
Of dawn, down the apple-branches, stair by stair,
With utmost, unforgettable, elegance and grace
Descended to the bare ground (never bare
Of small strewn seeds
For forced-down flyers at this treacherous time of year),
And richly and sweetly twittered there,
I pressed my forehead to the window, butting the cold glass
Till I feared it might break, disturbing the sparrows, so let the
     moment pass
When I had hoped to recapture the rapture of my dark dream;
I had heard as I awoke my own voice thinly scream,
"Where? in what street? (I knew the city) did they attack
You, bound for home?"
You were, of course, not there.
And I of course wept, remembering where I last had met you,
Yet clawed with desperate nails at the sliding dream, screaming
     not to lose, since I cannot forget you.

I felt the hot tears come;
Streaming with useless tears, which make the ears roar and the
  eyelids swell,
My blind face sought the window-sill
To cry on—frozen mourning melted by sly sleep,
Slapping hard-bought repose with quick successive blows until
  it whimper and outright weep.

The tide pulls twice a day,
The sunlit and the moonlit tides
Drag the rough ledge away
And bring back seaweed, little else besides.
Oh, do not weep these tears salter than the flung spray!—
Weepers are the sea's brides . . .
I mean this the drowning way.

Υ

Amorphous is the mind; its quality
Is in its fibre, not its form;
If it desire to fly it puts on wings,
Awkwardly, not like a bird
At first (though later); the rustle of a thing half-heard
Can twist it as iron at times is twisted by a wind-storm or word
    after word
Can pummel it for hours yet leave it like a leaf on a still day
    unstirred.

But a man's habit clings
And he will wear tomorrow what today he wears.

The mind is happy in the air, happy to be up there with
Learning feathers, but the man loathes it.

The mind cries "Up! Oh, up! Oh, let me try to fly!
Look! I can lift you!" but he smothers its cry;
Out of thrift, and fear of next year's feathers, he clothes it in
    last year's things
And tries his best to button across a keel-shaped breast a coat
    knobbed out by new wings.

For Warmth Alone, for Shelter Only

For warmth alone, for shelter only
From the cold anger of the eyeless wind,
That knows my whereabouts, and mainly
To be at your door when I go down
Is abroad at all tonight in town,
I left my phrase in air, and sinned,
Laying my head against your arm
A moment, and as suddenly
Withdrawing it, and sitting there,
Warmed a little but far from warm,
And the wind still waiting at the foot of the stair,
And much harm done, and the phrase in air.

The Agnostic

The tired agnostic longs for prayer
More than the blest can ever do:
Between the chinks in his despair,
From out his forest he peeps through
Upon a clearing sunned so bright
He cups his eyeballs from its light.

He for himself who would decide
What thing is black, what thing is white,
Whirls with the whirling spectrum wide,
Runs with the running spectrum through
Red, orange, yellow, green and blue
And purple,—turns and stays his stride
Abruptly, reaching left and right
To catch all colours into light—
But light evades him: still he stands
With rainbows streaming through his hands.

He knows how half his hours are spent
In blue or purple discontent,
In red or yellow hate or fright,
And fresh young green whereon a blight
Sits down in orange overnight.

Yet worships still the ardent sod
For every ripped and ribboned hue,
For warmth of sun and breath of air,
And beauty met with everywhere;
Not knowing why, not knowing who
Pumps in his breath and sucks it out,
Nor unto whom his praise is due.

Yet naught nor nobody obeys
But his own heart, which bids him, "Praise!"
This, knowing that doubled were his days
Could he but rid his mind of doubt—
Yet will not rid him, in such ways
Of awful dalliance with despair—
And, though denying, not betrays.

Y

The apple-trees bud, but I do not.
Who forgot
April?
Happiness, happiness, which once I held in my hand,
Does it persist?
Does it exist,
Perhaps, in some foreign land?

Did it expand
Somewhere into something that would twist my wrist?
Does it exist,
Sweeter than I could bear,
Anywhere?

———————o———————

There is no speed
In Indianapolis, or in Monte Carlo,
Which can exceed the awful speed of my thought.

These tiny Fiats and Bugattis
With the behind-them bespectacled

Looking like beetles, men who must go fast
In order to live, in order to outlast
Those that pile up on sand bags,
There is nothing so fast,
I find, as the motion of the mind.

———— ◦ ————

Why did you, June, June,
So suddenly
Arrive at noon
In the midst of July?

I was not prepared
For the deferred appearance
Of your purple-haired adherence
To all that we live for.

What can I give for
Your knowledge
Of when to expand
And when to contract—
This instructed, more academic college
Of when to act?

———— ◦ ————

Oh sovereign angel,
Wide winged stranger above a forgetful earth,
Care for me, care for me. Keep me unaware of danger
And not regretful
And not forgetful of my innocent birth.

If ever I should get warm
Again, which I somewhat doubt,
I shall light two candles,
One to St. Christopher
And one for me,
To keep us out
Of danger, and free from harm
In our adventurous voyage
Over cold
Unseen sea.

Υ

Black hair you'd say she had, or rather
Black crest, black nape and black lore-feather
Above the eye; eye black, and ring
About it white, white breast and wing;
Soft bill; (no predatory thing—
Three claws in front and one in back
But sparrow-fingered, for attack
Unfitted)—yet the questioning,
The desperate notes I did not hear,
Being pitched too high for human ear,
But seen so plainly in the eye
She turned upon me urgently
And watched me with as she went by
And close before me following,
Perching, and ever peering back,
Uttered, I know, some desperate cry,
I might have answered, had I heard:—
Ah, no; ah, no; poor female bird
With unmelodious throat and wing:

497

Sit on your eggs, by crimson king
Or gold made fertile; hatch them, bring
Beauty to birth, that it may sing
And leave you; be not haggard; cling
To what you have: a coloured thing
That grows more coloured every spring,
And whilst you warm his eggs, no lack
Will let you suffer: when they crack—
Feed them, and feed yourself; whilst he
Hangs from a thistle drunkenly,
Or loops his little flights between
The maple and the evergreen.
Utter your querulous chirp or quack;
And if his voice be anything,
Why, shut your lids and hear him sing,
And when he wants you, take him back.

Importuned through the mails, accosted over the telephone,
    overtaken by running footsteps, caught by the sleeve, the
    servant of strangers,
While amidst the haste and confusion lover and friend quietly
    step into the unreachable past,
I throw bright time to chickens in an untidy yard.

Through foul timidity, through a gross indisposition to excite
    the ill-will of even the most negligible,
Disliking voices raised in anger, faces with no love in them,
I avoid the looming visitor,
Flee him adroitly around corners,
Hating him, wishing him well;

Lest if he confront me I be forced to say what is in no wise
    true:
That he is welcome; that I am unoccupied;
And forced to sit while the potted roses wilt in the crate or the
    sonnet cools

Bending a respectful nose above such dried philosophies
As have hung in wreaths from the rafters of my house since
    I was a child.

Some trace of kindliness in this, no doubt,
There may be.
But not enough to keep a bird alive.

There is a flaw amounting to a fissure
In such behaviour.

An Ancient Gesture

I thought, as I wiped my eyes on the corner of my apron:
Penelope did this too.
And more than once: you can't keep weaving all day
And undoing it all through the night;
Your arms get tired, and the back of your neck gets tight;
And along towards morning, when you think it will never be
       light,
And your husband has been gone, and you don't know where,
       for years,
Suddenly you burst into tears;
There is simply nothing else to do.

And I thought, as I wiped my eyes on the corner of my apron:
This is an ancient gesture, authentic, antique,
In the very best tradition, classic, Greek;
Ulysses did this too.
But only as a gesture,—a gesture which implied
To the assembled throng that he was much too moved to speak.
He learned it from Penelope . . .
Penelope, who really cried.

Jesus to His Disciples

I have instructed you to follow me
What way I go;
The road is hard, and stony,—as I know;
Uphill it climbs, and from the crushing heat
No shelter will be found
Save in my shadow: wherefore follow me; the footprints of my
    feet
Will be distinct and clear;
However trodden on, they will not disappear.

And see ye not at last
How tall I am?—Even at noon I cast
A shadow like a forest far behind me on the ground.

Υ

Establishment is shocked. Stir no adventure
Upon this splitted granite.

I will no longer connive
At my own destruction:—I will not again climb,
Breaking my finger nails, out of reach of the reaching wave,
To save
What I hope will still be me
When I have slid on slime and clutched at slippery rock-weed,
    and had my face towed under
In scrubbing pebbles, under the weight of the wave and its
    thunder.
I decline to scratch at this cliff. *If* is not a word.
I will connive no more
With that which hopes and plans that I shall not survive:
Let the tide keep its distance;
Or advance, and be split for a moment by a thing very small but
    all resistance;
Then do its own chore.

503

Some Things Are Dark

Some things are dark—or think they are.
But, in comparison to me,
All things are light enough to see
In any place, at any hour.

For I am Nightmare: where I fly,
Terror and rain stand in the sky
So thick, you could not tell them from
That blackness out of which you come.

So much for "where I fly": but when
I strike, and clutch in claw the brain—
Erebus, to such brain, will seem
The thin blue dusk of pleasant dream.

Y

If it should rain—(the sneezy moon
Said: Rain)—then I shall hear it soon
From shingles into gutters fall . . .
And know, of what concerns me, all:

The garden will be wet till noon—
I may not walk—my temper leans
To myths and legends—through the beans
Till they are dried—lest I should spread
Diseases they have never had.

I hear the rain: it comes down straight.
Now I can sleep, I need not wait
To close the windows anywhere.

Tomorrow, it may be, I might
Do things to set the whole world right.
There's nothing I can do tonight.

The Parsi Woman

Beautiful Parsi woman in your pale silk veil
With the gold border, why do you watch the sky?
The sky is thick and cloudy with the bold strong wings
Of the vulture, that shall tear your breast and thigh,
On the tall Tower of Silence where you at length must lie.

Ah, but have not I,
I too at the end of the northern May
When the pasture slope was pink with the wild azalea
And fragrant with its breath,
Touched the brown treacherous earth with my living hand?—
Thrown me prone on my own green coffin-lid,
And smiled at the grass and had no thought of death?

You there with the tranquil lovely brow,
What do you see so high,—some beautiful thing?
The sun on the vulture's wing?

This book, when I am dead, will be
A little faint perfume of me.
People who knew me well will say,
"She really used to think that way."
I do not write it to survive
My mortal self, but, being alive
And full of curious thoughts today,
It pleases me, somehow, to say,
"This book when I am dead will be
A little faint perfume of me."

———————

Thoughts come so thickly to my head
These days, and will not be gainsaid,
Almost I think I am about
To end my thinking and pass out.
I have no heart to chide a thought
That with the careful blood is bought
Of one of my last moments here,
However barren it appear,—

Wherefore respectfully I write
Such dulness as I now indite.

———————

That need is mine which comes to each:
To speak aloud in honest speech
What doubts and dogmas have confined
The shadowy acres of his mind.

———————

If I, making my awkward way
Among my cluttered thoughts some day,
The lost and ominous key should find
To the sealed chamber of my mind,
Would I the secret room explore
And, knowing what I know, know more?

What fearful thing might not there be
Therein, to take away from me
The remnant of my little hour?—
Which, dark though it be, is not so dour
As in that chamber might be found;
Else should I now be underground.

It might be, now I think of it,
That such a key would nicely fit
The lock which Bluebeard set to prove
The patience of his ladies' love;
In which case, 'twould be fairly wise
To leave it lying where it lies.

———

Speaking of Bluebeard, might it be
The story is a pleasantry?—
What lovely fun! There in the vault
The obedient wives,—being those at fault—
While helped to half the kingdom she
Who had the sense to use the key!

(Maeterlinck had a web to weave
Across this legend, I believe;
But did not state his point so clearly
As I have done above, not nearly.
At least, that is to say, whatever
His point may be, said spicule never
Emerges far above the troubled

Face of the deep; if I have doubled
Upon him, as a consequence,
And gleaned away his general sense,
You can't blame *me*,—the wrong I do 'im
Is, as you might say, coming to 'im:
Who can't speak out in black and white
Deserves to lose his copyright.)

———

Why am I forever saying
Words I do not mean?—and laying
Ghosts of beauties that were dear,
With a laugh, or shrug, or sneer?
Does perhaps a balance stand
Between the Devil on one hand
And God on the other, which must be gained
As often as lost, and so maintained?—
And what I love as my own soul
I spit upon—to make me whole?

See, lest you grow too big for me,
Beauty, I prune your little tree!

———

I think that I would rather be
Blind than deaf; for frequently,
When birds were happy in the spring,
I've closed my eyes to hear them sing,
And felt the sun warm on my head,
And still could see some blue and red,
And all the things I ever saw
Remembered plain enough to draw.

But when, in order not to hear,
I've put a finger in each ear
At moments when I was a child,
The world stood still,—and I was wild!
'Twas like being chased in some bad dream;
Or silence following a scream.

I think that I could easily find
My way about, if I were blind.
Not in the city, it may be;
But in the woods, and by the sea.
No memory to my ear could teach

The sound of waves along the beach;
Though, hearing them, I could have guessed
The comb that curls along the crest,
And breaks and flattens and expands
Miraculously up the sands
In rapid-crawling sudsy water,
Like a white ink-stain through a blotter.

My sight, that was the activest
Of all the senses I possessed,
Would in its time have gathered most
For memory, if itself were lost.

Now, I could very easily tell
An apple-orchard by the smell,
And in my mind's eye see again
The rough bark blackened by the rain
And glistening, and the hardy big
Red and white blossoms on the twig.

But nothing could recall the sound
Of apples falling on the ground.

Though I should see an apple fall,
The sight of it could not recall
The sound. It would be like a stone
Into a bottomless cavern thrown,
That sends up no faint shout to tell
It reached the earth, and all is well.

I think if I should lose my eyes
My other senses all would rise
And walk beside me, bending down
To catch my brow's uncertain frown;
And when we came to something new
Or perilous to journey through,
Would lead me kindly by the hand;
And everyone would understand.

———

I do believe the most of me
Floats under water; and men see
Above the wave a jagged small
Mountain of ice, and that is all.
Only the depths of other peaks

May know my substance when it speaks,
And steadfast through the grinding jam
Remain aware of what I am.
Myself, I think, shall never know
How far beneath the wave I go.

——————

What it would be like to die . . .
What it would be like to lie
Knowing nothing,—the keen mind
Suddenly gone deaf and blind;
Not even knowing that it knows
Nothing at all; one must suppose
That this mind, which in its day
Mused on the mysterious way
Of stars and cancers in their courses,
On heat and light and other forces,
And through its little eye could see
A section of infinity,
Is at last—and yet, not so!—
Is not—everything we know.
Is not here and *is not* there,

Is not earth and *is not* air,
Is not even a keen mind
Suddenly gone deaf and blind,
Is not any possible thing
Itself could be conjecturing;
Nor cherishes in a new TO-BE
Its little self's integrity.

Here at last the miracle!—
The hen squeezed back into the shell,
The man crushed back into the womb
Whose wall he burst,—and plenty of room!
DEATH!—how monstrously he comes—
Outside all nature's axioms!

"Dust to dust!"—oh, happier far
The ashes of my body are,
Since all that's mortal of me goes
The deathless way of dew and rose!
Year by year the wasted plain
Eats its death and lives again;

And the dusty body heaves
Its death aside and puts forth leaves.
The mind, that sees its errand, must
In truth desire itself were dust.

When by-which-I-came-to-be
Shall uncreate as deftly me,
Where my irrelevant ashes lie
Write only this: THAT WHICH WAS I
NO LONGER HOLDS ITS LITTLE PLACE
AGAINST THE PUSHING LEAGUES OF SPACE.

—————

I read with varying degrees
Of bile the sage philosophies,
Since not a man has wit to purge
His pages of the Vital Urge.
At my head when I was young
Was Monad of all Monads flung;
And in my ears like any wind
Dubito Ergo Sum was dinned.
(When a chair was not a chair

Was when nobody else was there;
And Bergson's lump of sugar awed
My soul to see how slow it thawed!)

I, too, have mused upon the way
The sun comes up and makes the day,
The tide goes out and makes the shore,
And many, many matters more;
And coaxed till I was out of breath
My mind to take the hurdle, Death.
I, too, have writ my little book
On Things 'Twere Best to Overlook;
And struck a match and drawn a cork
And called a spade a salad-fork.
For men that are afraid to die
Must warm their hands before a lie;
The fire that's built of What is Known
Will chill the marrow in the bone.

Listen to a little story:
One day in a laboratory,

Where I was set to guess and grope,
I looked into a microscope.
I saw in perfect pattern sprawl
Something that was not there at all,
Something, perhaps, being utterly
Invisible to the naked eye,
By Descartes' doubt as all untrod
As furrows in the brain of God.
If, now, the naked eye can see
So little of the chemistry
By which itself is hale or blind,—
What, then, about the naked mind?

Think you a brain like as two peas
To any chattering chimpanzee's,
As 'twere a nut in the cheek shall nurse
The riddle of the universe?

Have we no patience, pray, to wait
Until that somewhat out-of-date,
Unwieldy instrument, the mind,

Shall be re-modeled and refined?
Or must we still abuse and vex
Our darkness with the Vital X,
Straining, with nothing given, to scan
The old equation: What is Man?

The sage philosopher at night,
When other men are breathing light,
Out of a troubled sleep I see
Start up in bed, holding the key!—
And wrap him in his dressing-gown,
And get him up and set him down,
And write enough to ease his head,
And rub his hands, and go to bed;—
And at the window, peering through,
All this time—the Bugaboo!

———————

I know a better way to spend
An hour, than itching on its end.
'Tis not, as peevish Omar sang,
To swill, and let the world go hang.

But tenderly and with high mirth
To hang up garlands on the earth,
Nor chide too much the generous whim
That sensed a god and honoured him.

Whether the moon be made of cheese,
Or eaten out by some disease,
And be the earth at center hot,
But cooling in, or be it not,
This fact holds true: the mind of man
Is desolate since its day began,
Divining more than it is able
To measure with its tiny table.

Oh, children, growing up to be
Adventurers into sophistry,
Forbear, forbear to be of those
That read the root to learn the rose;
Whose thoughts are like a tugging kite,
Anchored by day, drawn in at night.

Grieve not if from the mind be loosed
A wing that comes not home to roost;
There may be garnered yet of that
An olive-branch from Ararat.

———————

I was so afraid to die,
I walked in ague under the sky.
As sure as I fared forth alone,
There fell Death's shadow beside my own,
There hung his whisper at my ear:
"Now I'm here!—But now I'm here!"

Thus his swift and terrible ways
Were mildew on my living days,
And Death forbore to carry off
A wretch already dead enough.

I heard him in the heavy sound
Of traffic on the shaken ground;
I saw him on the girders where
Men with hammers walled in the air;

And in the awful tunnel built
Through the shifting river silt,
Where gentlemen with polished shoes
Ride at ease and read the news,
Dry and smug, dry and smug,
Far beneath a ferry and tug
That in the fog from off the sea
Pass and whistle mournfully,
There I smelled the steamy breath
Sighing from the lungs of Death.

In the evening I would sit
In my room and think of it,—
Think of fire that suddenly
Licks the wall, and none knows why,
And from the twentieth story hurls
To the pave the factory girls;
Think of ice-bergs rocking slow
Southward from the broken flow,—
Of a sailor on the deep
Roughly shaken out of sleep

By a mountain bright and dim,
Bending green eyes down on him.

When I see my netted veins
Blue and busy, while the grains
In the little glass of ME
Tumble to eternity,—
When I feel my body's heat
Surge beneath the icy sheet,
Body that in this same place,
With the sheet across its face,
Turned to ice inscrutably,
Will be lying soon maybe,
In my ear a voice will sigh,
"Here am I—I—I—!"
Bounding up in bed I shriek,
"Who is in this room?—Speak!"
And the clock ticks on the shelf.
And I know that Death himself
Came between the curtains there,

Laid his hand upon a chair,
Caught his image fleetingly
In the glass that mirrors me.

———————

Once upon a time I sat
Making verses, while the cat,
Half-asleep against my knee,
Clawed a cushion purringly.
As I watched the moving claws,
Musing wisely on the cause—
Early habit ruling yet
In this droll domestic pet—
Suddenly I was aware
That a Cat, as well, was there,
Through the slits in his round eyes
Watching me without surprise;
Cat, whose purring seemed to say,
"Some day—some day—"

Y

The sea at sunset can reflect,
And does, the thin flamingo cloud,
The pale-green rift beneath; the sky
Alone can say these things aloud;
The water ripples, and refracts
Celestial into water acts.
But this is lovely: you detect
The sky, from ocean's brief defect.

I left the island, left the sea,
Heartbroken for the twentieth time,—
"Beauty does not belong to me,"
I said, yet as I said it, knew
That this had never yet been true.
The sea was grey, the sea was blue,
The sea was white and streaked with spume,
Crowded with waves, but still had room
For wreckage; and the sea was green
Bursting against a reef unseen

Until the heavy swell sucked back,
Leaving the reef exposed and black.

In Vermont—and the stars so clear,
Seen through the dustless atmosphere,
That stars ahead both blazed and glowed
Only a foot above the road.
And then remorselessly appeared,
To eyes grown tired of lovely sights,
The flushing, soaring Northern Lights—
And still the eyes and mind must take
More wonder, and remain awake.

And then, again, the gleaming chasm
Began to vibrate, and I knew,
In spite of all that I could do,
I must endure the awful spasm
Of perfectness accomplished, sure
And terrible—so drove my eyes
Into the Northern-lighted skies;
And suffered Beauty to extent
Extreme, and with no merriment.

I sent my mind ahead to climb
The Mohawk Trail: which can be bad
In fog, and fog is what we had
Always; I spread the motor-map,
And left it lying on my lap.

Y

I, in disgust with the living, having read
Much of the accomplished dead,
Was nagged by the clucking of the robin, clucking her over-fed
Young off the nest—and what a night, I said,
Raining cats and dogs and blowing like hell,
To haul babies out of bed.

And I thought: their wings will be wet,
And heavy, in the long grass; and she will not let me help her,
    she is such a fuss-
Budget, and so stupid, trusting the hostile
Weather, and afraid of her friends. Oh, well.

"Afraid of her friends"? . . . I thought of a friendship extended
    to me,
And of my rejecting it, suspicious and wary.
And then I thought of the sea making
Between Ragged and Orr's,
And between their shores four miles of open water, and the
    wind blowing up, and a wicked swell, and me

Pitched and sliding and banged by the wave under the bow,
   and drenched with spray, and snug and content . . .
Because I knew that the sea
Was not concerned with me, might possibly
Drown me, but willed me no ill.

Y

How did I bear it—how could I possibly as a child,
On my narrow shoulders and pipe-stem legs have supported
The fragrance and the colour of the frangible hour, the deep
Taste of the shallow dish?—It is not as if
I had thought, being a child, that the beautiful thing would
    last: it passed while I looked at it,
Except, of course, in memory—memory is the seventh
Colour in the spectrum. But I knew about—when even then,
The grapevine growing over the grey rock—the shock
Of beauty seen, noticed, for the first time—
I remember it well—and I remember where I stood—on which
    side of the rock.

Already the triangular leaves on the grape-trellis are green; they
    have given me no time
To report their colour as it was when I first
Came upon them, wondering if the strawberry rhubarb was up,
    looking for the pretty, feared hoof-marks of deer
In the asparagus.

How did I bear it?—Now—grown up and encased
In the armour of custom, after years
Of looking at loveliness, forewarned and face to face, and no
     time and too prudent
At six in the morning to accept the unendurable embrace,

I come back from the garden into the kitchen, and take off my
     rubbers—the dew
Is heavy and high, wetting the sock above the shoe—but I
     cannot do
The housework yet.

Men Working

Charming, the movement of girls about a May-pole in May,
Weaving the coloured ribbons in and out,
Charming; youth is charming, youth is fair.

But beautiful the movement of men striking pikes
Into the end of a black pole, and slowly
Raising it out of the damp grass and up into the air.
The clean strike of the pike into the pole: beautiful.

Joe is the boss; but Ed or Bill will say,
"No, Joe; we can't get it that way—
We've got to take it from here. Are you okay
On your side, Joe?" "Yes," says the boss. "Okay."

The clean strike of the pike into the pole—"*That's it!*"
"*Ground your pikes!*"

The grounded pikes about the rising black pole, beautiful.
"Ed, you'd better get under here with me!" "I'm
Under!"

"That's it!"
"Ground your pikes!"

Joe says, "Now, boys, don't heave
Too hard—we've got her—but you, Ed, you and Mike,
You'll have to hold her from underneath while Bill
Shifts his pike—she wants to fall downhill;
We've got her all right, but we've got her on a slight
Slant."
"That's it!"—"Mike,
About six feet lower this time."
"That's it!"

"Ground your pikes!"

One by one the pikes are moved about the pole, more beautiful
Than coloured ribbons weaving.

The clean strike of the pike into the pole; each man
Depending on the skill
And the balance, both of body and of mind,

Of each of the others: in the back of each man's mind
The respect for the pole: it is forty feet high, and weighs
Two thousand pounds.

In the front of each man's mind: "She's going to go
Exactly where we want her to go: this pole
Is going to go into that seven-foot hole we dug
For her
To stand in."

This was in the deepening dusk of a July night.
They were putting in the poles: bringing the electric light.

Steepletop

I

Even you, Sweet Basil: even you,

Lemon Verbena: must exert yourselves now and somewhat
harden

Against untimely frost; I have hovered you and covered you and
kept going smudges,

Until I am close to worn-out. Now, you

Go about it. I have other things to do,

Writing poetry, for instance. And I, too,

Live in this garden.

II

Nothing could stand

All this rain.

The lilacs were drowned, browned before I had even smelled
them

Cool against my cheek, held down

A little by my hand.

Pain
Is seldom preventable, but is presentable
Even to strangers on a train—
But what the rain
Does to the lilacs—is something you must sigh and try
To explain.

III

Borage, forage for bees
And for those who love blue,
Why must you,
Having only been transplanted
From where you were not wanted
Either by the bee or by me
From under the sage, engage in this self-destruction?
I was tender about your slender tap-root.
I thought you would send out shoot after shoot
Of thick cucumber-smelling, hairy leaves.
But why anybody believes
Anything, I do not know. I thought I could trust you.

The Gardener in Haying-Time

I had a gardener. I had him until haying-time.
In haying-time they set him pitching hay.
I had two gardeners. I had them until haying-time.
In haying-time they set them pitching hay.
I had three gardeners. I had them until haying-time.
—Can life go on this way?

Y

Sky-coloured bird, blue wings with no more spots of spotless
    white
Dappled, than on a day in spring
When the brown meadows trickle with a hundred brooks two
    inches broad and wink and flash back light—
Dappled with no more white than on an all but cloudless sky
    makes clear blue deeper and more bright.

Exquisite glutton, azure coward with proud crest
And iridescent nape—
Mild milky mauve, chalcedony, then lustred, and all amethyst,
    then brushed with bronze, the half-green clustered with
    the ripe grape, under the lapis crest.
Dull-feathered bird today, pecking at ashes by the cinder-pit,
    your clanging tone alone makes known our northern jay
Sky-coloured—under a slaty sky sky-coloured still, slate-grey.

538

To a Snake

Poor dying thing; it was my dog, not I,
That did for you.
I gave you a wide arc, and moved to pass.

And yet, I was not sad that you should die;
You jarred me so; you were too motionless
And sudden, coiled there in the grass.

Now, you are coiled no longer. Now
Your splendid, streakèd back is to the ground.
Your beautiful, light-scarlet blood is spattered,
And shines in dreadful dew-drops all around.

And that white, ugly belly you had not confessed,—
So naked, so unscrolled with patterns—is at last exposed.

Oh—oh—I do not like to see
A fellow-mortal's final agony!
We shared this world all summer until now!
Now,—off you go.

539

All upside-down you lie, less looped than flung.
And all but done for.
And yet,—with head still raised; and that red, flickering tongue.

Y

I woke in the night and heard the wind, and it blowing half a
    gale.
"Blizzard, by gum!" I said to myself out loud, "What an
    elegant
Hissing and howling, what a roar!"
And I rose, half-rose, in bed, and
Listened to the wind, smelling new snow—
No smell like that—a smell neither sour nor sweet—
No fragrance, none at all, nothing to compete with, nothing to
    interfere
With the odourless clear passage of the smell of new snow
Through the nostrils. "Cold," I said;
And clawed up the extra blanket from the foot of the bed.
Lying there, coiled and cuddled within my own warmth,
Ephemeral but far from frail,
I listened to the winding-up from a sound almost not heard, to
    the yelling hurling
Thump against the house of an all-but-official gale
And thought, "Bad night for a sail

Except far out at sea . . ."

And somewhere something heavy bumped and rolled
And bumped, like a barrel of molasses loose in the hold.

Ϋ

Look how the bittersweet with lazy muscle moves aside
Great stones placed here by planning men not without sweat
 and pride.
And yet how beautiful this broken wall applied
No more to its first duty: to keep sheep or cattle in;
Bought up by Beauty now, with the whole calm abandoned
 countryside.

And how the bittersweet to meet the stunned admiring eye with
 all
The red and orange splendour of its fruit at the first stare
Unclasps its covering leaves, lets them all fall,
Strips to the twig, is bare.

See, too, the nightshade, the woody, the bittersweet, strangling
 the wall
For this, the beauty of berries, this scandalous, bright
Persimmon and tangerine comment on fieldstone, on granite and
 on quartz, by might

543

Of men and crowbars, and a rock for lever, and a rock above a
    rock wedged in, and the leverage right,
Wrested from the tough acres that in time must yield
And suffer plow and harrow and be a man's hay-field—
Wrested, hoisted, balanced on its edge, tipped, tumbled, clear
Of its smooth-walled cool hole lying, dark and damp side
    upward in the sun, inched and urged upon the stone-boat,
    hauled here.

Yet mark where the rowan, the mountain ash berries, hang
    bunched amid leaves like ferns,
Scarlet in clear blue air, and the tamarack turns
Yellow as mustard, and sheds its short needles to lie on the
    ground like light
Through the door of a hut in the forest to travellers miles off
    the road at night;
Where brilliant the briony glows in the hedge, frail, clustered,
    elliptical fruit;
Nightshade conserving in capsules transparent of jacinth and
    amber its jellies of ill-repute.

And only the cherries, that ripened for robins and cherry-birds, burned
With more ruddy a spark than the bark and the leaves of the cherry-tree, red in October turned.

Peaceful and slow, peaceful and slow,
Skillful and deft, in my own rhythm,
Happy about the house I go—
For the men are in town, and their noise gone with 'em.

Well I remember, long ago,
How still, in my girlish room, the night was—
Watching the moon from my window,
While cool on the empty bed her light was.

More than my heart to him I gave,
When I gave my heart in soft surrender—
Who now am the timid, laughed-at slave
Of a man unaware of this, and tender.

Never must he know how I feel,
Or how, at times, too loud his voice is—
When, just at the creak of his wagon-wheel
Cramped for the barn, my life rejoices!

He would be troubled; he could not learn
How small a part of myself I keep
To smell the meadows, or sun the churn,
When he's at market, or while he's asleep.

Intense and terrible, I think, must be the loneliness
Of infants—look at all
The Teddy-bears clasped in slumber in slatted cribs
Painted pale-blue or pink.
And all the Easter Bunnies, dirty and disreputable, that deface
The white pillow and the sterile, immaculate, sunny, turning
    pleasantly in space,
Dainty abode of Baby—try to replace them
With new ones, come Easter again, fluffy and white, and with a
    different smell;
Release with gentle force from the horrified embrace,
That hugs until the stitches give and the stuffing shows,
His only link with a life of his own, the only thing he really
    knows . . .
Try to sneak it out of sight.
If you wish to hear anger yell glorious
From air-filled lungs through a throat unthrottled
By what the neighbours will say;

If you wish to witness a human countenance contorted
And convulsed and crumpled by helpless grief and despair,
Then stand beside the slatted crib and say There, there, and
    take the toy away.

Pink and pale-blue look well
In a nursery. And for the most part Baby is really good:
He gurgles, he whimpers, he tries to get his toe to his mouth;
    he slobbers his food
Dreamily—cereals and vegetable juices—onto his bib:
He behaves as he should.

But do not for a moment believe he has forgotten Blackness;
    nor the deep
Easy swell; nor his thwarted
Design to remain for ever there;
Nor the crimson betrayal of his birth into a yellow glare.
The pictures painted on the inner eyelids of infants just before
    they sleep,
Are not in pastel.

Υ

Sometimes, oh, often, indeed, in the midst of ugly adversity, beautiful
Memories return.
You awake in wonder, you awake at half-past four,
Wondering what wonder is in store.
You reach for your clothes in the dark and pull them on, you have no time
Even to wash your face, you have to climb Megunticook.

You run through the sleeping town; you do not arouse
Even a dog, you are so young and so light on your feet.
What a way to live, what a way . . .
No breakfast, not even hungry. An apple, though,
In the pocket.
And the only people you meet are store-windows.

The path up the mountain is stony and in places steep,
And here it is really dark—wonderful, wonderful,
Wonderful—the smell of bark

And rotten leaves and dew! And nobody awake
In all the world but you!—
Who lie on a high cliff until your elbows ache,
To see the sun come up over Penobscot Bay.

Not for a nation:
Not the dividing, the estranging, thing
For;
Nor, in a world so small, the insulation
Of dream from dream—where dreams are links in the chain
Of a common hope; that man may yet regain
His dignity on earth—where before all
Eyes: small eyes of elephant and shark; still
Eyes of lizard grey in the sub-tropic noon,
Blowing his throat out into a scarlet, edged-with-cream in-
    credible balloon
Suddenly, and suddenly dancing, hoisting and lowering his body
    on his short legs on the hot stone window-sill;
And the eyes of the upturned, grooved and dusty, rounded,
    dull cut-worm
Staring upward at the spade,—
These, all these, and more, from the corner of the eye see man,
    infirm,
Tottering like a tree about to fall,—

Who yet had such high dreams—who not for this was made
    (or so said he),—nor did design to die at all.

Not for a nation,
Not the dividing, the estranging thing
For;
Nor, on a world so small, the insulation
Of dream from dream,
In what might be today, had we been better welders, a new
    chain for pulling down old buildings, uprooting the wrong
    trees; these
Not for;
Not for my country right or wrong;
Not for the drum or the bugle; not for the song
Which pipes me away from my home against my will along
    with the other children
To where I would not go
And makes me say what I promised never to say, and do the
    thing I am through with—
Into the Piper's Hill;
Not for the flag

Of any land because myself was born there
Will I give up my life.
But I will love that land where man is free,
And that will I defend.
"To the end?" you ask, "To the end?"—Naturally, to the end.

What is it to the world, or to me,
That I beneath an elm, not beneath a tamarisk-tree
First filled my lungs, and clenched my tiny hands already
    spurred and nailed
Against the world, and wailed
In anger and frustration that all my tricks had failed and I been
    torn
Out of the cave where I was hiding, to suffer in the world as I
    have done and I still do—
Never again—oh, no, no more on earth—ever again to find
    abiding-place.
Birth—awful birth . . .
Whatever the country, whatever the colour and race.

The colour and the traits of each,
The shaping of his speech,—

These can the elm, given a long time, alter; these,
Too, the tamarisk.
But if he starve, but if he freeze—
Early, in his own tongue, he knows;
And though with arms or bows or a dipped thorn
Blown through a tube, he fights—the brisk
Rattle of shot he is not slow to tell
From the sound of ripe seed bursting from a poddy shell;
And he whom, all his life, life has abused
Yet knows if he be justly or unjustly used.

I know these elms, this beautiful doorway: here
I am at home, if anywhere.
A natural fondness, an affection which need never be said,
Rises from the wooden sidewalks warm as the smell of new-
    baked bread
From a neighbour's kitchen. It is dusk. The sun goes down.
Sparsely strung along the street the thrifty lights appear.
It is pleasant. It is good.
I am very well-known here; here I am understood.
I can walk along the street, or turn into a path unlighted, with-
    out fear

Of poisonous snakes, or of any face in town.
Tall elms, my roots go down
As deep as yours into this soil, yes, quite as deep.
And I hear the rocking of my cradle. And I must not sleep.

Not for a nation; not for a little town,
Where, when the sun goes down, you may sit without fear
On the front porch, just out of reach of the arc-light, rocking,
With supper ready, wearing a pale new dress, and your baby
    near
In its crib, and your husband due to be home by the next
    trolley that you hear bumping into Elm Street—no:
But for a dream that was dreamt an elm-tree's life ago—
And longer, yes, much longer, and what I mean you know.

For the dream, for the plan, for the freedom of man as it was
    meant
To be;
Not for the structure set up so lustily, by rule of thumb
And over-night, bound to become
Loose, lop-sided, out of plumb,

But for the dream, for the plan, for the freedom of man as it
    was meant
To be
By men with more vision, more wisdom, more purpose, more
    brains
Than we,
(Possibly, possibly)
Men with more courage, men more unselfish, more intent
Than we, upon their dreams, upon their dream of Freedom,—
    Freedom not alone
For oneself, but for all, wherever the word is known,
In whatever tongue, or the longing in whatever spirit—
Men with more honour. (That remains
To be seen! That we shall see!)

Possibly. Possibly.

And if still these truths be held to be
Self-evident.

SONNETS

Thou art not lovelier than lilacs,—no,
Nor honeysuckle; thou art not more fair
Than small white single poppies,—I can bear
Thy beauty; though I bend before thee, though
From left to right, not knowing where to go,
I turn my troubled eyes, nor here nor there
Find any refuge from thee, yet I swear
So has it been with mist,—with moonlight so.
Like him who day by day unto his draught
Of delicate poison adds him one drop more
Till he may drink unharmed the death of ten,
Even so, inured to beauty, who have quaffed
Each hour more deeply than the hour before,
I drink—and live—what has destroyed some men.

Time does not bring relief; you all have lied
Who told me time would ease me of my pain!
I miss him in the weeping of the rain;
I want him at the shrinking of the tide;
The old snows melt from every mountain-side,
And last year's leaves are smoke in every lane;
But last year's bitter loving must remain
Heaped on my heart, and my old thoughts abide.
There are a hundred places where I fear
To go,—so with his memory they brim.
And entering with relief some quiet place
Where never fell his foot or shone his face
I say, "There is no memory of him here!"
And so stand stricken, so remembering him.

Mindful of you the sodden earth in spring,
And all the flowers that in the springtime grow;
And dusty roads, and thistles, and the slow
Rising of the round moon; all throats that sing
The summer through, and each departing wing,
And all the nests that the bared branches show;
And all winds that in any weather blow,
And all the storms that the four seasons bring.
You go no more on your exultant feet
Up paths that only mist and morning knew;
Or watch the wind, or listen to the beat
Of a bird's wings too high in air to view,—
But you were something more than young and sweet
And fair,—and the long year remembers you.

Not in this chamber only at my birth—
When the long hours of that mysterious night
Were over, and the morning was in sight—
I cried, but in strange places, steppe and firth
I have not seen, through alien grief and mirth;
And never shall one room contain me quite
Who in so many rooms first saw the light,
Child of all mothers, native of the earth.
So is no warmth for me at any fire
Today, when the world's fire has burned so low;
I kneel, spending my breath in vain desire,
At that cold hearth which one time roared so strong:
And straighten back in weariness, and long
To gather up my little gods and go.

If I should learn, in some quite casual way,
That you were gone, not to return again—
Read from the back-page of a paper, say,
Held by a neighbor in a subway train,
How at the corner of this avenue
And such a street (so are the papers filled)
A hurrying man, who happened to be you,
At noon today had happened to be killed—
I should not cry aloud—I could not cry
Aloud, or wring my hands in such a place—
I should but watch the station lights rush by
With a more careful interest on my face;
Or raise my eyes and read with greater care
Where to store furs and how to treat the hair.

Bluebeard

This door you might not open, and you did;
So enter now, and see for what slight thing
You are betrayed. . . . Here is no treasure hid,
No cauldron, no clear crystal mirroring
The sought-for Truth, no heads of women slain
For greed like yours, no writhings of distress;
But only what you see. . . . Look yet again:
An empty room, cobwebbed and comfortless.
Yet this alone out of my life I kept
Unto myself, lest any know me quite;
And you did so profane me when you crept
Unto the threshold of this room tonight
That I must never more behold your face.
This now is yours. I seek another place.

I do but ask that you be always fair,
That I for ever may continue kind;
Knowing me what I am, you should not dare
To lapse from beauty ever, nor seek to bind
My alterable mood with lesser cords:
Weeping and such soft matters but invite
To further vagrancy, and bitter words
Chafe soon to irremediable flight.
Wherefore I pray you if you love me dearly
Less dear to hold me than your own bright charms,
Whence it may fall that until death or nearly
I shall not move to struggle from your arms;
Fade if you must; I would but bid you be
Like the sweet year, doing all things graciously.

Love, though for this you riddle me with darts,
And drag me at your chariot till I die, —
Oh, heavy prince! Oh, panderer of hearts! —
Yet hear me tell how in their throats they lie
Who shout you mighty: thick about my hair,
Day in, day out, your ominous arrows purr,
Who still am free, unto no querulous care
A fool, and in no temple worshiper!
I, that have bared me to your quiver's fire,
Lifted my face into its puny rain,
Do wreathe you Impotent to Evoke Desire
As you are Powerless to Elicit Pain!
(Now will the god, for blasphemy so brave,
Punish me, surely, with the shaft I crave!)

I think I should have loved you presently,
And given in earnest words I flung in jest;
And lifted honest eyes for you to see,
And caught your hand against my cheek and breast;
And all my pretty follies flung aside
That won you to me, and beneath your gaze,
Naked of reticence and shorn of pride,
Spread like a chart my little wicked ways.
I, that had been to you, had you remained,
But one more waking from a recurrent dream,
Cherish no less the certain stakes I gained,
And walk your memory's halls, austere, supreme,
A ghost in marble of a girl you knew
Who would have loved you in a day or two.

x

Oh, think not I am faithful to a vow!

Faithless am I save to love's self alone.

Were you not lovely I would leave you now:

After the feet of beauty fly my own.

Were you not still my hunger's rarest food,

And water ever to my wildest thirst,

I would desert you—think not but I would!—

And seek another as I sought you first.

But you are mobile as the veering air,

And all your charms more changeful than the tide,

Wherefore to be inconstant is no care:

I have but to continue at your side.

So wanton, light and false, my love, are you,

I am most faithless when I most am true.

I shall forget you presently, my dear,
So make the most of this, your little day,
Your little month, your little half a year,
Ere I forget, or die, or move away,
And we are done forever; by and by
I shall forget you, as I said, but now,
If you entreat me with your loveliest lie
I will protest you with my favourite vow.
I would indeed that love were longer-lived,
And oaths were not so brittle as they are,
But so it is, and nature has contrived
To struggle on without a break thus far,—
Whether or not we find what we are seeking
Is idle, biologically speaking.

We talk of taxes, and I call you friend;
Well, such you are,—but well enough we know
How thick about us root, how rankly grow
Those subtle weeds no man has need to tend,
That flourish through neglect, and soon must send
Perfume too sweet upon us and overthrow
Our steady senses; how such matters go
We are aware, and how such matters end.
Yet shall be told no meagre passion here;
With lovers such as we forevermore
Isolde drinks the draught, and Guinevere
Receives the Table's ruin through her door,
Francesca, with the loud surf at her ear,
Lets fall the coloured book upon the floor.

Into the golden vessel of great song
Let us pour all our passion; breast to breast
Let other lovers lie, in love and rest;
Not we,—articulate, so, but with the tongue
Of all the world: the churning blood, the long
Shuddering quiet, the desperate hot palms pressed
Sharply together upon the escaping guest,
The common soul, unguarded, and grown strong.
Longing alone is singer to the lute;
Let still on nettles in the open sigh
The minstrel, that in slumber is as mute
As any man, and love be far and high,
That else forsakes the topmost branch, a fruit
Found on the ground by every passer-by.

Not with libations, but with shouts and laughter
We drenched the altars of Love's sacred grove,
Shaking to earth green fruits, impatient after
The launching of the coloured moths of Love.
Love's proper myrtle and his mother's zone
We bound about our irreligious brows,
And fettered him with garlands of our own,
And spread a banquet in his frugal house.
Not yet the god has spoken; but I fear
Though we should break our bodies in his flame,
And pour our blood upon his altar, here
Henceforward is a grove without a name,
A pasture to the shaggy goats of Pan,
Whence flee forever a woman and a man.

Only until this cigarette is ended,
A little moment at the end of all,
While on the floor the quiet ashes fall,
And in the firelight to a lance extended,
Bizarrely with the jazzing music blended,
The broken shadow dances on the wall,
I will permit my memory to recall
The vision of you, by all my dreams attended.
And then adieu,—farewell!—the dream is done.
Yours is a face of which I can forget
The colour and the features, every one,
The words not ever, and the smiles not yet;
But in your day this moment is the sun
Upon a hill, after the sun has set.

Once more into my arid days like dew,
Like wind from an oasis, or the sound
Of cold sweet water bubbling underground,
A treacherous messenger, the thought of you
Comes to destroy me; once more I renew
Firm faith in your abundance, whom I found
Long since to be but just one other mound
Of sand, whereon no green thing ever grew.
And once again, and wiser in no wise,
I chase your coloured phantom on the air,
And sob and curse and fall and weep and rise
And stumble pitifully on to where,
Miserable and lost, with stinging eyes,
Once more I clasp,—and there is nothing there.

No rose that in a garden ever grew,
In Homer's or in Omar's or in mine,
Though buried under centuries of fine
Dead dust of roses, shut from sun and dew
Forever, and forever lost from view,
But must again in fragrance rich as wine
The grey aisles of the air incarnadine
When the old summers surge into a new.
Thus when I swear, "I love with all my heart,"
'Tis with the heart of Lilith that I swear,
'Tis with the love of Lesbia and Lucrece;
And thus as well my love must lose some part
Of what it is, had Helen been less fair,
Or perished young, or stayed at home in Greece.

When I too long have looked upon your face,
Wherein for me a brightness unobscured
Save by the mists of brightness has its place,
And terrible beauty not to be endured,
I turn away reluctant from your light,
And stand irresolute, a mind undone,
A silly, dazzled thing deprived of sight
From having looked too long upon the sun.
Then is my daily life a narrow room
In which a little while, uncertainly,
Surrounded by impenetrable gloom,
Among familiar things grown strange to me
Making my way, I pause, and feel, and hark,
Till I become accustomed to the dark.

And you as well must die, belovèd dust,
And all your beauty stand you in no stead;
This flawless, vital hand, this perfect head,
This body of flame and steel, before the gust
Of Death, or under his autumnal frost,
Shall be as any leaf, be no less dead
Than the first leaf that fell,—this wonder fled,
Altered, estranged, disintegrated, lost.
Nor shall my love avail you in your hour.
In spite of all my love, you will arise
Upon that day and wander down the air
Obscurely as the unattended flower,
It mattering not how beautiful you were,
Or how belovèd above all else that dies.

Let you not say of me when I am old,
In pretty worship of my withered hands
Forgetting who I am, and how the sands
Of such a life as mine run red and gold
Even to the ultimate sifting dust, "Behold,
Here walketh passionless age!"—for there expands
A curious superstition in these lands,
And by its leave some weightless tales are told.
In me no lenten wicks watch out the night;
I am the booth where Folly holds her fair;
Impious no less in ruin than in strength,
When I lie crumbled to the earth at length,
Let you not say, "Upon this reverend site
The righteous groaned and beat their breasts
    in prayer."

Oh, my belovèd, have you thought of this:
How in the years to come unscrupulous Time,
More cruel than Death, will tear you from my kiss,
And make you old, and leave me in my prime?
How you and I, who scale together yet
A little while the sweet, immortal height
No pilgrim may remember or forget,
As sure as the world turns, some granite night
Shall lie awake and know the gracious flame
Gone out forever on the mutual stone;
And call to mind that on the day you came
I was a child, and you a hero grown?—
And the night pass, and the strange morning break
Upon our anguish for each other's sake!

As to some lovely temple, tenantless
Long since, that once was sweet with shivering brass,
Knowing well its altars ruined and the grass
Grown up between the stones, yet from excess
Of grief hard driven, or great loneliness,
The worshiper returns, and those who pass
Marvel him crying on a name that was, —
So is it now with me in my distress.
Your body was a temple to Delight;
Cold are its ashes whence the breath is fled;
Yet here one time your spirit was wont to move;
Here might I hope to find you day or night;
And here I come to look for you, my love,
Even now, foolishly, knowing you are dead.

Cherish you then the hope I shall forget
At length, my lord, Pieria?—put away
For your so passing sake, this mouth of clay,
These mortal bones against my body set,
For all the puny fever and frail sweat
Of human love,—renounce for these, I say,
The Singing Mountain's memory, and betray
The silent lyre that hangs upon me yet?
Ah, but indeed, some day shall you awake,
Rather, from dreams of me, that at your side
So many nights, a lover and a bride,
But stern in my soul's chastity, have lain,
To walk the world forever for my sake,
And in each chamber find me gone again!

When you, that at this moment are to me
Dearer than words on paper, shall depart,
And be no more the warder of my heart,
Whereof again myself shall hold the key;
And be no more—what now you seem to be—
The sun, from which all excellences start
In a round nimbus, nor a broken dart
Of moonlight, even, splintered on the sea;
I shall remember only of this hour—
And weep somewhat, as now you see me weep—
The pathos of your love, that, like a flower,
Fearful of death yet amorous of sleep,
Droops for a moment and beholds, dismayed,
The wind whereon its petals shall be laid.

That Love at length should find me out and bring
This fierce and trivial brow unto the dust,
Is, after all, I must confess, but just;
There is a subtle beauty in this thing,
A wry perfection; wherefore now let sing
All voices how into my throat is thrust,
Unwelcome as Death's own, Love's bitter crust,
All criers proclaim it, and all steeples ring.
This being done, there let the matter rest.
What more remains is neither here nor there.
That you requite me not is plain to see;
Myself your slave herein have I confessed:
Thus far, indeed, the world may mock at me;
But if I suffer, it is my own affair.

Love is not blind. I see with single eye
Your ugliness and other women's grace.
I know the imperfection of your face,—
The eyes too wide apart, the brow too high
For beauty. Learned from earliest youth am I
In loveliness, and cannot so erase
Its letters from my mind, that I may trace
You faultless, I must love until I die.
More subtle is the sovereignty of love:
So am I caught that when I say, "Not fair,"
'Tis but as if I said, "Not here—not there—
Not risen—not writing letters." Well I know
What is this beauty men are babbling of;
I wonder only why they prize it so.

I know I am but summer to your heart,
And not the full four seasons of the year;
And you must welcome from another part
Such noble moods as are not mine, my dear.
No gracious weight of golden fruits to sell
Have I, nor any wise and wintry thing;
And I have loved you all too long and well
To carry still the high sweet breast of Spring.
Wherefore I say: O love, as summer goes,
I must be gone, steal forth with silent drums,
That you may hail anew the bird and rose
When I come back to you, as summer comes.
Else will you seek, at some not distant time,
Even your summer in another clime.

xxviii

I pray you if you love me, bear my joy
A little while, or let me weep your tears;
I, too, have seen the quavering Fate destroy
Your destiny's bright spinning—the dull shears
Meeting not neatly, chewing at the thread,—
Nor can you well be less aware how fine,
How staunch as wire, and how unwarranted
Endures the golden fortune that is mine.
I pray you for this day at least, my dear,
Fare by my side, that journey in the sun;
Else must I turn me from the blossoming year
And walk in grief the way that you have gone.
Let us go forth together to the spring:
Love must be this, if it be anything.

Pity me not because the light of day
At close of day no longer walks the sky;
Pity me not for beauties passed away
From field and thicket as the year goes by;
Pity me not the waning of the moon,
Nor that the ebbing tide goes out to sea,
Nor that a man's desire is hushed so soon,
And you no longer look with love on me.
This have I known always: Love is no more
Than the wide blossom which the wind assails,
Than the great tide that treads the shifting shore,
Strewing fresh wreckage gathered in the gales:
Pity me that the heart is slow to learn
What the swift mind beholds at every turn.

Sometimes when I am wearied suddenly
Of all the things that are the outward you,
And my gaze wanders ere your tale is through
To webs of my own weaving, or I see
Abstractedly your hands about your knee
And wonder why I love you as I do,
Then I recall, "Yet *Sorrow* thus he drew";
Then I consider, "*Pride* thus painted he."
Oh, friend, forget not, when you fain would note
In me a beauty that was never mine,
How first you knew me in a book I wrote,
How first you loved me for a written line:
So are we bound till broken is the throat
Of Song, and Art no more leads out the Nine.

Oh, oh, you will be sorry for that word!
Give back my book and take my kiss instead.
Was it my enemy or my friend I heard,
"What a big book for such a little head!"
Come, I will show you now my newest hat,
And you may watch me purse my mouth and prink!
Oh, I shall love you still, and all of that.
I never again shall tell you what I think.
I shall be sweet and crafty, soft and sly;
You will not catch me reading any more:
I shall be called a wife to pattern by;
And some day when you knock and push the door,
Some sane day, not too bright and not too stormy,
I shall be gone, and you may whistle for me.

Here is a wound that never will heal, I know,
Being wrought not of a dearness and a death,
But of a love turned ashes and the breath
Gone out of beauty; never again will grow
The grass on that scarred acre, though I sow
Young seed there yearly and the sky bequeath
Its friendly weathers down, far underneath
Shall be such bitterness of an old woe.
That April should be shattered by a gust,
That August should be levelled by a rain,
I can endure, and that the lifted dust
Of man should settle to the earth again;
But that a dream can die, will be a thrust
Between my ribs forever of hot pain.

xxxiii

I shall go back again to the bleak shore
And build a little shanty on the sand,
In such a way that the extremest band
Of brittle seaweed will escape my door
But by a yard or two; and nevermore
Shall I return to take you by the hand;
I shall be gone to what I understand,
And happier than I ever was before.
The love that stood a moment in your eyes,
The words that lay a moment on your tongue,
Are one with all that in a moment dies,
A little under-said and over-sung.
But I shall find the sullen rocks and skies
Unchanged from what they were when I was young.

Say what you will, and scratch my heart to find
The roots of last year's roses in my breast;
I am as surely riper in my mind
As if the fruit stood in the stalls confessed.
Laugh at the unshed leaf, say what you will,
Call me in all things what I was before,
A flutterer in the wind, a woman still;
I tell you I am what I was and more.
My branches weigh me down, frost cleans the air,
My sky is black with small birds bearing south;
Say what you will, confuse me with fine care,
Put by my word as but an April truth—
Autumn is no less on me, that a rose
Hugs the brown bough and sighs before it goes.

What's this of death, from you who never will die?
Think you the wrist that fashioned you in clay,
The thumb that set the hollow just that way
In your full throat and lidded the long eye
So roundly from the forehead, will let lie
Broken, forgotten, under foot some day
Your unimpeachable body, and so slay
The work he most had been remembered by?
I tell you this: whatever of dust to dust
Goes down, whatever of ashes may return
To its essential self in its own season,
Loveliness such as yours will not be lost,
But, cast in bronze upon his very urn,
Make known him Master, and for what good reason.

I see so clearly now my similar years
Repeat each other, shod in rusty black,
Like one hack following another hack
In meaningless procession, dry of tears,
Driven empty, lest the noses sharp as shears
Of gutter-urchins at a hearse's back
Should sniff a man died friendless, and attack
With silly scorn his deaf triumphant ears;
I see so clearly how my life must run
One year behind another year until
At length these bones that leap into the sun
Are lowered into the gravel, and lie still,
I would at times the funeral were done
And I abandoned on the ultimate hill.

Your face is like a chamber where a king
Dies of his wounds, untended and alone,
Stifling with courteous gesture the crude moan
That speaks too loud of mortal perishing,
Rising on elbow in the dark to sing
Some rhyme now out of season but well known
In days when banners in his face were blown
And every woman had a rose to fling.
I know that through your eyes which look on me
Who stand regarding you with pitiful breath,
You see beyond the moment's pause, you see
The sunny sky, the skimming bird beneath,
And, fronting on your windows hopelessly,
Black in the noon, the broad estates of Death.

The light comes back with Columbine; she brings
A touch of this, a little touch of that,
Coloured confetti, and a favour hat,
Patches, and powder, dolls that work by strings
And moons that work by switches, all the things
That please a sick man's fancy, and a flat
Spry convalescent kiss, and a small pat
Upon the pillow,—paper offerings.
The light goes out with her; the shadows sprawl.
Where she has left her fragrance like a shawl
I lie alone and pluck the counterpane,
Or on a dizzy elbow rise and hark—
And down like dominoes along the dark
Her little silly laughter spills again!

xxxix

Lord Archer, Death, whom sent you in your stead?
What faltering prentice fumbled at your bow,
That now should wander with the insanguine dead
In whom forever the bright blood must flow?
Or is it rather that impairing Time
Renders yourself so random, or so dim?
Or are you sick of shadows and would climb
A while to light, a while detaining him?
For know, this was no mortal youth, to be
Of you confounded, but a heavenly guest,
Assuming earthly garb for love of me,
And hell's demure attire for love of jest:
Bringing me asphodel and a dark feather,
He will return, and we shall laugh together!

xl

Loving you less than life, a little less
Than bitter-sweet upon a broken wall
Or brush-wood smoke in autumn, I confess
I cannot swear I love you not at all.
For there is that about you in this light—
A yellow darkness, sinister of rain—
Which sturdily recalls my stubborn sight
To dwell on you, and dwell on you again.
And I am made aware of many a week
I shall consume, remembering in what way
Your brown hair grows about your brow and cheek,
And what divine absurdities you say:
Till all the world, and I, and surely you,
Will know I love you, whether or not I do.

I, being born a woman and distressed
By all the needs and notions of my kind,
Am urged by your propinquity to find
Your person fair, and feel a certain zest
To bear your body's weight upon my breast:
So subtly is the fume of life designed,
To clarify the pulse and cloud the mind,
And leave me once again undone, possessed.
Think not for this, however, the poor treason
Of my stout blood against my staggering brain,
I shall remember you with love, or season
My scorn with pity,—let me make it plain:
I find this frenzy insufficient reason
For conversation when we meet again.

What lips my lips have kissed, and where, and why,
I have forgotten, and what arms have lain
Under my head till morning; but the rain
Is full of ghosts tonight, that tap and sigh
Upon the glass and listen for reply,
And in my heart there stirs a quiet pain
For unremembered lads that not again
Will turn to me at midnight with a cry.
Thus in the winter stands the lonely tree,
Nor knows what birds have vanished one by one,
Yet knows its boughs more silent than before:
I cannot say what loves have come and gone,
I only know that summer sang in me
A little while, that in me sings no more.

Still will I harvest beauty where it grows:
In coloured fungus and the spotted fog
Surprised on foods forgotten; in ditch and bog
Filmed brilliant with irregular rainbows
Of rust and oil, where half a city throws
Its empty tins; and in some spongy log
Whence headlong leaps the oozy emerald frog. . . .
And a black pupil in the green scum shows.
Her the inhabiter of divers places
Surmising at all doors, I push them all.
Oh, you that fearful of a creaking hinge
Turn back forevermore with craven faces,
I tell you Beauty bears an ultra fringe
Unguessed of you upon her gossamer shawl!

How healthily their feet upon the floor
Strike down! These are no spirits, but a band
Of children, surely, leaping hand in hand
Into the air in groups of three and four,
Wearing their silken rags as if they wore
Leaves only and light grasses, or a strand
Of black elusive seaweed oozing sand,
And running hard as if along a shore.
I know how lost forever, and at length
How still these lovely tossing limbs shall lie,
And the bright laughter and the panting breath;
And yet, before such beauty and such strength,
Once more, as always when the dance is high,
I am rebuked that I believe in death.

Euclid alone has looked on Beauty bare.
Let all who prate of Beauty hold their peace,
And lay them prone upon the earth and cease
To ponder on themselves, the while they stare
At nothing, intricately drawn nowhere
In shapes of shifting lineage; let geese
Gabble and hiss, but heroes seek release
From dusty bondage into luminous air.
O blinding hour, O holy, terrible day,
When first the shaft into his vision shone
Of light anatomized! Euclid alone
Has looked on Beauty bare. Fortunate they
Who, though once only and then but far away,
Have heard her massive sandal set on stone.

Sonnets from an Ungrafted Tree

I

So she came back into his house again
And watched beside his bed until he died,
Loving him not at all. The winter rain
Splashed in the painted butter-tub outside,
Where once her red geraniums had stood,
Where still their rotted stalks were to be seen;
The thin log snapped; and she went out for wood,
Bareheaded, running the few steps between
The house and shed; there, from the sodden eaves
Blown back and forth on ragged ends of twine,
Saw the dejected creeping-jinny vine,
(And one, big-aproned, blithe, with stiff blue sleeves
Rolled to the shoulder that warm day in spring,
Who planted seeds, musing ahead to their far blos-
    soming).

II

The last white sawdust on the floor was grown
Gray as the first, so long had he been ill;
The axe was nodding in the block; fresh-blown
And foreign came the rain across the sill,
But on the roof so steadily it drummed
She could not think a time it might not be—
In hazy summer, when the hot air hummed
With mowing, and locusts rising raspingly,
When that small bird with iridescent wings
And long incredible sudden silver tongue
Had just flashed (and yet maybe not!) among
The dwarf nasturtiums—when no sagging springs
Of shower were in the whole bright sky, somehow
Upon this roof the rain would drum as it was drum-
    ming now.

III

She filled her arms with wood, and set her chin
Forward, to hold the highest stick in place,
No less afraid than she had always been
Of spiders up her arms and on her face,
But too impatient for a careful search
Or a less heavy loading, from the heap
Selecting hastily small sticks of birch,
For their curled bark, that instantly will leap
Into a blaze, nor thinking to return
Some day, distracted, as of old, to find
Smooth, heavy, round, green logs with a wet, gray rind
Only, and knotty chunks that will not burn,
(That day when dust is on the wood-box floor,
And some old catalogue, and a brown, shriveled
    apple core).

IV

The white bark writhed and sputtered like a fish
Upon the coals, exuding odorous smoke.
She knelt and blew, in a surging desolate wish
For comfort; and the sleeping ashes woke
And scattered to the hearth, but no thin fire
Broke suddenly, the wood was wet with rain.
Then, softly stepping forth from her desire,
(Being mindful of like passion hurled in vain
Upon a similar task, in other days)
She thrust her breath against the stubborn coal,
Bringing to bear upon its hilt the whole
Of her still body . . . there sprang a little blaze . . .
A pack of hounds, the flame swept up the flue!—
And the blue night stood flattened against the window,
    staring through.

l

A wagon stopped before the house; she heard
The heavy oilskins of the grocer's man
Slapping against his legs. Of a sudden whirred
Her heart like a frightened partridge, and she ran
And slid the bolt, leaving his entrance free;
Then in the cellar way till he was gone
Hid, breathless, praying that he might not see
The chair sway she had laid her hand upon
In passing. Sour and damp from that dark vault
Arose to her the well-remembered chill;
She saw the narrow wooden stairway still
Plunging into the earth, and the thin salt
Crusting the crocks; until she knew him far,
So stood, with listening eyes upon the empty dough-
 nut jar.

li

Then cautiously she pushed the cellar door
And stepped into the kitchen—saw the track
Of muddy rubber boots across the floor,
The many paper parcels in a stack
Upon the dresser; with accustomed care
Removed the twine and put the wrappings by,
Folded, and the bags flat, that with an air
Of ease had been whipped open skillfully,
To the gape of children. Treacherously dear
And simple was the dull, familiar task.
And so it was she came at length to ask:
How came the soda there? The sugar here?
Then the dream broke. Silent, she brought the mop,
And forced the trade-slip on the nail that held his
    razor strop.

VII

One way there was of muting in the mind
A little while the ever-clamorous care;
And there was rapture, of a decent kind,
In making mean and ugly objects fair:
Soft-sooted kettle-bottoms, that had been
Time after time set in above the fire,
Faucets, and candlesticks, corroded green,
To mine again from quarry; to attire
The shelves in paper petticoats, and tack
New oilcloth in the ringed-and-rotten's place,
Polish the stove till you could see your face,
And after nightfall rear an aching back
In a changed kitchen, bright as a new pin,
An advertisement, far too fine to cook a supper in.

VIII

She let them leave their jellies at the door
And go away, reluctant, down the walk.
She heard them talking as they passed before
The blind, but could not quite make out their talk
For noise in the room—the sudden heavy fall
And roll of a charred log, and the roused shower
Of snapping sparks; then sharply from the wall
The unforgivable crowing of the hour.
One instant set ajar, her quiet ear
Was stormed and forced by the full rout of day:
The rasp of a saw, the fussy cluck and bray
Of hens, the wheeze of a pump, she needs must hear;
She inescapably must endure to feel
Across her teeth the grinding of a backing wagon wheel.

liv

Not over-kind nor over-quick in study
Nor skilled in sports nor beautiful was he,
Who had come into her life when anybody
Would have been welcome, so in need was she.
They had become acquainted in this way:
He flashed a mirror in her eyes at school;
By which he was distinguished; from that day
They went about together, as a rule.
She told, in secret and with whispering,
How he had flashed a mirror in her eyes;
And as she told, it struck her with surprise
That this was not so wonderful a thing.
But what's the odds?—It's pretty nice to know
You've got a friend to keep you company everywhere
    you go.

x

She had forgotten how the August night
Was level as a lake beneath the moon,
In which she swam a little, losing sight
Of shore; and how the boy, who was at noon
Simple enough, not different from the rest,
Wore now a pleasant mystery as he went,
Which seemed to her an honest enough test
Whether she loved him, and she was content.
So loud, so loud the million crickets' choir . . .
So sweet the night, so long-drawn-out and late . . .
And if the man were not her spirit's mate,
Why was her body sluggish with desire?
Stark on the open field the moonlight fell,
But the oak tree's shadow was deep and black and
    secret as a well.

XI

It came into her mind, seeing how the snow
Was gone, and the brown grass exposed again,
And clothes-pins, and an apron—long ago,
In some white storm that sifted through the pane
And sent her forth reluctantly at last
To gather in, before the line gave way,
Garments, board-stiff, that galloped on the blast
Clashing like angel armies in a fray,
An apron long ago in such a night
Blown down and buried in the deepening drift,
To lie till April thawed it back to sight,
Forgotten, quaint and novel as a gift—
It struck her, as she pulled and pried and tore,
That here was spring, and the whole year to be lived
    through once more.

XII

Tenderly, in those times, as though she fed
An ailing child—with sturdy propping up
Of its small, feverish body in the bed,
And steadying of its hands about the cup—
She gave her husband of her body's strength,
Thinking of men, what helpless things they were,
Until he turned and fell asleep at length,
And stealthily stirred the night and spoke to her.
Familiar, at such moments, like a friend,
Whistled far off the long, mysterious train,
And she could see in her mind's vision plain
The magic World, where cities stood on end . . .
Remote from where she lay—and yet—between,
Save for something asleep beside her, only the window
   screen.

XIII

From the wan dream that was her waking day,
Wherein she journeyed, borne along the ground
Without her own volition in some way,
Or fleeing, motionless, with feet fast bound,
Or running silent through a silent house
Sharply remembered from an earlier dream,
Upstairs, down other stairs, fearful to rouse,
Regarding him, the wide and empty scream
Of a strange sleeper on a malignant bed,
And all the time not certain if it were
Herself so doing or some one like to her,
From this wan dream that was her daily bread,
Sometimes, at night, incredulous, she would wake—
A child, blowing bubbles that the chairs and carpet
did not break!

XIV

She had a horror he would die at night.
And sometimes when the light began to fade
She could not keep from noticing how white
The birches looked—and then she would be afraid,
Even with a lamp, to go about the house
And lock the windows; and as night wore on
Toward morning, if a dog howled, or a mouse
Squeaked in the floor, long after it was gone
Her flesh would sit awry on her. By day
She would forget somewhat, and it would seem
A silly thing to go with just this dream
And get a neighbor to come at night and stay.
But it would strike her sometimes, making the tea:
She had kept that kettle boiling all night long, for company.

lx

There was upon the sill a pencil mark,
Vital with shadow when the sun stood still
At noon, but now, because the day was dark,
It was a pencil mark upon the sill.
And the mute clock, maintaining ever the same
Dead moment, blank and vacant of itself,
Was a pink shepherdess, a picture frame,
A shell marked Souvenir, there on the shelf.
Whence it occurred to her that he might be,
The mainspring being broken in his mind,
A clock himself, if one were so inclined,
That stood at twenty minutes after three—
The reason being for this, it might be said,
That things in death were neither clocks nor people,
but only dead.

lxi

XVI

The doctor asked her what she wanted done
With him, that could not lie there many days.
And she was shocked to see how life goes on
Even after death, in irritating ways;
And mused how if he had not died at all
'Twould have been easier—then there need not be
The stiff disorder of a funeral
Everywhere, and the hideous industry,
And crowds of people calling her by name
And questioning her, she'd never seen before,
But only watching by his bed once more
And sitting silent if a knocking came . . .
She said at length, feeling the doctor's eyes,
"I don't know what you do exactly when a person
    dies."

XVII

Gazing upon him now, severe and dead,
It seemed a curious thing that she had lain
Beside him many a night in that cold bed,
And that had been which would not be again.
From his desirous body the great heat
Was gone at last, it seemed, and the taut nerves
Loosened forever. Formally the sheet
Set forth for her today those heavy curves
And lengths familiar as the bedroom door.
She was as one who enters, sly, and proud,
To where her husband speaks before a crowd,
And sees a man she never saw before—
The man who eats his victuals at her side,
Small, and absurd, and hers: for once, not hers,
    unclassified.

FINIS

lxiii

Life, were thy pains as are the pains of hell,
So hardly to be borne, yet to be borne,
And all thy boughs more grim with wasp and thorn
Than armoured bough stood ever; too chill to spell
With the warm tongue, and sharp with broken shell
Thy ways, whereby in wincing haste forlorn
The desperate foot must travel, blind and torn,
Yet must I cry: So be it; it is well.
So fair to me thy vineyards, nor less fair
Than the sweet heaven my fathers hoped to gain;
So bright this earthly blossom spiked with care,
This harvest hung behind the boughs of pain,
Needs must I gather, guessing by the stain
I bleed, but know not wherefore, know not where.

Grow not too high, grow not too far from home,
Green tree, whose roots are in the granite's face!
Taller than silver spire or golden dome
A tree may grow above its earthy place,
And taller than a cloud, but not so tall
The root may not be mother to the stem,
Lifting rich plenty, though the rivers fall,
To the cold sunny leaves to nourish them.
Have done with blossoms for a time, be bare;
Split rock; plunge downward; take heroic soil,—
Deeper than bones, no pasture for you there;
Deeper than water, deeper than gold and oil:
Earth's fiery core alone can feed the bough
That blooms between Orion and the Plough.

lxv

Not that it matters, not that my heart's cry
Is potent to deflect our common doom,
Or bind to truce in this ambiguous room
The planets of the atom as they ply;
But only to record that you and I,
Like thieves that scratch the jewels from a tomb,
Have gathered delicate love in hardy bloom
Close under Chaos,—I rise to testify.
This is my testament: that we are taken;
Our colours are as clouds before the wind;
Yet for a moment stood the foe forsaken,
Eyeing Love's favour to our helmet pinned;
Death is our master,—but his seat is shaken;
He rides victorious,—but his ranks are thinned.

lxvi
Sonnet to Gath

Country of hunchbacks!—where the strong, straight
   spine,
Jeered at by crooked children, makes his way
Through by-streets at the kindest hour of day,
Till he deplore his stature, and incline
To measure manhood with a gibbous line;
Till out of loneliness, being flawed with clay,
He stoop into his neighbour's house and say,
"Your roof is low for me—the fault is mine."
Dust in an urn long since, dispersed and dead
Is great Apollo; and the happier he;
Since who amongst you all would lift a head
At a god's radiance on the mean door-tree,
Saving to run and hide your dates and bread,
And cluck your children in about your knee?

lxvii

To Inez Milholland

Read in Washington, November eighteenth, 1923, at the unveiling
of a statue of three leaders in the cause of Equal Rights for Women

Upon this marble bust that is not I

Lay the round, formal wreath that is not fame;

But in the forum of my silenced cry

Root ye the living tree whose sap is flame.

I, that was proud and valiant, am no more;—

Save as a dream that wanders wide and late,

Save as a wind that rattles the stout door,

Troubling the ashes in the sheltered grate.

The stone will perish; I shall be twice dust.

Only my standard on a taken hill

Can cheat the mildew and the red-brown rust

And make immortal my adventurous will.

Even now the silk is tugging at the staff:

Take up the song; forget the epitaph.

lxviii

To Jesus on His Birthday

For this your mother sweated in the cold,
For this you bled upon the bitter tree:
A yard of tinsel ribbon bought and sold;
A paper wreath; a day at home for me.
The merry bells ring out, the people kneel;
Up goes the man of God before the crowd;
With voice of honey and with eyes of steel
He drones your humble gospel to the proud.
Nobody listens. Less than the wind that blows
Are all your words to us you died to save.
O Prince of Peace! O Sharon's dewy Rose!
How mute you lie within your vaulted grave.
The stone the angel rolled away with tears
Is back upon your mouth these thousand years.

lxix

On Hearing a Symphony of Beethoven

Sweet sounds, oh, beautiful music, do not cease!
Reject me not into the world again.
With you alone is excellence and peace,
Mankind made plausible, his purpose plain.
Enchanted in your air benign and shrewd,
With limbs a-sprawl and empty faces pale,
The spiteful and the stingy and the rude
Sleep like the scullions in the fairy-tale.
This moment is the best the world can give:
The tranquil blossom on the tortured stem.
Reject me not, sweet sounds! oh, let me live,
Till Doom espy my towers and scatter them,
A city spell-bound under the aging sun,
Music my rampart, and my only one.

lxx
Fatal Interview
I

What thing is this that, built of salt and lime
And such dry motes as in the sunbeam show,
Has power upon me that do daily climb
The dustless air?—for whom those peaks of snow
Whereup the lungs of man with borrowed breath
Go labouring to a doom I may not feel,
Are but a pearled and roseate plain beneath
My wingèd helmet and my wingèd heel.
What sweet emotions neither foe nor friend
Are these that clog my flight? what thing is this
That hastening headlong to a dusty end
Dare turn upon me these proud eyes of bliss?
Up, up, my feathers!—ere I lay you by
To journey barefoot with a mortal joy.

II

This beast that rends me in the sight of all,
This love, this longing, this oblivious thing,
That has me under as the last leaves fall,
Will glut, will sicken, will be gone by spring.
The wound will heal, the fever will abate,
The knotted hurt will slacken in the breast;
I shall forget before the flickers mate
Your look that is today my east and west.
Unscathed, however, from a claw so deep
Though I should love again I shall not go:
Along my body, waking while I sleep,
Sharp to the kiss, cold to the hand as snow,
The scar of this encounter like a sword
Will lie between me and my troubled lord.

lxxii

III

No lack of counsel from the shrewd and wise
How love may be acquired and how conserved
Warrants this laying bare before your eyes
My needle to your north abruptly swerved;
If I would hold you, I must hide my fears
Lest you be wanton, lead you to believe
My compass to another quarter veers,
Little surrender, lavishly receive.
But being like my mother the brown earth
Fervent and full of gifts and free from guile,
Liefer would I you loved me for my worth,
Though you should love me but a little while,
Than for a philtre any doll can brew, —
Though thus I bound you as I long to do.

IV

Nay, learnèd doctor, these fine leeches fresh
From the pond's edge my cause cannot remove:
Alas, the sick disorder in my flesh
Is deeper than your skill, is very love.
And you, good friar, far liefer would I think
Upon my dear, and dream him in your place,
Than heed your *ben'cites* and heavenward sink
With empty heart and noddle full of grace.
Breathes but one mortal on the teeming globe
Could minister to my soul's or body's needs—
Physician minus physic, minus robe;
Confessor minus Latin, minus beads.
Yet should you bid me name him, I am dumb;
For though you summon him, he would not come.

v

Of all that ever in extreme disease
"Sweet Love, sweet cruel Love, have pity!" cried,
Count me the humblest, hold me least of these
That wear the red heart crumpled in the side,
In heaviest durance, dreaming or awake,
Filling the dungeon with their piteous woe;
Not that I shriek not till the dungeon shake,
"Oh, God! Oh, let me out! Oh, let me go!"
But that my chains throughout their iron length
Make such a golden clank upon my ear,
But that I would not, boasted I the strength,
Up with a terrible arm and out of here
Where thrusts my morsel daily through the bars
This tall, oblivious gaoler eyed with stars.

VI

Since I cannot persuade you from this mood
Of pale preoccupation with the dead,
Not for my comfort nor for your own good
Shift your concern to living bones instead;
Since that which Helen did and ended Troy
Is more than I can do though I be warm,
Have up your buried girls, egregious boy,
And stand with them against the unburied storm.
When you lie wasted and your blood runs thin,
And what's to do must with dispatch be done,
Call Cressid, call Elaine, call Isolt in!—
More bland the ichor of a ghost should run
Along your dubious veins than the rude sea
Of passion pounding all day long in me.

VII

Night is my sister, and how deep in love,
How drowned in love and weedily washed ashore,
There to be fretted by the drag and shove
At the tide's edge, I lie—these things and more:
Whose arm alone between me and the sand,
Whose voice alone, whose pitiful breath brought near,
Could thaw these nostrils and unlock this hand,
She could advise you, should you care to hear.
Small chance, however, in a storm so black,
A man will leave his friendly fire and snug
For a drowned woman's sake, and bring her back
To drip and scatter shells upon the rug.
No one but Night, with tears on her dark face,
Watches beside me in this windy place.

VIII

Yet in an hour to come, disdainful dust,
You shall be bowed and brought to bed with me.
While the blood roars, or when the blood is rust
About a broken engine, this shall be.
If not today, then later; if not here
On the green grass, with sighing and delight,
Then under it, all in good time, my dear,
We shall be laid together in the night.
And ruder and more violent, be assured,
Than the desirous body's heat and sweat
That shameful kiss by more than night obscured
Wherewith at length the scornfullest mouth is met.
Life has no friend; her converts late or soon
Slide back to feed the dragon with the moon.

IX

When you are dead, and your disturbing eyes
No more as now their stormy lashes lift
To lance me through—as in the morning skies
One moment, plainly visible in a rift
Of cloud, two splendid planets may appear
And purely blaze, and are at once withdrawn,
What time the watcher in desire and fear
Leans from his chilly window in the dawn—
Shall I be free, shall I be once again
As others are, and count your loss no care?
Oh, never more, till my dissolving brain
Be powerless to evoke you out of air,
Remembered morning stars, more fiercely bright
Than all the Alphas of the actual night!

lxxix

x

Strange thing that I, by nature nothing prone
To fret the summer blossom on its stem,
Who know the hidden nest, but leave alone
The magic eggs, the bird that cuddles them,
Should have no peace till your bewildered heart
Hung fluttering at the window of my breast,
Till I had ravished to my bitter smart
Your kiss from the stern moment, could not rest.
"Swift wing, sweet blossom, live again in air!
Depart, poor flower; poor feathers you are free!"
Thus do I cry, being teased by shame and care
That beauty should be brought to terms by me;
Yet shamed the more that in my heart I know,
Cry as I may, I could not let you go.

XI

Not in a silver casket cool with pearls
Or rich with red corundum or with blue,
Locked, and the key withheld, as other girls
Have given their loves, I give my love to you;
Not in a lovers'-knot, not in a ring
Worked in such fashion, and the legend plain—
Semper fidelis, where a secret spring
Kennels a drop of mischief for the brain:
Love in the open hand, no thing but that,
Ungemmed, unhidden, wishing not to hurt,
As one should bring you cowslips in a hat
Swung from the hand, or apples in her skirt,
I bring you, calling out as children do:
"Look what I have!—And these are all for you."

XII

Olympian gods, mark now my bedside lamp
Blown out; and be advised too late that he
Whom you call sire is stolen into the camp
Of warring Earth, and lies abed with me.
Call out your golden hordes, the harm is done:
Enraptured in his great embrace I lie;
Shake heaven with spears, but I shall bear a son
Branded with godhead, heel and brow and thigh.
Whom think not to bedazzle or confound
With meteoric splendours or display
Of blackened moons or suns or the big sound
Of sudden thunder on a silent day;
Pain and compassion shall he know, being mine,—
Confusion never, that is half divine.

XIII

I said, seeing how the winter gale increased,
Even as waxed within us and grew strong
The ancient tempest of desire, "At least,
It is the season when the nights are long.
Well flown, well shattered from the summer hedge
The early sparrow and the opening flowers!—
Late climbs the sun above the southerly edge
These days, and sweet to love those added hours."
Alas, already does the dark recede,
And visible are the trees against the snow.
Oh, monstrous parting, oh, perfidious deed,
How shall I leave your side, how shall I go? . . .
Unnatural night, the shortest of the year,
Farewell! 'Tis dawn. The longest day is here.

XIV

Since of no creature living the last breath
Is twice required, or twice the ultimate pain,
Seeing how to quit your arms is very death,
'Tis likely that I shall not die again;
And likely 'tis that Time whose gross decree
Sends now the dawn to clamour at our door,
Thus having done his evil worst to me,
Will thrust me by, will harry me no more.
When you are corn and roses and at rest
I shall endure, a dense and sanguine ghost,
To haunt the scene where I was happiest,
To bend above the thing I loved the most;
And rise, and wring my hands, and steal away
As I do now, before the advancing day.

xv

My worship from this hour the Sparrow-Drawn
Alone will cherish, and her arrowy child,
Whose groves alone in the inquiring dawn
Rise tranquil, and their altars undefiled.
Seaward and shoreward smokes a plundered land
To guard whose portals was my dear employ;
Razed are its temples now; inviolate stand
Only the slopes of Venus and her boy.
How have I stripped me of immortal aid
Save theirs alone,—who could endure to see
Forsworn Aeneas with conspiring blade
Sever the ship from shore (alas for me)
And make no sign; who saw, and did not speak,
The brooch of Troilus pinned upon the Greek.

XVI

I dreamed I moved among the Elysian fields,
In converse with sweet women long since dead;
And out of blossoms which that meadow yields
I wove a garland for your living head.
Danae, that was the vessel for a day
Of golden Jove, I saw, and at her side,
Whom Jove the Bull desired and bore away,
Europa stood, and the Swan's featherless bride.
All these were mortal women, yet all these
Above the ground had had a god for guest;
Freely I walked beside them and at ease,
Addressing them, by them again addressed,
And marvelled nothing, for remembering you,
Wherefore I was among them well I knew.

XVII

Sweet love, sweet thorn, when lightly to my heart
I took your thrust, whereby I since am slain,
And lie disheveled in the grass apart,
A sodden thing bedrenched by tears and rain,
While rainy evening drips to misty night,
And misty night to cloudy morning clears,
And clouds disperse across the gathering light,
And birds grow noisy, and the sun appears—
Had I bethought me then, sweet love, sweet thorn,
How sharp an anguish even at the best,
When all's requited and the future sworn,
The happy hour can leave within the breast,
I had not so come running at the call
Of one who loves me little, if at all.

XVIII

Shall I be prisoner till my pulses stop
To hateful Love and drag his noisy chain,
And bait my need with sugared crusts that drop
From jeweled fingers neither kind nor clean?—
Mewed in an airless cavern where a toad
Would grieve to snap his gnat and lay him down,
While in the light along the rattling road
Men shout and chaff and drive their wares to town?...
Perfidious Prince, that keep me here confined,
Doubt not I know the letters of my doom:
How many a man has left his blood behind
To buy his exit from this mournful room
These evil stains record, these walls that rise
Carved with his torment, steamy with his sighs.

XIX

My most distinguished guest and learnèd friend,
The pallid hare that runs before the day
Having brought your earnest counsels to an end
Now have I somewhat of my own to say:
That it is folly to be sunk in love,
And madness plain to make the matter known,
These are no mysteries you are verger of;
Everyman's wisdoms these are, and my own.
If I have flung my heart unto a hound
I have done ill, it is a certain thing;
Yet breathe I freer, walk I the more sound
On my sick bones for this brave reasoning?
Soon must I say, "'Tis prowling Death I hear!"
Yet come no better off, for my quick ear.

xx

Think not, nor for a moment let your mind,
Wearied with thinking, doze upon the thought
That the work's done and the long day behind,
And beauty, since 'tis paid for, can be bought.
If in the moonlight from the silent bough
Suddenly with precision speak your name
The nightingale, be not assured that now
His wing is limed and his wild virtue tame.
Beauty beyond all feathers that have flown
Is free; you shall not hood her to your wrist,
Nor sting her eyes, nor have her for your own
In any fashion; beauty billed and kissed
Is not your turtle; tread her like a dove—
She loves you not; she never heard of love.

XXI

Gone in good sooth you are: not even in dream
You come. As if the strictures of the light,
Laid on our glances to their disesteem,
Extended even to shadows and the night;
Extended even beyond that drowsy sill
Along whose galleries open to the skies
All maskers move unchallenged and at will,
Visor in hand or hooded to the eyes.
To that pavilion the green sea in flood
Curves in, and the slow dancers dance in foam;
I find again the pink camellia-bud
On the wide step, beside a silver comb. . . .
But it is scentless; up the marble stair
I mount with pain, knowing you are not there.

XXII

Now by this moon, before this moon shall wane
I shall be dead or I shall be with you!
No moral concept can outweigh the pain
Past rack and wheel this absence puts me through;
Faith, honour, pride, endurance, what the tongues
Of tedious men will say, or what the law—
For which of these do I fill up my lungs
With brine and fire at every breath I draw?
Time, and to spare, for patience by and by,
Time to be cold and time to sleep alone;
Let me no more until the hour I die
Defraud my innocent senses of their own.
Before this moon shall darken, say of me:
She's in her grave, or where she wants to be.

XXIII

I know the face of Falsehood and her tongue
Honeyed with unction, plausible with guile,
Are dear to men, whom count me not among,
That owe their daily credit to her smile;
Such have been succoured out of great distress
By her contriving, if accounts be true:
Their deference now above the board, I guess,
Discharges what beneath the board is due.
As for myself, I'd liefer lack her aid
Than eat her presence; let this building fall:
But let me never lift my latch, afraid
To hear her simpering accents in the hall,
Nor force an entrance past mephitic airs
Of stale patchouli hanging on my stairs.

XXIV

Whereas at morning in a jeweled crown
I bit my fingers and was hard to please,
Having shook disaster till the fruit fell down
I feel tonight more happy and at ease:
Feet running in the corridors, men quick-
Buckling their sword-belts bumping down the stair,
Challenge, and rattling bridge-chain, and the click
Of hooves on pavement—this will clear the air.
Private this chamber as it has not been
In many a month of muffled hours; almost,
Lulled by the uproar, I could lie serene
And sleep, until all's won, until all's lost,
And the door's opened and the issue shown,
And I walk forth Hell's mistress . . . or my own.

XXV

Peril upon the paths of this desire
Lies like the natural darkness of the night,
For me unpeopled; let him hence retire
Whom as a child a shadow could affright;
And fortune speed him from this dubious place
Where roses blenched or blackened of their hue,
Pallid and stemless float on undulant space,
Or clustered hidden shock the hand with dew.
Whom as a child the night's obscurity
Did not alarm, let him alone remain,
Lanterned but by the longing in the eye,
And warmed but by the fever in the vein,
To lie with me, sentried from wrath and scorn
By sleepless Beauty and her polished thorn.

XXVI

Women have loved before as I love now;
At least, in lively chronicles of the past—
Of Irish waters by a Cornish prow
Or Trojan waters by a Spartan mast
Much to their cost invaded—here and there,
Hunting the amorous line, skimming the rest,
I find some woman bearing as I bear
Love like a burning city in the breast.
I think however that of all alive
I only in such utter, ancient way
Do suffer love; in me alone survive
The unregenerate passions of a day
When treacherous queens, with death upon the tread,
Heedless and wilful, took their knights to bed.

XXVII

Moon, that against the lintel of the west
Your forehead lean until the gate be swung,
Longing to leave the world and be at rest,
Being worn with faring and no longer young,
Do you recall at all the Carian hill
Where worn with loving, loving late you lay,
Halting the sun because you lingered still,
While wondering candles lit the Carian day?
Ah, if indeed this memory to your mind
Recall some sweet employment, pity me,
That with the dawn must leave my love behind,
That even now the dawn's dim herald see!
I charge you, goddess, in the name of one
You loved as well: endure, hold off the sun.

XXVIII

When we are old and these rejoicing veins
Are frosty channels to a muted stream,
And out of all our burning there remains
No feeblest spark to fire us, even in dream,
This be our solace: that it was not said
When we were young and warm and in our prime,
Upon our couch we lay as lie the dead,
Sleeping away the unreturning time.
O sweet, O heavy-lidded, O my love,
When morning strikes her spear upon the land,
And we must rise and arm us and reprove
The insolent daylight with a steady hand,
Be not discountenanced if the knowing know
We rose from rapture but an hour ago.

XXIX

Heart, have no pity on this house of bone:
Shake it with dancing, break it down with joy.
No man holds mortgage on it; it is your own;
To give, to sell at auction, to destroy.
When you are blind to moonlight on the bed,
When you are deaf to gravel on the pane,
Shall quavering caution from this house instead
Cluck forth at summer mischief in the lane?
All that delightful youth forbears to spend
Molestful age inherits, and the ground
Will have us; therefore, while we're young, my friend—
The Latin's vulgar, but the advice is sound.
Youth, have no pity; leave no farthing here
For age to invest in compromise and fear.

xxx

Love is not all: it is not meat nor drink
Nor slumber nor a roof against the rain;
Nor yet a floating spar to men that sink
And rise and sink and rise and sink again;
Love can not fill the thickened lung with breath,
Nor clean the blood, nor set the fractured bone;
Yet many a man is making friends with death
Even as I speak, for lack of love alone.
It well may be that in a difficult hour,
Pinned down by pain and moaning for release,
Or nagged by want past resolution's power,
I might be driven to sell your love for peace,
Or trade the memory of this night for food.
It well may be. I do not think I would.

XXXI

When we that wore the myrtle wear the dust,
And years of darkness cover up our eyes,
And all our arrogant laughter and sweet lust
Keep counsel with the scruples of the wise;
When boys and girls that now are in the loins
Of croaking lads, dip oar into the sea,—
And who are these that dive for copper coins?
No longer we, my love, no longer we—
Then let the fortunate breathers of the air,
When we lie speechless in the muffling mould,
Tease not our ghosts with slander, pause not there
To say that love is false and soon grows cold,
But pass in silence the mute grave of two
Who lived and died believing love was true.

XXXII

Time, that is pleased to lengthen out the day
For grieving lovers parted or denied,
And pleased to hurry the sweet hours away
From such as lie enchanted side by side,
Is not my kinsman; nay, my feudal foe
Is he that in my childhood was the thief
Of all my mother's beauty, and in woe
My father bowed, and brought our house to grief.
Thus, though he think to touch with hateful frost
Your treasured curls, and your clear forehead line,
And so persuade me from you, he has lost;
Never shall he inherit what was mine.
When Time and all his tricks have done their worst,
Still will I hold you dear, and him accurst.

XXXIII

Sorrowful dreams remembered after waking
Shadow with dolour all the candid day;
Even as I read, the silly tears out-breaking
Splash on my hands and shut the page away. . . .
Grief at the root, a dark and secret dolour,
Harder to bear than wind-and-weather grief,
Clutching the rose, draining its cheek of colour,
Drying the bud, curling the opened leaf.
Deep is the pond—although the edge be shallow,
Frank in the sun, revealing fish and stone,
Climbing ashore to turtle-head and mallow—
Black at the centre beats a heart unknown.
Desolate dreams pursue me out of sleep;
Weeping I wake; waking, I weep, I weep.

XXXIV

Most wicked words!-forbear to speak them out.
Utter them not again; blaspheme no more
Against our love with maxims learned from Doubt:
Lest Death should get his foot inside the door.
We are surrounded by a hundred foes;
And he that at your bidding joins our feast,
I stake my heart upon it, is one of those,
Nor in their councils does he sit the least.
Hark not his whisper: he is Time's ally,
Kinsman to Death, and leman of Despair:
Believe that I shall love you till I die;
Believe; and thrust him forth; and arm the stair;
And top the walls with spikes and splintered glass
That he pass gutted should again he pass.

XXXV

Clearly my ruined garden as it stood
Before the frost came on it I recall—
Stiff marigolds, and what a trunk of wood
The zinnia had, that was the first to fall;
These pale and oozy stalks, these hanging leaves
Nerveless and darkened, dripping in the sun,
Cannot gainsay me, though the spirit grieves
And wrings its hands at what the frost has done.
If in a widening silence you should guess
I read the moment with recording eyes,
Taking your love and all your loveliness
Into a listening body hushed of sighs . . .
Though summer's rife and the warm rose in season,
Rebuke me not: I have a winter reason.

XXXVI

Hearing your words, and not a word among them
Tuned to my liking, on a salty day
When inland woods were pushed by winds that flung
 them
Hissing to leeward like a ton of spray,
I thought how off Matinicus the tide
Came pounding in, came running through the Gut,
While from the Rock the warning whistle cried,
And children whimpered, and the doors blew shut;
There in the autumn when the men go forth,
With slapping skirts the island women stand
In gardens stripped and scattered, peering north,
With dahlia tubers dripping from the hand:
The wind of their endurance, driving south,
Flattened your words against your speaking mouth.

XXXVII

Believe, if ever the bridges of this town,
Whose towers were builded without fault or stain,
Be taken, and its battlements go down,
No mortal roof shall shelter me again;
I shall not prop a branch against a bough
To hide me from the whipping east or north,
Nor tease to flame a heap of sticks, who now
Am warmed by all the wonders of the earth.
Do you take ship unto some happier shore
In such event, and have no thought for me,
I shall remain;—to share the ruinous floor
With roofs that once were seen far out at sea;
To cheer a mouldering army on the march . . .
And beg from spectres by a broken arch.

XXXVIII

You say: "Since life is cruel enough at best;"
You say: "Considering how our love is cursed,
And housed so bleakly that the sea-gull's nest
Were better shelter, even as better nursed
Between the breaker and the stingy reeds
Ragged and coarse that hiss against the sand
The gull's brown chick, and hushed in all his needs,
Than our poor love so harried through the land—
You being too tender, even with all your scorn,
To line his cradle with the world's reproof,
And I too devious, too surrendered, born
Too far from home to hunt him even a roof
Out of the rain—" Oh, tortured voice, be still!
Spare me your premise: leave me when you will.

XXXIX

Love me no more, now let the god depart,
If love be grown so bitter to your tongue!
Here is my hand; I bid you from my heart
Fare well, fare very well, be always young.
As for myself, mine was a deeper drouth:
I drank and thirsted still; but I surmise
My kisses now are sand against your mouth,
Teeth in your palm and pennies on your eyes.
Speak but one cruel word, to shame my tears;
Go, but in going, stiffen up my back
To meet the yelping of the mustering years—
Dim, trotting shapes that seldom will attack
Two with a light who match their steps and sing:
To one alone and lost, another thing.

XL

You loved me not at all, but let it go;
I loved you more than life, but let it be.
As the more injured party, this being so,
The hour's amenities are all to me—
The choice of weapons; and I gravely choose
To let the weapons tarnish where they lie;
And spend the night in eloquent abuse
Of senators and popes and such small fry
And meet the morning standing, and at odds
With heaven and earth and hell and any fool
Who calls his soul his own, and all the gods,
And all the children getting dressed for school . . .
And you will leave me, and I shall entomb
What's cold by then in an adjoining room.

XLI

I said in the beginning, did I not?—
Prophetic of the end, though unaware
How light you took me, ignorant that you thought
I spoke to see my breath upon the air:
If you walk east at daybreak from the town
To the cliff's foot, by climbing steadily
You cling at noon whence there is no way down
But to go toppling backward to the sea.
And not for birds nor birds'-eggs, so they say,
But for a flower that in these fissures grows,
Forms have been seen to move throughout the day
Skyward; but what its name is no one knows.
'Tis said you find beside them on the sand
This flower, relinquished by the broken hand.

XLII

O ailing Love, compose your struggling wing!
Confess you mortal; be content to die.
How better dead, than be this awkward thing
Dragging in dust its feathers of the sky;
Hitching and rearing, plunging beak to loam,
Upturned, disheveled, uttering a weak sound
Less proud than of the gull that rakes the foam,
Less kind than of the hawk that scours the ground.
While yet your awful beauty, even at bay,
Beats off the impious eye, the outstretched hand,
And what your hue or fashion none can say,
Vanish, be fled, leave me a wingless land . . .
Save where one moment down the quiet tide
Fades a white swan, with a black swan beside.

XLIII

Summer, be seen no more within this wood;
Nor you, red Autumn, down its paths appear;
Let no more the false mitrewort intrude
Nor the dwarf cornel nor the gentian here;
You too be absent, unavailing Spring,
Nor let those thrushes that with pain conspire
From out this wood their wild arpeggios fling,
Shaking the nerves with memory and desire.
Only that season which is no man's friend,
You, surly Winter, in this wood be found;
Freeze up the year; with sleet these branches bend
Though rasps the locust in the fields around.
Now darken, sky! Now shrieking blizzard, blow!—
Farewell, sweet bank; be blotted out with snow.

XLIV

If to be left were to be left alone,
And lock the door and find one's self again—
Drag forth and dust Penates of one's own
That in a corner all too long have lain;
Read Brahms, read Chaucer, set the chessmen out
In classic problem, stretch the shrunken mind
Back to its stature on the rack of thought—
Loss might be said to leave its boon behind.
But fruitless conference and the interchange
With callow wits of bearded *cons* and *pros*
Enlist the neutral daylight, and derange
A will too sick to battle for repose.
Neither with you nor with myself, I spend
Loud days that have no meaning and no end.

XLV

I know my mind and I have made my choice;
Not from your temper does my doom depend;
Love me or love me not, you have no voice
In this, which is my portion to the end.
Your presence and your favours, the full part
That you could give, you now can take away:
What lies between your beauty and my heart
Not even you can trouble or betray.
Mistake me not—unto my inmost core
I do desire your kiss upon my mouth;
They have not craved a cup of water more
That bleach upon the deserts of the south;
Here might you bless me; what you cannot do
Is bow me down, who have been loved by you.

XLVI

Even in the moment of our earliest kiss,

When sighed the straitened bud into the flower,

Sat the dry seed of most unwelcome this;

And that I knew, though not the day and hour.

Too season-wise am I, being country-bred,

To tilt at autumn or defy the frost:

Snuffing the chill even as my fathers did,

I say with them, "What's out tonight is lost."

I only hoped, with the mild hope of all

Who watch the leaf take shape upon the tree,

A fairer summer and a later fall

Than in these parts a man is apt to see,

And sunny clusters ripened for the wine:

I tell you this across the blackened vine.

XLVII

Well, I have lost you; and I lost you fairly;
In my own way, and with my full consent.
Say what you will, kings in a tumbrel rarely
Went to their deaths more proud than this one went.
Some nights of apprehension and hot weeping
I will confess; but that's permitted me;
Day dried my eyes; I was not one for keeping
Rubbed in a cage a wing that would be free.
If I had loved you less or played you slyly
I might have held you for a summer more,
But at the cost of words I value highly,
And no such summer as the one before.
Should I outlive this anguish—and men do—
I shall have only good to say of you.

XLVIII

Now by the path I climbed, I journey back.
The oaks have grown; I have been long away.
Taking with me your memory and your lack
I now descend into a milder day;
Stripped of your love, unburdened of my hope,
Descend the path I mounted from the plain;
Yet steeper than I fancied seems the slope
And stonier, now that I go down again.
Warm falls the dusk; the clanking of a bell
Faintly ascends upon this heavier air;
I do recall those grassy pastures well:
In early spring they drove the cattle there.
And close at hand should be a shelter, too,
From which the mountain peaks are not in view.

XLIX

There is a well into whose bottomless eye,
Though I were flayed, I dare not lean and look,
Sweet once with mountain water, now gone dry,
Miraculously abandoned by the brook
Wherewith for years miraculously fed
It kept a constant level cold and bright,
Though summer parched the rivers in their bed;
Withdrawn these waters, vanished overnight.
There is a word I dare not speak again,
A face I never again must call to mind;
I was not craven ever nor blenched at pain,
But pain to such degree and of such kind
As I must suffer if I think of you,
Not in my senses will I undergo.

L

The heart once broken is a heart no more,
And is absolved from all a heart must be;
All that it signed or chartered heretofore
Is cancelled now, the bankrupt heart is free;
So much of duty as you may require
Of shards and dust, this and no more of pain,
This and no more of hope, remorse, desire,
The heart once broken need support again.
How simple 'tis, and what a little sound
It makes in breaking, let the world attest:
It struggles, and it fails; the world goes round,
And the moon follows it. Heart in my breast,
'Tis half a year now since you broke in two;
The world's forgotten well, if the world knew.

LI

If in the years to come you should recall,
When faint at heart or fallen on hungry days,
Or full of griefs and little if at all
From them distracted by delights or praise;
When failing powers or good opinion lost
Have bowed your neck, should you recall to mind
How of all men I honoured you the most,
Holding you noblest among mortal-kind:
Might not my love——although the curving blade
From whose wide mowing none may hope to hide,
Me long ago below the frosts had laid——
Restore you somewhat to your former pride?
Indeed I think this memory, even then,
Must raise you high among the run of men.

LII

Oh, sleep forever in the Latmian cave,
Mortal Endymion, darling of the Moon!
Her silver garments by the senseless wave
Shouldered and dropped and on the shingle strewn,
Her fluttering hand against her forehead pressed,
Her scattered looks that trouble all the sky,
Her rapid footsteps running down the west—
Of all her altered state, oblivious lie!
Whom earthen you, by deathless lips adored,
Wild-eyed and stammering to the grasses thrust,
And deep into her crystal body poured
The hot and sorrowful sweetness of the dust:
Whereof she wanders mad, being all unfit
For mortal love, that might not die of it.

FINIS

Two Sonnets in Memory

(NICOLA SACCO — BARTOLOMEO VANZETTI)

Executed August 23, 1927

I

As men have loved their lovers in times past

And sung their wit, their virtue and their grace,

So have we loved sweet Justice to the last,

Who now lies here in an unseemly place.

The child will quit the cradle and grow wise

And stare on beauty till his senses drown;

Yet shall be seen no more by mortal eyes

Such beauty as here walked and here went down.

Like birds that hear the winter crying plain

Her courtiers leave to seek the clement south;

Many have praised her, we alone remain

To break a fist against the lying mouth

Of any man who says this was not so:

Though she be dead now, as indeed we know.

II

Where can the heart be hidden in the ground
And be at peace, and be at peace forever,
Under the world, untroubled by the sound
Of mortal tears, that cease from pouring never?
Well for the heart, by stern compassion harried,
If death be deeper than the churchmen say,—-
Gone from this world indeed what's graveward carried,
And laid to rest indeed what's laid away.
Anguish enough while yet the indignant breather
Have blood to spurt upon the oppressor's hand;
Who would eternal be, and hang in ether
A stuffless ghost above his struggling land,
Retching in vain to render up the groan
That is not there, being aching dust's alone?

Enormous moon, that rise behind these hills
Heavy and yellow in a sky unstarred
And pale, your girth by purple fillets barred
Of drifting cloud, that as the cool sky fills
With planets and the brighter stars, distills
To thinnest vapour and floats valley-ward,
You flood with radiance all this cluttered yard,
The sagging fence, the chipping window sills.
Grateful at heart as if for my delight
You rose, I watch you through a mist of tears,
Thinking how man, who gags upon despair,
Salting his hunger with the sweat of fright
Has fed on cold indifference all these years,
Calling it kindness, calling it God's care.

Now let the mouth of wailing for a time
Be shut, ye happy mourners; and return
To the marked door, the ribbon and the fern,
Without a tear. The good man in his prime,
The pretty child, the Gone—from a fair clime
Above the ashes of the solemn urn
Behold you; wherefore, then, these hearts that burn
With hot remorse, these cheeks the tears begrime?
Grief that is grief and worthy of that word
Is ours alone for whom no hope can be
That the loved eyes look down and understand.
Ye true believers, trusters in the Lord,
Today bereft, tomorrow hand in hand,
Think ye not shame to show your tears to me?

Thou famished grave, I will not fill thee yet,
Roar though thou dost, I am too happy here;
Gnaw thine own sides, fast on; I have no fear
Of thy dark project, but my heart is set
On living—I have heroes to beget
Before I die; I will not come anear
Thy dismal jaws for many a splendid year;
Till I be old, I aim not to be eat.
I cannot starve thee out: I am thy prey
And thou shalt have me; but I dare defend
That I can stave thee off; and I dare say,
What with the life I lead, the force I spend,
I'll be but bones and jewels on that day,
And leave thee hungry even in the end.

Now that the west is washed of clouds and clear,
The sun gone under and his beams laid by,
You, that require a quarter of the sky
To shine alone in: prick the dusk, appear,
Beautiful Venus! The dense atmosphere
Cannot diffuse your rays, you blaze so high,
Lighting with loveliness a crisp and dry
Cold evening in the autumn of the year.
The pilot standing by his broken plane
In the unheard-of mountains, looks on you, .
And warms his heart a moment at your light . . .
Benignant planet, sweet, familiar sight . . .
Thinking he may be found, he may again
See home, breaks the stale buttered crust in two.

I too beneath your moon, almighty Sex,
Go forth at nightfall crying like a cat,
Leaving the lofty tower I laboured at
For birds to foul and boys and girls to vex
With tittering chalk; and you, and the long necks
Of neighbours sitting where their mothers sat
Are well aware of shadowy this and that
In me, that's neither noble nor complex.
Such as I am, however, I have brought
To what it is, this tower; it is my own;
Though it was reared To Beauty, it was wrought
From what I had to build with: honest bone
Is there, and anguish; pride; and burning thought;
And lust is there, and nights not spent alone.

When did I ever deny, though this was fleeting,
That this was love? When did I ever, I say,
With iron thumb put out the eyes of day
In this cold world where charity lies bleating
Under a thorn, and none to give him greeting,
And all that lights endeavour on its way
Is the teased lamp of loving, the torn ray
Of the least kind, the most clandestine meeting?
As God's my judge, I do cry holy, holy,
Upon the name of love however brief,
For want of whose ill-trimmed, aspiring wick
More days than one I have gone forward slowly
In utter dark, scuffling the drifted leaf,
Tapping the road before me with a stick.

Be sure my coming was a sharp offense
And trouble to my mother in her bed;
And harsh to me must be my going hence,
Though I were old and spent and better dead;
Between the awful spears of birth and death
I run a grassy gauntlet in the sun;
And curdled in me is my central pith,
Remembering there is dying to be done.
O Life, my little day, at what a cost
Have you been purchased! What a bargain's here!
(And yet, thou canny Lender, thou hast lost:
Thumb thy fat book until my debt appear:
So . . . art thou stuck? . . . thou canst not strike that through
  through
For the small dying that a man can do!)

Not only love plus awful grief,
The ardent and consuming pain
Of all who loved and who remain
To tend alone the buried brief
Eternal, propping laurel-leaf
And frozen rose above the slain,—
But pity lest they die again
Makes of the mind an iron sheaf
Of bundled memories. Ah, bright ghost,
Who shadow all I have and do,
Be gracious in your turn, be gone!
Suffice it that I loved you most.
I would be rid of even you,
And see the world I look upon.

Czecho-Slovakia

If there were balm in Gilead, I would go
To Gilead for your wounds, unhappy land,
Gather you balsam there, and with this hand,
Made deft by pity, cleanse and bind and sew
And drench with healing, that your strength might
  grow,
(Though love be outlawed, kindness contraband)
And you, O proud and felled, again might stand;
But where to look for balm, I do not know.
The oils and herbs of mercy are so few;
Honour's for sale; allegiance has its price;
The barking of a fox has bought us all;
We save our skins a craven hour or two.—
While Peter warms him in the servants' hall
The thorns are platted and the cock crows twice.

Count them unclean, these tears that turn no mill,
This salty flux of sorrow from the heart;
Count them unclean, and grant me one day still
To weep, in an avoided room apart.
I shall come forth at length with reddened lid
Transparent, and thick mouth, and take the
   plough . . .
That other men may hope, as I once did;
That other men may weep, as I do now.
I am beside you, I am at your back
Firing our bridges, I am in your van;
I share your march, your hunger; all I lack
Is the sure song I cannot sing, you can.
You think we build a world; I think we leave
Only these tools, wherewith to strain and grieve.

Three Sonnets in Tetrameter

I

See how these masses mill and swarm
And troop and muster and assail:
God!—We could keep this planet warm
By friction, if the sun should fail.
Mercury, Saturn, Venus, Mars:
If no prow cuts your arid seas,
Then in your weightless air no wars
Explode with such catastrophes
As rock our planet all but loose
From its frayed mooring to the sun.
Law will not sanction such abuse
Forever; when the mischief's done,
Planets, rejoice, on which at night
Rains but the twelve-ton meteorite.

II

His stalk the dark delphinium
Unthorned into the tending hand
Releases . . . yet that hour will come . . .
And must, in such a spiny land.
The silky, powdery mignonette
Before these gathering dews are gone
May pierce me—does the rose regret
The day she did her armour on?
In that the foul supplants the fair,
The coarse defeats the twice-refined,
Is food for thought, but not despair:
All will be easier when the mind
To meet the brutal age has grown
An iron cortex of its own.

III

No further from me than my hand
Is China that I loved so well;
Love does not help to understand
The logic of the bursting shell.

Perfect in dream above me yet
Shines the white cone of Fuji-San;
I wake in fear, and weep and sweat . . .
Weep for Yoshida, for Japan.

Logic alone, all love laid by,
Must calm this crazed and plunging star:
Sorrowful news for such as I,
Who hoped—with men just as they are,

Sinful and loving—to secure
A human peace that might endure.

Upon this age, that never speaks its mind,
This furtive age, this age endowed with power
To wake the moon with footsteps, fit an oar
Into the rowlocks of the wind, and find
What swims before his prow, what swirls behind—
Upon this gifted age, in its dark hour,
Rains from the sky a meteoric shower
Of facts . . . they lie unquestioned, uncombined.
Wisdom enough to leech us of our ill
Is daily spun; but there exists no loom
To weave it into fabric; undefiled
Proceeds pure Science, and has her say; but still
Upon this world from the collective womb
Is spewed all day the red triumphant child.

My earnestness, which might at first offend,
Forgive me, for the duty it implies:
I am the convoy to the cloudy end
Of a most bright and regal enterprise;
Which under angry constellations, ill-
Mounted and under-rationed and unspurred,
Set forth to find if any country still
Might do obeisance to an honest word.
Duped and delivered up to rascals; bound
And bleeding, and his mouth stuffed; on his knees;
Robbed and imprisoned; and adjudged unsound;
I have beheld my master, if you please.
Forgive my earnestness, who at his side
Received his swift instructions, till he died.

I must not die of pity; I must live;
Grow strong, not sicken; eat, digest my **food**,
That it may build me, and in doing good
To blood and bone, broaden the sensitive
Fastidious pale perception: we contrive
Lean comfort for the starving, who intrude
Upon them with our pots of pity; brewed
From stronger meat must be the broth we give.
Blue, bright September day, with here and there
On the green hills a maple turning red,
And white clouds racing in the windy air!—
If I would help the weak, I must be fed
In wit and purpose, pour away despair
And rinse the cup, eat happiness like bread.

How innocent of me and my dark pain
In the clear east, unclouded save for one
Flamingo-coloured feather, combed and spun
Into fine spirals, with ephemeral stain
To dye the morning rose after the rain,
Rises the simple and majestic sun,
His azure course, well-known and often-run
With patient brightness to pursue again.
The gods are patient; they are slaves of Time
No less than we, and longer, at whose call
Must Phoebus rise and mount his dewy car,
And lift the reins and start the ancient climb;
Could we learn patience, though day-creatures all,
Our day should see us godlier than we are.

Epitaph for the Race of Man

I

Before this cooling planet shall be cold,
Long, long before the music of the Lyre,
Like the faint roar of distant breakers rolled
On reefs unseen, when wind and flood conspire
To drive the ship inshore—long, long, I say,
Before this ominous humming hits the ear,
Earth will have come upon a stiller day,
Man and his engines be no longer here.
High on his naked rock the mountain sheep
Will stand alone against the final sky,
Drinking a wind of danger new and deep,
Staring on Vega with a piercing eye,
And gather up his slender hooves and leap
From crag to crag down Chaos, and so go by.

II

When Death was young and bleaching bones were few,
A moving hill against the risen day
The dinosaur at morning made his way,
And dropped his dung upon the blazing dew;
Trees with no name that now are agate grew
Lushly beside him in the steamy clay;
He woke and hungered, rose and stalked his prey,
And slept contented, in a world he knew.
In punctual season, with the race in mind,
His consort held aside her heavy tail,
And took the seed; and heard the seed confined
Roar in her womb; and made a nest to hold
A hatched-out conqueror . . . but to no avail:
The veined and fertile eggs are long since cold.

III

Cretaceous bird, your giant claw no lime
From bark of holly bruised or mistletoe
Could have arrested, could have held you so
Through fifty million years of jostling time;
Yet cradled with you in the catholic slime
Of the young ocean's tepid lapse and flow
Slumbered an agent, weak in embryo,
Should grip you straitly, in its sinewy prime.
What bright collision in the zodiac brews,
What mischief dimples at the planet's core
For shark, for python, for the dove that coos
Under the leaves?—what frosty fate's in store
For the warm blood of man,—man, out of ooze
But lately crawled, and climbing up the shore?

IV

O Earth, unhappy planet born to die,
Might I your scribe and your confessor be,
What wonders must you not relate to me
Of Man, who when his destiny was high
Strode like the sun into the middle sky
And shone an hour, and who so bright as he,
And like the sun went down into the sea,
Leaving no spark to be remembered by.
But no; you have not learned in all these years
To tell the leopard and the newt apart;
Man, with his singular laughter, his droll tears,
His engines and his conscience and his art,
Made but a simple sound upon your ears:
The patient beating of the animal heart.

v

When Man is gone and only gods remain
To stride the world, their mighty bodies hung
With golden shields, and golden curls outflung
Above their childish foreheads; when the plain
Round skull of Man is lifted and again
Abandoned by the ebbing wave, among
The sand and pebbles of the beach,—what tongue
Will tell the marvel of the human brain?
Heavy with music once this windy shell,
Heavy with knowledge of the clustered stars;
The one-time tenant of this draughty hall
Himself, in learned pamphlet, did foretell,
After some aeons of study jarred by wars,
This toothy gourd, this head emptied of all.

VI

See where Capella with her golden kids
Grazes the slope between the east and north:
Thus when the builders of the pyramids
Flung down their tools at nightfall and poured forth
Homeward to supper and a poor man's bed,
Shortening the road with friendly jest and slur,
The risen She-Goat showing blue and red
Climbed the clear dusk, and three stars followed her.
Safe in their linen and their spices lie
The kings of Egypt; even as long ago
Under these constellations, with long eye
And scented limbs they slept, and feared no foe.
Their will was law; their will was not to die:
And so they had their way; or nearly so.

VII

He heard the coughing tiger in the night
Push at his door; close by his quiet head
About the wattled cabin the soft tread
Of heavy feet he followed, and the slight
Sigh of the long banana leaves; in sight
At last and leaning westward overhead
The Centaur and the Cross now heralded
The sun, far off but marching, bringing light.
What time the Centaur and the Cross were spent,
Night and the beast retired into the hill,
Whereat serene and undevoured he lay,
And dozed and stretched and listened and lay still,
Breathing into his body with content
The temperate dawn before the tropic day.

VIII

Observe how Miyanoshita cracked in two
And slid into the valley; he that stood
Grinning with terror in the bamboo wood
Saw the earth heave and thrust its bowels through
The hill, and his own kitchen slide from view,
Spilling the warm bowl of his humble food
Into the lap of horror; mark how lewd
This cluttered gulf,—'twas here his paddy grew.
Dread and dismay have not encompassed him;
The calm sun sets; unhurried and aloof
Into the riven village falls the rain;
Days pass; the ashes cool; he builds again
His paper house upon oblivion's brim,
And plants the purple iris in its roof.

IX

He woke in terror to a sky more bright
Than middle day; he heard the sick earth groan,
And ran to see the lazy-smoking cone
Of the fire-mountain, friendly to his sight
As his wife's hand, gone strange and full of fright;
Over his fleeing shoulder it was shown
Rolling its pitchy lake of scalding stone
Upon his house that had no feet for flight.
Where did he weep? Where did he sit him down
And sorrow, with his head between his knees?
Where said the Race of Man, "Here let me drown"?
"Here let me die of hunger"?—"let me freeze"?
By nightfall he has built another town:
This boiling pot, this clearing in the trees.

x

The broken dike, the levee washed away,
The good fields flooded and the cattle drowned,
Estranged and treacherous all the faithful ground,
And nothing left but floating disarray
Of tree and home uprooted,—was this the day
Man dropped upon his shadow without a sound
And died, having laboured well and having found
His burden heavier than a quilt of clay?
No, no. I saw him when the sun had set
In water, leaning on his single oar
Above his garden faintly glimmering yet . . .
There bulked the plough, here washed the updrifted
    weeds . . .
And scull across his roof and make for shore,
With twisted face and pocket full of seeds.

XI

Sweeter was loss than silver coins to spend,
Sweeter was famine than the belly filled;
Better than blood in the vein was the blood spilled;
Better than corn and healthy flocks to tend
And a tight roof and acres without end
Was the barn burned and the mild creatures killed,
And the back aging fast, and all to build:
For then it was, his neighbour was his friend.
Then for a moment the averted eye
Was turned upon him with benignant beam,
Defiance faltered, and derision slept;
He saw as in a not unhappy dream
The kindly heads against the horrid sky,
And scowled, and cleared his throat and spat, and
    wept.

XII

Now forth to meadow as the farmer goes
With shining buckets to the milking-ground,
He meets the black ant hurrying from his mound
To milk the aphis pastured on the rose;
But no good-morrow, as you might suppose,
No nod of greeting, no perfunctory sound
Passes between them; no occasion's found
For gossip as to how the fodder grows.
In chilly autumn on the hardening road
They meet again, driving their flocks to stall,
Two herdsmen, each with winter for a goad;
They meet and pass, and never a word at all
Gives one to t'other. On the quaint abode
Of each, the evening and the first snow fall.

XIII

His heatless room the watcher of the stars
Nightly inhabits when the night is clear;
Propping his mattress on the turning sphere,
Saturn his rings or Jupiter his bars
He follows, or the fleeing moons of Mars,
Till from his ticking lens they disappear. . .
Whereat he sighs, and yawns, and on his ear
The busy chirp of Earth remotely jars.
Peace at the void's heart through the wordless night,
A lamb cropping the awful grasses, grazed;
Earthward the trouble lies, where strikes his light
At dawn industrious Man, and unamazed
Goes forth to plough, flinging a ribald stone
At all endeavour alien to his own.

XIV

Him not the golden fang of furious heaven,
Nor whirling Aeolus on his awful wheel,
Nor foggy specter ramming the swift keel,
Nor flood, nor earthquake, nor the red tongue even
Of fire, disaster's dog—him, him bereaven
Of all save the heart's knocking, and to feel
The air upon his face: not the great heel
Of headless Force into the dust has driven.
These sunken cities, tier on tier, bespeak
How ever from the ashes with proud beak
And shining feathers did the phoenix rise,
And sail, and send the vulture from the skies . . .
That in the end returned; for Man was weak
Before the unkindness in his brother's eyes.

xv

Now sets his foot upon the eastern sill
Aldebaran, swiftly rising, mounting high,
And tracks the Pleiads down the crowded sky,
And drives his wedge into the western hill;
Now for the void sets forth, and further still,
The questioning mind of Man . . . that by and by
From the void's rim returns with swooning eye,
Having seen himself into the maelstrom spill.
O race of Adam, blench not lest you find
In the sun's bubbling bowl anonymous death,
Or lost in whistling space without a mind
To monstrous Nothing yield your little breath:
You shall achieve destruction where you stand,
In intimate conflict, at your brother's hand.

XVI

Alas for Man, so stealthily betrayed,
Bearing the bad cell in him from the start,
Pumping and feeding from his healthy heart
That wild disorder never to be stayed
When once established, destined to invade
With angry hordes the true and proper part,
Till Reason joggles in the headsman's cart,
And Mania spits from every balustrade.
Would he had searched his closet for his bane,
Where lurked the trusted ancient of his soul,
Obsequious Greed, and seen that visage plain;
Would he had whittled treason from his side
In his stout youth and bled his body whole,
Then had he died a king, or never died.

XVII

Only the diamond and the diamond's dust
Can render up the diamond unto Man;
One and invulnerable as it began
Had it endured, but for the treacherous thrust
That laid its hard heart open, as it must,
And ground it down and fitted it to span
A turbaned brow or fret an ivory fan,
Lopped of its stature, pared of its proper crust.
So Man, by all the wheels of heaven unscored,
Man, the stout ego, the exuberant mind
No edge could cleave, no acid could consume,—
Being split along the vein by his own kind,
Gives over, rolls upon the palm abhorred,
Is set in brass on the swart thumb of Doom.

XVIII

Here lies, and none to mourn him but the sea,
That falls incessant on the empty shore,
Most various Man, cut down to spring no more;
Before his prime, even in his infancy
Cut down, and all the clamour that was he,
Silenced; and all the riveted pride he wore,
A rusted iron column whose tall core
The rains have tunnelled like an aspen tree.
Man, doughty Man, what power has brought you low,
That heaven itself in arms could not persuade
To lay aside the lever and the spade
And be as dust among the dusts that blow?
Whence, whence the broadside? whose the heavy
     blade? . . .
Strive not to speak, poor scattered mouth; I know.

FINIS

Those hours when happy hours were my estate,—
Entailed, as proper, for the next in line,
Yet mine the harvest, and the title mine—
Those acres, fertile, and the furrow straight,
From which the lark would rise—all of my late
Enchantments, still, in brilliant colours, shine,
But striped with black, the tulip, lawn and vine,
Like gardens looked at through an iron gate.
Yet not as one who never sojourned there
I view the lovely segments of a past
I lived with all my senses, well aware
That this was perfect, and it would not last:
I smell the flower, though vacuum-still the air;
I feel its texture, though the gate is fast.

Not, to me, less lavish—though my dreams have been
    splendid—
Than dreams, have been the hours of the actual day:
Never, awaking, did I awake to say:
"Nothing could be like that," when a dream was ended.
Colours, in dream; ecstasy, in dream extended
Beyond the edge of sleep—these, in their way,
Approach, come even close, yet pause, yet stay,
In the high presence of request by its answer attended.
Music, and painting, poetry, love, and grief,
Had they been more intense, I could not have borne,—
Yet, not, I think, through stout endurance lacked;
Rather, because the budding and the falling leaf
Were one, and wonderful,—not to be torn
Apart: I ask of dream: seem like the fact.

Tranquility at length, when autumn comes,
Will lie upon the spirit like that haze
Touching far islands on fine autumn days
With tenderest blue, like bloom on purple plums;
Harvest will ring, but not as summer hums,
With noisy enterprise—to broaden, raise,
Proceed, proclaim, establish: autumn stays
The marching year one moment; stills the drums.

Then sits the insistent cricket in the grass;
But on the gravel crawls the chilly bee;
And all is over that could come to pass
Last year; excepting this: the mind is free
One moment, to compute, refute, amass,
Catalogue, question, contemplate, and see.

clxii

Sonnet in Dialectic

And is indeed truth beauty?—at the cost
Of all else that we cared for, can this be?—
To see the coarse triumphant, and to see
Honour and pity ridiculed, and tossed
Upon a poked-at fire; all courage lost
Save what is whelped and fattened by decree
To move among the unsuspecting free
And trap the thoughtful, with their thoughts engrossed?
Drag yet that stream for Beauty, if you will;
And find her, if you can; finding her drowned
Will not dismay your ethics,—you will still
To one and all insist she has been found . . .
And haggard men will smile your praise, until,
Some day, they stumble on her burial-mound.

To hold secure the province of Pure Art,—
What if the crude and weighty task were mine?—
For him who runs, cutting the pen less fine
Than formerly, and in the indignant heart
Dipping it straight? (to issue thence a dart,
And shine no more except as weapons shine)
The deeply-loved, the laboured, polished line
Eschew for ever?—this to be my part?
Attacked that Temple is which must not fall—
Under whose ancient shade Calliope,
Thalia, Euterpe, the nine Muses all
Went once about their happy business free:
Could I but write the Writing on the Wall!—
What matter, if one poet cease to be.

And if I die, because that part of me
Which part alone of me had chance to live,
Chose to be honour's threshing-floor, a sieve
Where right through wrong might make its way, and be;
If from all taint of indignation, free
Must be my art, and thereby fugitive
From all that threatens it—why—let me give
To moles my dubious immortality.
For, should I cancel by one passionate screed
All that in chaste reflection I have writ,
So that again not ever in bright need
A man shall want my verse and reach for it,
I and my verses will be dead indeed,—
That which we died to champion, hurt no whit.

It is the fashion now to wave aside
As tedious, obvious, vacuous, trivial, trite,
All things which do not tickle, tease, excite
To some subversion, or in verbiage hide
Intent, or mock, or with hot sauce provide
A dish to prick the thickened appetite;
Straightforwardness is wrong, evasion right;
It is correct, *de rigueur,* to deride.
What fumy wits these modern wags expose,
For all their versatility: Voltaire,
Who wore to bed a night-cap, and would close,
In fear of drafts, all windows, could declare
In antique stuffiness, a phrase that blows
Still through men's smoky minds, and clears the air.

Alcestis to her husband, just before,
with his tearful approbation, she dies
in order that he may live.

Admetus, from my marrow's core I do
Despise you: wherefore pity not your wife,
Who, having seen expire her love for you
With heaviest grief, today gives up her life.
You could not with your mind imagine this:
One might surrender, yet continue proud.
Not having loved, you do not know: the kiss
You sadly beg, is impious, not allowed.
Of all I loved,—how many girls and men
Have loved me in return?—speak!—young or old—
Speak!—sleek or famished, can you find me then
One form would flank me, as this night grows cold?
I am at peace, Admetus—go and slake
Your grief with wine. I die for my own sake.

What chores these churls do put upon the great,
What chains, what harness; the unfettered mind,
At dawn, in all directions flying blind
Yet certain, might accomplish, might create
What all men must consult or contemplate,—
Save that the spirit, earth-born and born kind,
Cannot forget small questions left behind,
Nor honest human impulse underrate:
Oh, how the speaking pen has been impeded,
To its own cost and to the cost of speech,
By specious hands that for some thinly-needed
Answer or autograph, would claw a breach
In perfect thought . . . till broken thought receded
And ebbed in foam, like ocean down a beach.

I will put Chaos into fourteen lines
And keep him there; and let him thence escape
If he be lucky; let him twist, and ape
Flood, fire, and demon—his adroit designs
Will strain to nothing in the strict confines
Of this sweet Order, where, in pious rape,
I hold his essence and amorphous shape,
Till he with Order mingles and combines.
Past are the hours, the years, of our duress,
His arrogance, our awful servitude:
I have him. He is nothing more nor less
Than something simple not yet understood;
I shall not even force him to confess;
Or answer. I will only make him good.

Come home, victorious wounded!—let the dead,
The out-of-it, the more victorious still,
Hold in the cold the hot-contested hill,
Hold by the sand the abandoned smooth beach-head;—
Maimed men, whose scars must be exhibited
To all the world, though much against your will—
And men whose bodies bear no marks of ill,
Being twisted only in the guts and head:
Come home! come home!—not to the home you long
To find,—and which your valour had achieved
Had virtue been but right, and evil wrong!—
We have tried hard, and we have greatly grieved:
Come home and help us!—you are hurt but strong!
—And we—we are bewildered—and bereaved.

Read history: so learn your place in Time;
And go to sleep: all this was done before;
We do it better, fouling every shore;
We disinfect, we do not probe, the crime.
Our engines plunge into the seas, they climb
Above our atmosphere: we grow not more
Profound as we approach the ocean's floor;
Our flight is lofty, it is not sublime.
Yet long ago this Earth by struggling men
Was scuffed, was scraped by mouths that bubbled mud;
And will be so again, and yet again;
Until we trace our poison to its bud
And root, and there uproot it: until then,
Earth will be warmed each winter by man's blood.

Read history: thus learn how small a space
You may inhabit, nor inhabit long
In crowding Cosmos—in that confined place
Work boldly; build your flimsy barriers strong;
Turn round and round, make warm your nest; among
The other hunting beasts, keep heart and face,—
Not to betray the doomed and splendid race
You are so proud of, to which you belong.
For trouble comes to all of us: the rat
Has courage, in adversity, to fight;
But what a shining animal is man,
Who knows, when pain subsides, that is not that,
For worse than that must follow—yet can write
Music; can laugh; play tennis; even plan.

My words that once were virtuous and expressed
Nearly enough the mortal joys I knew,
Now that I sit to supper with the blest
Come haltingly, are very poor and few.
Whereof you speak and wherefore the bright walls
Resound with silver mirth I am aware,
But I am faint beneath the coronals
Of living vines you set upon my hair.
Angelic friends that stand with pointed wings
Sweetly demanding, in what dulcet tone,
How fare I in this heaven of happy things,—
I cannot lift my words against your own.
Forgive the downcast look, the lyre unstrung;
Breathing your presence, I forget your tongue.

Now sits the autumn cricket in the grass,
And on the gravel crawls the chilly bee;
Near to its close and none too soon for me
Draws the dull year, in which has come to pass
The changing of the happy child I was
Into this quiet creature people see
Stitching a seam with careful industry
To deaden you, who died on Michaelmas.
Ages ago the purple aconite
Laid its dark hoods about it on the ground,
And roses budded small and were content;
Swallows are south long since and out of sight;
With you the phlox and asters also went;
Nor can my laughter anywhere be found.

And must I then, indeed, Pain, live with you
All through my life?—sharing my fire, my bed,
Sharing—oh, worst of all things!—the same head?—
And, when I feed myself, feeding you, too?
So be it, then, if what seems true, is true:
Let us to dinner, comrade, and be fed;—
I cannot die till you yourself are dead,
And, with you living, I can live life through.
Yet have you done me harm, ungracious guest,
Spying upon my ardent offices
With frosty look; robbing my nights of rest;
And making harder things I did with ease.
You will die with me: but I shall, at best,
Forgive you with restraint, for deeds like these.

If I die solvent—die, that is to say,
In full possession of my critical mind,
Not having cast, to keep the wolves at bay
In this dark wood—till all be flung behind—
Wit, courage, honour, pride, oblivion
Of the red eyeball and the yellow tooth;
Nor sweat nor howl nor break into a run
When loping Death's upon me in hot sooth;
'Twill be that in my honoured hands I bear
What's under no condition to be spilled
Till my blood spills and hardens in the air:
An earthen grail, a humble vessel filled
To its low brim with water from that brink
Where Shakespeare, Keats and Chaucer learned to drink.

Grief that is grief and properly so hight
Has lodging in the orphaned brain alone,
Whose nest is cold, whose wings are now his own
And thinly feathered for the perchless flight
Between the owl and ermine; overnight
His food is reason, fodder for the grown,
His range is north to famine, south to fright.
When Constant Care was manna to the beak,
And Love Triumphant downed the hovering breast,
Vainly the cuckoo's child might nudge and speak
In ugly whispers to the indignant nest:
How even a feathered heart had power to break,
And thud no more above their huddled rest.

Felicity of Grief!—even Death being kind,
Reminding us how much we dared to love!
There, once, the challenge lay,—like a light glove
Dropped as through carelessness—easy to find
Means and excuse for being somewhat blind
Just at that moment; and why bend above,
Take up, such certain anguish for the mind?
Ah, you who suffer now as I now do,
Seeing, of Life's dimensions, not one left
Save Time—long days somehow to be lived through:
Think—of how great a thing were you bereft
That it should weigh so now!—and that you knew
Always, its awkward contours, and its heft.

What rider spurs him from the darkening east
As from a forest, and with rapid pound
Of hooves, now light, now louder on hard ground,
Approaches, and rides past with speed increased,
Dark spots and flecks of foam upon his beast?
What shouts he from the saddle, turning 'round,
As he rides on?—"Greetings!"—I made the sound;
"Greetings from Nineveh!"—it seemed, at least.
Did someone catch the object that he flung?
He held some object on his saddle-bow,
And flung it towards us as he passed; among
The children then it fell most likely; no,
'Tis here: a little bell without a tongue.
Listen; it has a faint voice even so.

INDEX OF TITLES AND FIRST LINES

Y

752

About the book

About the author

Read on

Photos,
Letters
& More...

"Night Is My Sister"
Edna St. Vincent Millay and the Poetry of Nature

By Holly Peppe

OPEN ANY BOOK of Edna St. Vincent Millay's poems at random and you're certain to find a reference to nature: natural phenomena, and the natural course of events, provided a context for the poet's changing feelings, situations, and moods. Whatever her subject—love, loss, faith, patriotism, war, or personal freedom—nature and its archetypes endured for her; nature structured her world. With its predictable, seasonal cycles of life and death, growth and decay, nature offered Millay a rich source for imagery and symbolism and served as an organizing principle in her poetry and in her life.

Many of Millay's early lyrics are hymns exalting nature's grandeur: "O world, I cannot hold thee close enough! / Thy winds, thy wide grey skies!" In "Renascence," the visionary poem that launched her career, the poet's spiritual crisis is intensified by her passionate devotion to nature and her unwillingness to leave the beauty of the earth behind. In an allegorical "Journey" through life, written at age twenty-one, she finds herself "following Care along the dusty road," beckoned by the sounds of birds and "creeks at dusk," welcomed by "eager vines" and "flushed apple-trees." Though the path is difficult, she rejoices that as "far as passionate eye can reach, / . . . / The

world is mine: blue hill, still silver lake, /
Broad field, bright flower, and the long
white road."

Nature serves as Millay's touchstone for
happiness—"I will be the gladdest thing /
Under the sun! / I will touch a hundred
flowers / And not pick one"—and for
sorrow—"Dark, Dark, is all I find for
metaphor." In "Bean-stalk," she portrays
the precarious but thrilling process of
writing a poem as a dizzying climb up a
beanstalk into the "light so sheer and
sunny" that even the "little dirty city"
appears "dazzling bright and pretty."
Yet her youthful exuberance is tempered
by the reality that nature shows no regard
for human loss or grief. Of her lost
beloved, she writes, "There will be rose
and rhododendron / When you are dead
and under ground; / . . . / Spring will not
ail nor autumn falter; / Nothing will know
that you are gone."

Millay traced her devotion to nature to
her childhood on the Maine coast, where
she and her two younger sisters, Norma
and Kathleen, spent hours by the sea and
learned the names of flowers, plants, and
medicinal herbs from their mother, Cora,
a private nurse who used the herbs to treat
her patients. Even as a child, Millay was
moved by "the grapevine growing over
the grey rock—the shock / Of beauty seen,
noticed, for the first time—"

After graduating from Vassar in 1917,
she moved to New York, where her writing
career flourished, despite her preference for
traditional poetic form over the Modernist
tendencies of the day. Hailed as "America's
Poet of the Future" by the *New York* ▶

Times, she lived as a free spirit—bohemian in lifestyle, progressive in her convictions about women's rights and social equality, and noncommittal with her many suitors. Yet in private moments she longed to return to the coast of Maine: "I am weary of words and people," she wrote, "sick of the city, wanting the sea."

In 1923, Edna St. Vincent Millay became the first woman to receive the Pulitzer Prize in poetry. That same year, at a house party with her writer friends, she was paired in a dramatic skit with Eugen Boissevain, a Dutch merchant she had met briefly in 1918 after the death of his wife, the suffrage leader Inez Milholland. The skit, which featured Millay and Eugen as a couple in love, soon translated into reality and they were married within a few months. In Eugen, Millay had found a soul mate who shared her deep emotional bond with nature. In her first poem dedicated to him, she wrote: "I am in love with him to whom a hyacinth is dearer / Than I shall ever be dear."

In 1925, after a honeymoon tour around the world, Millay and Eugen purchased a seven-hundred-acre berry farm in Austerlitz, New York, naming it Steepletop after the steeplebush, a pink flowering shrub that grew wild in the hills and meadows around the farmhouse. Over the next several years, in transforming the house and property to suit their own tastes and whims, they planted herb, flower, rose, and vegetable gardens; built an outdoor bar, a barn, and guesthouses; dug a swimming pool (in which they and their guests swam au naturel); and created Japanese-style outdoor garden "rooms" accessible through wooden doors mounted between trees.

Eugen assumed many of the household chores so his wife would have time to study and write in an upstairs library and in a small pine writing cabin just up the hill from the house. An avid naturalist, Millay meticulously collected and pressed hundreds of specimens of wildflowers and, in true writer form, kept detailed diaries of every bird she sighted and every flower and herb she planted. After a morning spent transplanting lilac bushes, she wrote gleefully, "We pulled up the lilacs by the roots of their hair!!" and after a few hours weeding in the hot sun, she reported: "Did all my weeding without a stitch and got a marvelous tan."

In her self-deprecating "Portrait by a Neighbour," Millay mused about what it meant to be a lazy gardener:

> She digs in her garden
>   With a shovel and a spoon,
> She weeds her lazy lettuce
>   By the light of the moon,
>
>   . . .
>
> Her lawn looks like a meadow,
>   And if she mows the place
> She leaves the clover standing
>   And the Queen Anne's lace!

And in "Counting-out Rhyme," she found delight, and consonance, in the nomenclature of trees:

> Silver bark of beech, and sallow
> Bark of yellow birch and yellow
>   Twig of willow.
>
> Stripe of green in moosewood maple,
> Color seen in leaf of apple,
>   Bark of popple.

But Millay missed the sea, and in 1933 she and Eugen bought Ragged Island, a small property off the coast of Maine that soon became her sanctuary from the pressures and demands of literary fame. Her moments of solitude there also inspired new poems: "There, thought unbraids itself, and the mind becomes single. / There you row with tranquil oars, and the ocean / Shows no scars from the cutting of your placid keel; / Care becomes senseless there; pride and promotion / Remote; you only look; you scarcely feel."

Millay felt a strong affinity for the Romantic poets, identifying with their reverence for nature and unwavering belief in the ▶

5

individual. She also shared their fascination for fantasy and the supernatural, manifested in her own array of strange characters with mysterious origins. In "The Singing-Woman from the Wood's Edge," a part-human, part-sylvan being narrates her life story in a lilting voice: "Teethed on a crucifix and cradled under water, / What should I be but the fiend's god-daughter? / And who should be my playmates but the adder and the frog, / That was got beneath a furze-bush and born in a bog?" In "Wraith," a ghostly visitor, "thin as thread, with exquisite fingers" and "glimmering eyes," haunts the poet's house, rattling the windows and doors. Another specter, "The Little Ghost," dressed in a flowing white gown, ruffled white hat, and lacy gloves, returns to visit her garden and, finding it tended by the poet, smiles with approval before disappearing through "a gate that once was there."

Nature takes center stage in one of Millay's finest works, a seventeen-sonnet sequence titled *Sonnets from an Ungrafted Tree*, based on a true story told to Millay by her mother. A New England farm wife, having left an unfulfilling marriage, returns to her husband's side many years later to care for him on his deathbed, "loving him not at all." As the sequence progresses, the mood of suspense and spiritual heaviness magnifies the wife's taut emotional state. Nature images—earth, air, water, trees, and birds—comprise a physical world to which the woman is closely bound, while her imagination and dreams create an equally lush but terrifying mental landscape.

Tense and fearful in "the presence of death," she sees her past in "the painted butter-tub . . . , / Where once her red geraniums had stood," and recalls how, as a young, hopeful wife, she had planted seeds, "musing ahead to their far blossoming." Now, her senses heightened, rain drumming "steady" on the roof, her heart beating "like a frightened partridge," she feels trapped by her husband's eerily silent presence, waiting for his death to set her free.

In a series of flashbacks, the woman revisits their courtship, recalling "the August night / . . . level as a lake beneath the moon" when, "her body sluggish with desire," she believed "the boy, who was at noon / . . . not different from the rest" might be "her spirit's mate." Millay's sinister natural imagery foreshadows the doomed relationship ahead: "Stark on the open field the moonlight fell, / But the oak tree's shadow was deep and black and secret as a well."

The woman's "horror he would die at night" dissipates as her husband slips away and she begins to imagine him as an inanimate object, like a "mute clock, maintaining ever the same / Dead moment." Though "from his desirous body the great heat / Was gone at last," her own life is about to be renewed: "It struck her . . . / That here was spring, and the whole year to be lived through once more."

In *Fatal Interview,* a sequence of fifty-two sonnets, the changing seasons serve as a timepiece for the life cycle of a failed love affair and the framework for a narrative structure that references the Greek myth of Endymion and Selene the Moon Goddess. This sequence was inspired by Millay's love affair with George Dillon, a twenty-one-year-old aspiring poet she met in Chicago in 1928 on one of her national reading tours. Their relationship fueled Millay's poetry but strained her marriage: "The scar of this encounter like a sword / Will lie between me and my troubled lord."

The poet's passionate encounter—the "fatal interview"—leaves her grappling with feelings of rejection and despair when her lover loses interest. Like the goddess Selene, who fell hopelessly in love with the sleeping shepherd boy Endymion, the poet desires the "unconscious man," though she knows he cannot satisfy her needs. Throughout the sequence, Millay reverses the gender roles found in traditional love poetry by portraying the female lover as desirous and the man as unattainable. The poet finally finds comfort in the female forces of nature, citing the integrity of her own natural heritage, her "mother the brown earth / Fervent and full of gifts and free from guile." When the man refuses to acknowledge the pain he has caused her, she turns to nature for protection: "Night is my sister, . . . / . . . / No one but Night with tears on her dark face, / Watches beside me in this windy place." Finally, she beckons a third female ally, Beauty, to keep her safe from "wrath and scorn." Unlike Selene, the poet need not go mad with longing for an unresponsive lover; instead, flanked by Night and Beauty, she declares that she will "love again." ▶

Millay's metaphor for the thwarted love affair is the destruction of a flower garden after the first frost. Though her "spirit grieves / And wrings its hands at what the frost has done," the grotesque images of dead plants—"these pale and oozy stalks, these hanging leaves / Nerveless and darkened, dripping in the sun"—cannot deny her the joyous memory of their former glory: "Clearly my ruined garden as it stood / Before the frost came on it I recall—/ Stiff marigolds, and what a trunk of wood / The zinnia had . . ." Similarly, the poet, having survived the loss of her lover by acknowledging that her primary, archetypal bond is with nature and not another human being, can look back and savor the memories of her "summer" love affair.

Edna St. Vincent Millay lived and wrote at Steepletop for twenty-five years. In 1950, the last year of her life, mourning the recent loss of her beloved Eugen, she chose to remain there alone, relying on the familiar scenes and cycles of nature to inspire, ground, and calm her. Still, she felt "scared the way [she] used to be as a child" as she imagined life without him. "I am exploring strange and uncharted country," she wrote to a friend. "I am the first one that ever lost Eugen."

Among the unfinished poems found in Millay's notebooks after her death were three penciled lines she had circled, as if to remind herself that even in grief, the natural world must be held in the highest esteem:

I will control myself, or go inside.
I will not flaw perfection with my grief.
Handsome, this day: no matter who has died. ∽

Edna St. Vincent Millay's Preface to *Distressing Dialogues* by Nancy Boyd (her pen name)

MISS BOYD HAS ASKED ME to write a preface to these dialogues, with which, having followed them eagerly as they appeared from time to time in the pages of Vanity Fair, I was already familiar. I am no friend of prefaces, but if there must be one to this book, it should come from me, who was its author's earliest admirer. I take pleasure in recommending to the public these excellent small satires, from the pen of one in whose work I have a never-failing interest and delight.

Edna St. Vincent Millay
Tokyo, May 6, 1924

A Selection of Letters

All excerpts from Millay's letters are taken from Letters of Edna St. Vincent Millay, *edited by Allan Ross Macdougall (Camden, Maine: Down East Books, 1952).*

To the Millay Family

135 East 52nd Street
New York City
Tuesday Morning
[April 8, 1913]

Dearest Darlings—
    I just this minute got a check for twenty-five dollars from Mitchell Kennerly for two little poems I sent him. I am going to indorse it and send it home after I've looked at it a little while. He says "I am delighted to have them and shall print them in early numbers of the Forum. I should like to talk to you about your work, and hope you will come and see me."
    Have just got a letter from some of you but haven't had the time to read it.
    O, Mother and girls!
                                —Vincent

To Norma Millay

New York
Sunday
[June 1917]

Dear Norma,—
    Tell Mother it is all right,—the class made such a fuss that they let me come

back, & I graduated [from Vassar] in my cap & gown along with the rest. Tell her it had nothing to do with money;—all my bills have been settled for some time.— Commencement went off beautifully & I had a wonderful time. Tell her this at once if you can. I didn't get the Milwaukee season, so I'm staying here & just looking around for a job. If I get one soon enough, & it doesn't begin for a short time perhaps I shall come home when [younger sister] Kathleen does, but otherwise I shall just stay on here until I get something to do, probably. You see I have to start right in working as soon as I can get a job,—& I may not be able to come home at all. We mustn't be foolish about these things.

***

I have sold *October-November* to *The Yale Review*, a fine magazine.

If I got an engagement for the fall then I could come home & do some writing, which I am very anxious to do, this summer. But I *can't* come home unless I have something sure here to come back to,—you understand.

***

I am feeling much rested,—& all keyed up to go to work—but, oh, I am so homesick to see you, dear, & Mother,—& the garden & everything!—Never mind, if I have good luck I shall come home,— unless I have to begin work at once.

***

Please write my darling, darling, darling, sister.

Vincent
(Edna St. Vincent Millay A.B.!)

To Harriet Monroe

139 Waverly Place,
New York City.
March 1st, 1918

Dear Harriet Monroe,—
    Spring is here,—and I could be very happy, except that I am broke. Would you mind paying me *now* instead of on publication for those so stunning verses of mine which you have? I am become very, very thin, and have taken to smoking Virginia tobacco.

Wistfully yours,
Edna St. Vincent Millay

P.S. I am *awfully* broke. Would you mind paying me a lot?

To Arthur Davison Ficke

[October 24, 1930]

Dearest Artie:
    It's not true that life is one damn thing after another—it's one damn thing over & over—there's the rub—first you get sick—then you get sicker—then you get not quite so sick—then you get hardly sick at all—then you get a little sicker—then you get a lost sicker—then you get not quite so sick—oh, hell

Love from
Little Wince.

To Eugen Jan Boissevain

Chicago & Northeastern Station
10:25 A.M. Wednesday [January, 1924]

Darling:—
    . . .
    It's wonderful to write to you, my
dearest. It takes the sting out of almost
anything, I find. I wanted you so last
night. I was pretty unhappy. And of
course I was tired too.—I had to get
up early this morning, because I made a
sudden decision to check out of the Hotel
Windermere . . . so I had to pack . . .
& I had to take a 10:30 train.
    . . .
    It's amusing to think how entirely,
totally, ABSOLUTELY different everything
would be if you were in this chair beside
me.—It makes me laugh, it's so funny that
there could be such a difference. Oh, it will
be so lovely when we go around the earth
together!—I told some people that we are
going to Java & China in March.—Why
not?—For we are, we are!—Aren't we?
    . . .
    There's a man getting off at this
[train] station. . . . The porter just
brushed him off, standing just in front
of me. This is the porter's little trick. He
brushes the dust from the man getting
off at this station, onto the man getting
off at the next station,—& business
flourishes.—Well, darling, I have poured
out all my troubles.—none of them
matters, when I think of you.—

                                    Edna.

To Cass Canfield

Steepletop, Austerlitz, N.Y.
May 10th, 1948

Dear Cass:
    Enclosed is a copy of my letter to
Arthur Rushmore, in reply to his of
several weeks ago. I cannot do what he
suggests. So, once again, Harper's makes
me a proposition which I must turn
down. I feel very bad about it, always
turning you down.
    ***

    I think it only fair to tell you, fair to my
publishers and to myself, that if only you
and Rushmore and all the rest of you nice
people down there at Harper's, would
just for a little while stop nagging me,
I might be able to get some work done.
It is perfectly natural and understandable
that you should try to think up schemes
for making people buy more of my
books,—new combinations, new
material combined with old, etc.
I do not blame you; I sympathize fully.
But on the other hand it is a fact, that
you harass me so, you run me so ragged,
with your one proposition after another,
propositions which, more often than not,
I feel unhappily obliged to turn down,
that you destroy all my serenity of mind.
And surely this is unwise: you do not get
anywhere; and you impede me. If you
really want a book from me, why not stop
worrying me for a while, and give me a
chance to write it?

On which genial and diplomatic note,
I close.

Trusting, however, in closing, that for
one year more it may be said of me by
Harpers & Brothers, that although
I reject their proposals, I welcome
their advances.

Sincerely,

Edna.

Steepletop, Austerlitz, N.Y.
April 4th, 1950

Dear Cass:

I meant to write you at once, after
sending you that telegram. For I realized,
the moment it had gone, how abrupt
and chilly it might sound, unless it were
followed at once by a letter explaining it.
But I have had little time for writing
letters.

The reason I wired you not to come
that Friday, was because it suddenly
occurred to me that that day would
be the day after Thanksgiving day;
and I was not at all sure how I should get
through that day, the first Thanksgiving
Day I had ever spent alone. I got through
it all right, and all the other happy
holidays, too, by simply by-passing
them. (I love that expression.) The
only thing I did by way of observance,
was to sit at the piano on Christmas
Eve, and play and sing some Christmas
Carols. And on New Year's Eve, I rang
up Eugen's family in Holland. None of ▶

them had received any word from me
at all, since that one shocking cablegram.
And New Year's Eve, which they call
Old Year's Eve, is a very solemn occasion
with them, not like our gay and rowdy
drunken tooting. The family assembles,
and talks about what has happened in
the year that has passed. And I knew
that they would talk of Eugen with
heavy heartache; and that they would
be worrying about me. For they love
me as if I were their own kin; as I do
them.

I should like very much to see you,
and I will let you know as soon as the
roads are open. The weather this winter
has been phenomenally bad. Spring is at
least six weeks later than usual, and the
roads are just now beginning to thaw,
and are like quicksand. John Pinnie has
to walk here every morning, to do the
chores. Please forgive me for not writing
sooner.

> Affectionately,
> Edna.

To Mrs. Lena Reusch

*The following note was left one morning
in the autumn of 1950 for Mrs. Ruesch,
a neighbor who helped keep the house.*

Dear Lena:
The iron is set too high. Don't put
it on where it says "Linen"—or it will
scorch the linen. Try it on "Rayon"—
and then, perhaps on "Woollen." And

be careful not to *burn your fingers* when you shift it from one heat to another.

It is 5:30, and I have been working all night. I am going to bed.

Goodmorning—

E.St.V.M ⌒

A Selection of Photographs

Edna St. Vincent Millay was born in Camden, Maine, on February 22, 1892.

The poet's mother, Cora Buzzell Millay, worked as a visiting nurse while Edna (whom everyone called Vincent) and her sisters, Norma and Kathleen, were growing up.

Millay's high school graduation photo, 1909, Camden, Maine.

Millay, fresh from the country, newly arrived in Manhattan.

Early portrait of the young poet.

On July 18, 1923, Millay married Dutch merchant Eugen
Boissevain in the garden of a private home in Croton-on-
Hudson, New York.

On her older sister's wedding day, Norma fashioned a wedding
veil from mosquito netting taken from the front porch.

A Selection of Photographs *(continued)*

Always happy to pose for the camera, Millay is flanked by two loves of her life, Arthur Davison Ficke (left) and her devoted husband, Eugen Boissevain.

PRIVATE LANDS

NO TRESPASSING

All Persons are warned against HUNTING, FISHING or TRAPPING hereon or TRESPASSING hereon for any purpose.

Estate of Edna St. Vincent Millay
Austerlitz, N.Y.

After Millay and Eugen purchased Steepletop in 1925, they posted notices to guard their privacy on the seven-hundred-acre farm.

A Selection of Photographs *(continued)*

A famous shot of Millay picketing in Boston in April 1927 for the release of Italian immigrant anarchists Sacco and Vanzetti.

Millay and Eugen, with one of their first cars, out for a drive in the country.

Millay the poet, circa 1924.

The three sisters: Vincent, Norma, and Kathleen in Maine, circa 1924–25.

Millay in her thirties, having become a famous poet.

Millay in her later years.

Recommended Reading

Poetry

Edna St. Vincent Millay. *Collected Lyrics* (Harper Perennial, 1981)

Elizabeth Barnett, editor. *Collected Sonnets of Edna St. Vincent Millay* (Harper Perennial, 1988)

Holly Peppe, editor. *Edna St. Vincent Millay: Early Poems* (Penguin Books, 1998)

Colin Falck, editor. *Edna St. Vincent Millay: Selected Poems* (Harper Perennial, 1999)

J. D. McClatchy, editor. *Edna St. Vincent Millay: Selected Poems* (American Poets Project, 7: Library of America, 2003)

Biographies

Daniel Mark Epstein. *What Lips My Lips Have Kissed: The Loves and Love Poems of Edna St. Vincent Millay* (Henry Holt & Company, 2001)

Nancy Milford. *Savage Beauty: The Life of Edna St. Vincent Millay* (Random House, 2001)

About the Poet and Her Era

Marion Meade. *Bobbed Hair and Bathtub Gin: Writers Running Wild in the Twenties* (Doubleday, 2004)

The Edna St. Vincent Millay Society

The Edna St. Vincent Millay Society, founded in 1978 as a nonprofit educational organization, is dedicated to preserving Millay's literary work, personal belongings, and real property for the enjoyment of present and future generations.

Steepletop, an 1892 Victorian farmhouse and seven-hundred-acre farm in Austerlitz, New York, was the poet's permanent home for the second half of her life. Under the stewardship of the Society, both the house, designated as a National Historic Landmark, and the surrounding gardens are undergoing a full restoration. In 2010, sixty years after the poet's death, the house was opened to the public for the first time.

Visitors will be amazed to discover how Millay lived and where she found inspiration in her quintessential New England homestead. For more information please visit www.millay.org or call 518-392-3362.